THE UNDERSIDE OF AMERICAN HISTORY: OTHER READINGS

72 - 81

154-164

194-205

281-193

The Underside of American History: Other Readings

Edited by
Thomas R. Frazier

Under the general editorship of
JOHN MORTON BLUM

HARCOURT BRACE JOVANOVICH, INC.

New York   Chicago   San Francisco   Atlanta   Dallas

Thomas R. Frazier is an Associate Professor of History at the Bernard M. Baruch College of the City University of New York.

This book is based on *The Underside of American History: Other Readings,*
Volumes I and II, © 1971 by Harcourt Brace Jovanovich, Inc.

Printed in the United States of America

ISBN   0–15–378100–9

Contents

6 / Women

Introduction

The United States was conceived in a cloud of conflict—conflict of ideas, conflict of economic and political systems, conflict of peoples with different cultural backgrounds, different needs, and different ambitions. Our history is the story of many peoples and unsteady progress. Yet traditional history textbooks often trace the development of this country as though it were the gradual, almost natural, growth of a single people into a unified nation. Historians have concentrated on what they considered the dominant themes in American life—themes that almost always centered on the dominant groups of Americans. In the process they have sometimes overlooked vital aspects of the American past, neglecting whole groups within the nation. For the past decade these groups have been insistently advancing their claims to be recognized and given their place in the story of our nation. Today the part of the past that has remained hidden—the "underside" of American history—is forcing itself into the public consciousness.

This book provides an introduction to some of the neglected groups and their place in American history. It presents a selection of *un*traditional readings in American history. The stress is on the failings of the system. The focus is not on the victors, but on the victims. The result, of course, is not a balanced view of our history, but an attempt to correct the existing imbalance. These notes and these readings, unless they are considered within a larger context, provide a harsher view of American history than might be warranted. They are, however, an essential part of the whole story, and they must be taken into account in any attempt to reach a valid assessment of the American past.

In this work, six different oppressed groups are studied in

turn. This topical arrangement enables you to concentrate on the individual groups, one at a time. Within each topic the arrangement is chronological—within every section the essays follow a historical sequence.

Each topic deals with a group that is still being oppressed in the United States today. No attempt is made in this book to provide solutions to the many problems of oppression, although some of the readings suggest solutions in particular situations. The programs of the various organized movements for liberation are often indefinite and shifting, but one thing is clear: all the groups feel that they must have the opportunity for self-determination and control over the institutions that govern their lives. If the United States is to achieve a truly cohesive national identity, it must be a changed one; it must become a genuinely pluralistic nation, able to acknowledge and accept the rights of different racial, ethnic, religious, and sex groups within its boundaries.

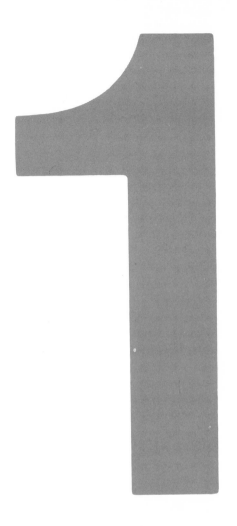

Indians

Tecumseh, the Greatest Indian

ALVIN M. JOSEPHY, JR.

The Indians met the advance of white settlers in various ways. During the colonial period and in the early years of the American nation, some Indians hoped to halt the white man through military action. However, the peace treaties that followed military encounters were regularly ignored by whites, and endless armed conflict was out of the question. Some Indians considered the possibility of seeking admission to the union as separate Indian states. Though this may sound like a vain hope, it did not appear to be so at the time. Article VI of the Delaware Treaty of September 17, 1778, for example, contained the following statement:

> The United States do engage to guarantee to the aforesaid nation of Delawares, and their heirs, all their territorial rights in the fullest and most ample manner as it hath been bound by former treaties, as long as they the said Delaware nation shall abide by and hold fast the chain of friendship now entered into. And it is further agreed on between the contracting parties should it for the future be found conducive for the mutual interest of both parties to invite any other tribes who have been friends to the interest of the United States, to join the present confederation, and to form a state whereof the Delaware nation shall be the head, and have a representation in Congress: Provided, nothing contained in this article to be considered as conclusive until it meets with the approbation of Congress.

Indian unity also seemed to hold out genuine possibilities. However, the history of the Indian nations in America is anything but the story of increasing cooperation. Although there were some confederations among Indian groups, such as those of the Creek and the Iroquois, not even the presence of a common enemy led to the formation of permanent alliances. Pan-Indianism met the fate of similar movements the world over —Pan-Slavism, Pan-Arabism, Pan-Africanism, all have demonstrated a low degree of cohesiveness and effectiveness.

Early in the nineteenth century, a movement led by Tecumseh and his brother the Shawnee Prophet came closer than any other to uniting the various Indian nations on the western frontier of the United States. Using a combination of political leadership and religious vision, these two Indian leaders were well on the way to developing a broad-based alliance of Indian nations stretching from Canada to the Gulf Coast. Had they had more time to develop the administrative machinery that would have strengthened the alliance and led, perhaps, to a permanent confederation, they might indeed have presented an obstacle to westward expansion. As it was, the disaster at Tippecanoe in 1811 led Tecumseh to split with his brother, and the onset of the War of 1812 brought the Indians into conflict. Tecumseh and many of his followers fought for the British, hoping thus to gain British support in negotiating a peace that would recognize three nations in North America—the British, the American, and the Indian. In the end, however, the British betrayed their Indian allies and left them defenseless against the Americans. Tecumseh himself was killed in battle, and the weakened remains of his alliance were pushed west of the Mississippi to await the inevitable tide of white settlers.

The following pages describe Tecumseh's attempt to unify the Indians after their defeat at the hands of the United States forces under Anthony Wayne at the Battle of Fallen Timbers in 1794.

The peace envisioned for the Northwest Territory by Wayne's treaty lasted little more than a decade, and was never more than a truce. As Tecumseh had foreseen, the line established at Greenville between the races could not halt conflict. Though the Indians acknowledged white possession of southern Ohio, many of them continued to

"Tecumseh, the Greatest Indian" from *The Patriot Chiefs: A Chronicle of American Indian Resistance* by Alvin M. Josephy, Jr., copyright © 1958, 1961 by Alvin M. Josephy, Jr. Reprinted by permission of The Viking Press, Inc., and International Famous Agency.

live and hunt on their former lands, and they were in constant friction with frontier settlers. Moreover, as whites continued to come down the Ohio River, they began to press for the opening of new Indian lands, and in 1800, as if preparing to slice another large piece from the natives' domain, the government established administrative machinery for a Territory of Indiana, west of Ohio.

During this period another tragedy struck the Indians. Traders and settlers brought liquor into the region in huge quantities, and native bands in close contact with the whites could not resist it. They traded land, possessions, and their services for the alcohol, and almost overnight large segments of once proud and dignified tribes became demoralized in drunkenness and disease. As poverty and death claimed the natives, whole bands disappeared, and the weakened survivors clung together in ragged misery. The Miamis, who in 1791 had helped to destroy St. Clair's army, became, in the view of William Henry Harrison, "a poor, miserable drunken set, diminishing every year." The Piankashaws and Weas, almost extinct, were "the most depraved wretches on earth," and the Chippewas, who had fought nobly under Pontiac, were described as "frightful drunkards." Almost every tribe in the Northwest, including the Potawatomis, Kickapoos, Ottawas, Peorias, Kaskaskias, and Winnebagos, felt the effects of the firewater, and as their bands were reduced to poverty they were forced to steal from the whites to stay alive.

Tribes that remained farthest from contact with the traders, such as the Shawnees, retained their independence and strength. Tecumseh himself refused to drink whisky, and preached angrily against its use by his followers. Nevertheless, the liquor trade continued to threaten his people in Indiana. Despite his opposition, as well as government attempts to stop whisky sales to natives, unscrupulous traders managed to sneak more than six thousand gallons up the Wabash River annually for a trade of no more than six hundred warriors. One of the Shawnees who became most noted among his own people as a depraved drunk was Tecumseh's younger brother, Laulewasika. A loud-mouthed idler and loafer, he had lost an eye in an accident and wore a handkerchief over the empty socket. For years he drank heavily and lived in laziness. Then, suddenly, in 1805, he was influenced by the great religious revival taking place among white settlers on the frontier, and particularly by itinerant Shaker preachers, whose jerking, dancing, and excessive physical activity stirred mystic forces within him.

During a frightening epidemic of sickness among the Shawnees,

Laulewasika was overcome by a "deep and awful sense" of his own wickedness, and fell into the first of many trances, during which he thought he met the Indian Master of Life. The latter showed him the horrible torments and sufferings of persons doomed by drink, and then pointed out another path, "beautiful, sweet, and pleasant," reserved for abstainers. Laulewasika's regeneration was instantaneous. He began to preach against the use of liquor, and the intensity of his words drew followers to him. As he continued to have trances and commune with the Master of Life, he changed his name to Tenskwatawa, "the open door," which he took from the saying of Jesus, "I am the door." He allied himself to Tecumseh, and gradually under the war chief's influence broadened his doctrine of abstinence into an anti-white code that urged Indians to return to the ways of their fathers and end inter-tribal wars. Like other native prophets who had arisen among the Indians in earlier days of crisis, Tenskwatawa soon became a dynamic force for opposition to the whites, but many of his sermons were the words of Tecumseh, who now saw, more than ever before, that the Indians must maintain their self-respect and dignity if they were to have the strength to halt another westward advance by the whites. The two brothers joined forces and moved to Greenville, Ohio, at the very place where the chiefs had signed their treaty with Wayne in 1795; there they built a large frame meeting house and fifty or sixty cabins for their converts.

The Prophet's emotional appeals traveled quickly across the Northwest Territory, and he soon gained followers from almost every tribe. His growing influence and the dangerous concentration of natives around him disturbed General Harrison at his territorial headquarters in Vincennes, and he began to scoff publicly at the Shawnee, hoping that ridicule would undermine the natives' belief in him. He made little progress, however, and in April 1806 he challenged Tenskwatawa to perform a miracle. "If he is really a prophet," he wrote to one group of Indians, "ask him to cause the sun to stand still, the moon to alter its course, the rivers to cease to flow, or the dead to rise from their graves. If he does these things, you may then believe he has been sent from God."

Harrison's challenge was disastrous. From some white source, perhaps from a British agent in the North, the Prophet learned that a total eclipse of the sun would occur on June 16. In a bold and boastful response to Harrison, he proclaimed to the Indians that he would make the sun darken, and on the designated day a huge crowd of natives assembled at Greenville. Moving into their center, Tenskwatawa pointed commandingly at the sun, and at 11:32 in the morning, the moon began to darken the sun's face. The Indians were stricken with awe. As night descended over the gathering the Prophet called to the Master of Life to bring back the sun. In a moment light began to reappear. With the return of full daylight the Prophet's reputation and power were assured. Word of the miracle electrified the tribes of the Northwest, and as far away as Minnesota entire bands gave their loyalty to the Shawnee's code. But it was only the beginning.

Miracle begat miracle, and as agents of the Prophet traveled from tribe to tribe, carrying sacred strings of beans to peoples as remote as the Arikaras, Sioux, Mandans, and Blackfeet on the upper Missouri and the plains of central Canada, the Indians accepted any new wonder that was credited to the mystic Shawnee. In the Northwest Territory particularly, the Prophet's preachings inspired the natives with new pride and purpose, and as Tecumseh hoped, helped to strengthen the feeling of unity among them. Moreover, as Tenskwatawa's personal power increased, he began to stir his followers with demagogic appeals against Christianized Indians and others who weakened the native cause by their friendship for the whites. Violence flared at first against Christian Delawares in Indiana, and soon spread to the Wyandots, Kickapoos, and other tribes, where the Prophet's followers slew natives who were considered bewitched or under the influence of white men. Several hundred Indians were killed before Tecumseh personally stopped the purge. But an idea had been launched, and Tecumseh now continued it by peaceful methods, encouraging and aiding the transfer of power within tribes from weak and venal chiefs who were too friendly to the Americans to young warriors who had promised loyalty to himself and his brother.

Harrison became alarmed as his agents sent reports of the tribes that had deposed their old chiefs and gone over to the Prophet. Tension between Great Britain and the United States, ever-present since the end of the Revolution, had reached a critical point again, and Harrison and most western settlers were certain that the British in Canada were the real troublemakers behind Tenskwatawa. "I really fear that this said Prophet is an engine set to work by the British for some bad purpose," Harrison wrote the Secretary of War on July 11, 1807. As the clouds of international conflict continued to travel across the Appalachians from Washington, the settlers' dread of a new frontier war with the English and Indians heightened, and they looked on the

Prophet's successes with increasing suspicion and hostility. Gradually Tecumseh felt the growing animosity toward the natives, and recognized its ultimate consequences. In their fear of the British, the Americans would again attack the Indians, and try to drive them out of more of their lands. He saw only one hope—a dream which had been influenced by his knowledge of both the Iroquois League and the formation of the United States, and which he had long nourished for the Indians during his many travels and frontier fights. The unity among the Indians which he and his brothers were beginning to achieve must be broadened and strengthened. All the tribes must be brought together to be ready to fight as a single people in defense of their common lands. To avoid premature conflict he ordered Tenskwatawa to evacuate Greenville, which was too close to settlers in Ohio, and move his center westward to a tract of land that the Potawatomi and Kickapoo Indians had offered him in Indiana. The site lay along the west bank of the Tippecanoe River; its name was an English corruption of a Potawatomi word that meant "great clearing." In May 1808, at the stream's confluence with the Wabash River, Tenskwatawa and the families of eighty of his followers raised the mission house and bark dwellings of a new Prophet's Town. As soon as it was established, Tecumseh and his brother, accompanied by several companions and attendants, set out on horseback to unite the tribes for defense.

Forty-five years before, Pontiac had sent deputies to urge the chiefs and their warriors to war against the English. Now Tecumseh himself, already a war chief of great prestige, appeared at village after village, exciting the people with the presence of the Prophet and himself, and appealing for their support with thrilling patriotic oratory. At many places, chiefs who had signed the Treaty of Greenville and wanted no more war with the Americans opposed him, and he suffered many rebuffs. Elsewhere, whole tribes responded with enthusiasm to his speeches or divided their loyalties between their old chiefs and eager, young warriors who agreed with Tecumseh's appeals. In Illinois he won the Potawatomis to him, and rode away with a new and influential companion, a young Ottawa chief named Shabbona, who had married into the Potawatomi nation. In Wisconsin the civil chiefs of the Sauk and Foxes opposed the mission, but Tecumseh gained another resolute convert in a war leader named Black Hawk, who would one day fight his own war against the Americans. Most of the Menominees and Winnebagos near Green Bay pledged support, and back in Indiana the Kickapoos and Ottawas also agreed to join if war came. The Mississinewa and Miami Indians, who still looked to Little Turtle for leadership, had by now degenerated into weak and dissolute peoples, and Tecumseh made no impression on them. But almost the whole tribe of Wyandots and many villages of Delawares, Weas, Chippewas, Illinois, and Piankashaws, smarting under the frustrations of debauchery and idleness, found new pride in the Shawnee's patriotic appeals and promised to take up arms again in defense of their lands.

After covering the Northwest country, Tecumseh turned south and west, and in 1809, accompanied by a small band of followers, visited dozens of tribes, from the Seminoles in Florida to the Osages in Missouri. He received attention and sympathy and made many friends, and among most of the peoples he visited he managed to sow the seeds of future action against the Americans. Before the end of the year he was back in the North and heading into New York State, where he tried in vain to enlist the Iroquois tribes in his alliance. After being rebuffed by the Senecas and Onondagas he returned to Indiana and rejoined the Prophet on the Tippecanoe River. Despite his tireless journeys, he still had much work to do to achieve the unity he envisioned. He had to revisit many of the tribes he had met, make new appeals to those who had turned him down, and secure more binding agreements with his allies. But he had already made remarkable progress. From Lake Superior to the Gulf of Mexico he had laid the groundwork for the common defense of the Indians' country by the greatest military alliance in native history.

While he had been away the situation had worsened in Indiana. The war scare had abated, but additional pressures were threatening the natives. There were now more than twenty thousand Americans in southern Indiana, and if they were to receive statehood, for which they were clamoring, they would have to secure more Indian land on which to support a larger white population. The politically ambitious Governor Harrison was as aggressive as any of the settlers, and during the summer of 1809 he decided to force the Indians into a new cession. He sent his agents to Little Turtle and a host of the older and weaker chiefs and, armed with maps of central Indiana, met them at Fort Wayne in September. Harrison's letters reveal that he had little conscience in his dealings with the Indians, and that he was not above deceit. He "mellowed" the chiefs with alcohol, and after he had placed considerable pressure on them, they proved obliging. For $7,000 in cash and an annuity of $1,750, they ceded three million acres of land in Indiana, much of it owned by tribes that were not even present.

The new cession enraged Tecumseh, who heard about it while he was returning from New York. Included in the ceded territory were some of the Shawnees' best hunting grounds. Moreover, while he had been trying to unite the Indians in defense of the country they still owned, Indians behind his back had sold more of it, demonstrating once more that as long as individual tribes and chiefs were allowed to sell land as their own the Americans would find weak and greedy traitors to the native cause. More determined than ever, Tecumseh circulated word that Indian country was the common property of all the tribes, and that he and his allies would refuse to recognize the latest piece of treachery. Angry Indians who agreed with him flocked to the Tippecanoe, and in the spring of 1810 Tecumseh had a force of a thousand warriors at the Prophet's Town, training to repel, if necessary, any attempt by Americans to settle the newly ceded lands.

The hostile preparations disturbed Harrison, and he was further concerned by reports that the Wyandots, Creeks, and Choctaws were in sympathy with the Shawnees, and that a force of eleven hundred Sauk, Foxes, and Winnebagos was marching to the Prophet's Town. Harrison still thought that Tenskwatawa was the main agitator of the native opposition, and in an attempt to calm him he sent a messenger to the Tippecanoe settlement, inviting the Prophet to visit the President of the United States in Washington. Early in August he was surprised to learn from his agent that the Prophet's brother Tecumseh was the real leader of the Indians, and that the two men were coming to see him at Vincennes.

On August 11, 1810, the Shawnee brothers, accompanied by several hundred armed and painted warriors, swept down the Wabash River in a fleet of eighty canoes. At Fort Knox, three miles north of Vincennes, an Army captain observed them and reported that, true enough, "they were headed by the brother of the Prophet—Tecumseh —who, perhaps, is one of the finest-looking men I ever saw." Preliminaries and rain delayed the council for several days, but when it began it was tense and dramatic. In a grove near the governor's mansion Tecumseh and Harrison faced one another, both strong, willful leaders of national forces that had met in head-on collision. The two men were proud and suspicious, and as their followers stood nervously in the background, eyeing each other for sign of treachery, the air bristled with hostility. Tecumseh spoke first, beginning slowly, but soon pouring out his words in such swift and passionate flights of oratory that the interpreter had difficulty following him.

The Shawnee first reviewed the history of Indian-white relations in the Ohio Valley, and reminded Harrison of every wrong suffered by the natives at the hands of the Americans. Now, he told the governor, he was trying to unite the Indians, but the American leader was fomenting enmities among them. Tecumseh's words were lofty and eloquent, but we have only the interpreter's stilted translation of his ideas. "You endeavor to make distinctions," the translation of the speech reads.

> You endeavor to prevent the Indians from doing what we, their leaders, wish them to do—unite and consider their land the common property. . . . I am a Shawnee. My forefathers were warriors. Their son is a warrior. From them I take only my existence. From my tribe I take nothing. I have made myself what I am. And I would that I could make the red people as great as the conceptions of my mind, when I think of the Great Spirit that rules over all. I would not then come to Governor Harrison to ask him to tear the treaty. But I would say to him, Brother, you have liberty to return to your own country.

Several times Tecumseh turned to his dream of uniting the tribes in order to halt the whites. "The way, the only way to stop this evil," he told Harrison,

> is for all the red men to unite in claiming a common and equal right in the land, as it was at first, and should be now—for it never was divided, but belongs to all. No tribe has a right to sell, even to each other, much less to strangers, who demand all, and will take no less. . . . Sell a country! Why not sell the air, the clouds and the great sea, as well as the earth? Did not the Great Spirit make them all for the use of his children?

Toward the end of his speech, he apparently tried to nettle Harrison. "How can we have confidence in the white people?" he asked him. "When Jesus Christ came upon the earth, you killed Him, and nailed Him to a cross. You thought He was dead, but you were mistaken. You have Shakers among you, and you laugh and make light of their worship." Finally he pointed to the United States as a model for the natives. "The states," he said, "have set the example of forming a union among all the fires [states]—why should they censure the Indians for following it?" He ended brusquely. "I shall now be glad to know immediately what is your determination about the land."

Harrison began his reply by insisting that Tecumseh had no right to contest the sale of land in Indiana, because the Shawnee homeland had been in Georgia. The Indian chief stirred angrily, recognizing the deliberate evasion of his thesis that Indian land everywhere belonged to all natives. As Harrison went on he became more impatient, and tension among the onlookers began to mount. Suddenly Harrison asserted that the United States had always been fair in its dealings with Indians. Tecumseh leaped to his feet and shouted, "It is false! He lies!" As he poured his wrath on Harrison, the governor unsheathed his sword and started forward. Several whites aimed their guns, and the Indians behind Tecumseh drew their tomahawks. For an instant a fight seemed imminent. Then Harrison coolly declared the council adjourned and strode to his house. As the other whites followed him, Tecumseh motioned his warriors back to their camp.

The next morning Tecumseh's temper had subsided, and he sent his apologies to Harrison. The governor accepted them, and visited the chief's camp. Tecumseh was in a good mood, and the two men sat down together on a bench. Gradually the Indian kept pushing against Harrison, forcing the American to move closer to one end. Finally, as Harrison was about to be shoved off, he objected, and Tecumseh laughed, pointing out that that was what the American settlers were doing to the Indians.

The council reconvened the same day, but accomplished nothing, and Tecumseh and his party soon left Vincennes and returned to the Prophet's Town. Harrison had made no concessions to the natives. He sent the War Department the Indians' complaint that "the Americans had driven them from the seacoast, and would shortly, if not stopped, push them into the lakes," and though he added, "they were determined to make a stand where they were," the prospect that such a stand might be made did not seem to worry him. Six weeks later, alluding to Northwest Territory lands that the Indians still held, he asked the members of the Indiana legislature, "Is one of the fairest portions of the globe to remain in a state of nature, the haunt of a few wretched savages, when it seems destined, by the Creator, to give support to a large population, and to be the sea of civilization, of science, and true religion?"

The issue was joined. Harrison's attitude served notice that he intended to keep pressing for more Indian land, and Tecumseh knew that to stop him he had to hurry his alliances and strengthen the natives' will to resist. Once more the Shawnee leader made rapid visits to the tribes of Ohio, Indiana, and Michigan, delivering passionate pleas for his confederation. On November 15, 1810, he even crossed to the Canadian side of the Detroit River and at the British post of Fort Malden addressed a council of Potawatomis, Ottawas, Sauk, Foxes, and Winnebagos. Harrison and most of the settlers were confident now that the British were instigating Tecumseh, though this time the reverse was actually the case. Documentary evidence, found in later days, showed clearly that before the War of 1812 the British Government definitely opposed any Indian action that would imperil English relations with the United States or disrupt the lucrative Great Lakes fur trade, and that from Downing Street to Fort Malden British officials were irritated by Tecumseh's activities and tried to discourage his agitation against the Americans. Nevertheless, appearances convinced the settlers that unless something was soon done, the Indians with British assistance would again threaten the entire Ohio Valley. To Harrison the best defense was vigorous offense, and in 1811 he decided that the time had come to smash the Prophet's Town and scatter the leaders of Indian opposition.

All he needed was an overt act by the natives to justify his invasion of the Indians' country, and in July 1811 he gained his excuse when Potawatomis killed some white men in Illinois. Harrison claimed at once that they were followers of the Prophet, and demanded that the Shawnees on the Tippecanoe surrender them to him for justice. In reply, Tecumseh and the Prophet again visited Vincennes for a personal meeting with the American leader. They refused to deliver the Potawatomis, and once more the council ended in an impasse. The Prophet returned to his center on the Tippecanoe, and Tecumseh, accompanied by twenty-four warriors, set off down the Wabash River, bound on a second attempt to unite the southern tribes behind him. As soon as the Indian leader had disappeared, Harrison began preparations for his expedition to the Tippecanoe. "I hope," he wrote the Secretary of War regarding the departed Tecumseh, "before his return that that part of the fabrick which he considered complete will be demolished and even its foundations rooted up."

Tecumseh's second southern journey was an heroic and memorable effort; in six months it took him down the Ohio and Mississippi Rivers to the present site of Memphis, through Tennessee to Mississippi, Alabama, Georgia, and Florida, back north again across Georgia to the Carolinas, through the full length of Tennessee to the Ozark Mountains of Arkansas and Missouri, north into Iowa, and eventually back home. Once more he hurried from village to village, visiting strong interior tribes such as the Choctaws, Chickasaws, Cherokees, Creeks, Osages, and Iowas, and pleading with them for a united war against the Americans. Generally he met with opposition, and was disappointed. Great councils, sometimes numbering more than five thousand natives, gathered to listen to him, and white traders and Indian agents who also managed to be present reported the fervor and eloquence with which the Shawnee spoke.

His words "fell in avalanches from his lips," General Sam Dale said. "His eyes burned with supernatural lustre, and his whole frame trembled with emotion. His voice resounded over the multitude—now sinking in low and musical whispers, now rising to the highest key, hurling out his words like a succession of thunderbolts. . . . I have heard many great orators, but I never saw one with the vocal powers of Tecumseh." Wearing only a breechclout and moccasins, with lines of red war paint beneath his eyes, the Shawnee stood alone with his followers amid the throngs and cried to the Indians to stop their inter-tribal wars, to unite in a single nation as the states had done, and to fight together for all their land before it was too late. Old chiefs listened to him uneasily, and argued back. They would not unite with old, hereditary enemies. They would not give up their autonomy in a federation that would make them subordinate to strangers. The kind of union that Tecumseh talked about was for white men, not Indians. And besides, it was already too late.

In historic debates with the greatest chiefs of the South, Tecumseh continued to plead his cause, and on several occasions white agents who were present were able to record some of his thoughts, but again in the flowery language of awkward translations:

> Where today are the Pequot? Where the Narrangansett, the Mohican, the Pokanoket and many other once powerful tribes of our people? They have vanished before the avarice and oppression of the white man, as snow before a summer sun. . . . Will we let ourselves be destroyed in our turn without making an effort worthy of our race? Shall we, without a struggle, give up our homes, our country bequeathed to us by the Great Spirit, the graves of our dead and everything that is dear and sacred to us? I know you will cry with me, Never! Never!

The white observer, writing down the speech, had difficulty translating the Indian's expressions, but as the Shawnee continued the meaning of his words was not lost. "That people," he warned his listeners, "will continue longest in the enjoyment of peace who timely prepare to vindicate themselves and manifest a determination to protect themselves whenever they are wronged."

Again and again young warriors shouted their approval, and small groups promised to strike the Americans when Tecumseh gave them the signal. But the older leaders were wary and afraid. Some of them were receiving annuities and gifts from the Americans, some saw only ruin in Tecumseh's plans, and some thought that their people could do well enough by themselves. Only the Creeks and Seminoles, already smoldering with hatred for the Americans, provided the Shawnee with hope. To them he gave bundles of red-painted sticks. When they received word from him they were to start throwing one stick away each day, and when all were gone it would be the day on which all the tribes in every part of the frontier would commence a simultaneous attack on the whites.

Disappointed by his failures in the South, Tecumseh returned to the Tippecanoe River early in 1812, only to be met by news of a more stunning setback at home. During the Shawnee leader's absence, Harrison had finally struck at the Prophet's Town. At the head of an army of almost a thousand men the American governor had marched up the Wabash River, and on the night of November 6, 1811, had camped near the Indian settlement at the mouth of the Tippecanoe. The ominous arrival of the hostile force alarmed the Indians; at first, without Tecumseh to direct them, they were undecided what to do. A band of Winnebagos, bolder than the others, argued for an immediate attack on the invading whites, and finally won Tenskwatawa's approval. In the early hours of morning, some 450 natives crawled through the darkness toward the Americans. Harrison had placed his men in an unbroken line around the three sides of his triangular-shaped camp, and shortly before four o'clock a sentry on the northern perimeter saw an Indian moving in the gloom and shot him. In an instant the whooping natives were on their feet, charging toward the whites. The Americans met them with blazing musketry, and only a few of the Indians were able to crash into the camp, where Harrison's men battled them in hand-to-hand struggles. The rest were chased back, and though they launched a series of rushes at other sides of the camp they failed to break through. As the sky lightened they finally withdrew among the trees, and kept up a desultory fire from cover during the day. By the second day they had all disappeared, and Harrison moved his men, unopposed, into the abandoned Prophet's Town. He fired the buildings and destroyed all the natives' possessions, including their stores of food.

The number of Indian dead in the battle was never known, though it was estimated to be between 25 and 40. Harrison lost 61 killed and 127 wounded, but on his return to the settlements he announced that he had won a great victory and wrote to the Secretary of War that "the Indians have never sustained so severe a defeat since their acquaintance with the white people." The importance of the battle was soon exaggerated beyond reality, and in the flush of excitement many of the western settlers began to think that Harrison had beaten Tecumseh himself. The facts of what had been little more than an inconclusive swipe at a small segment of Tecumseh's followers never fully caught up with the legend of a dramatic triumph, and in 1840 the magic of Tippecanoe's memory still worked well enough to help elect Harrison to the Presidency.

Indian Removal
and Land Allotment
in the South

MARY E. YOUNG

Much has been written about the removal of the Cherokee
Indian nation from Georgia. One reason is that this episode
furnishes a dramatic illustration of conflict between the executive and judicial branches of the government, represented by
President Andrew Jackson and Chief Justice John Marshall. But
the removal of the Creeks, Choctaws, and Chickasaws from the
South has been less widely noted, although it offers valuable
insights into conflicts between red and white culture in the
United States as well as into the government's method of
handling Indian affairs.

Unlike the Indians of the old Northwest who joined together
to fight under Tecumseh, the Five Civilized Tribes of the South
—the Cherokee, Choctaw, Creek, Chickasaw, and Seminole
nations—adopted the goal of assimilation. By tradition these
Indians were village agriculturalists rather than nomads, so it
was relatively easy for them to adjust to white ways. Many of
them embraced white culture completely, drawing up constitutions, accepting the white man's religion and style of dress, and
even owning Negro slaves. Only the Seminoles maintained a
warrior tradition. The other nations settled down to farm their
rich lands, feeling secure under the eighteenth-century treaties.
By denying their own cultural traditions, the Indians eliminated
much of the basis for white displeasure. Yet they stood in the
way of the advancing white frontier, and methods of removing
them were found. Ironically, they were ultimately dispossessed
as a result of a cultural difference that remained between them
and the colonists—a difference in the idea of land ownership.

When the English colonists first arrived in the New World,
they brought with them the recently developed Anglo-Saxon

17

notion of private ownership. In fact, many of the white settlers had themselves been driven off land in the Old World during the eighteenth century as a result of the consolidation of communally held lands into large, single-owner estates. Thus the colonists believed that land could be permanently and exclusively owned by individuals. In contrast, the Indians understood possession of the land as a matter of use rather than ownership. Since the New World seemed to contain plenty of land for all, the Indians originally greeted the white man hospitably.

As white settlers occupied more and more land and barred the Indians from their claims, the implications of exclusive ownership became clear. Even then, however, the Indians rarely grasped the notion of individual land ownership. Rather, they considered their land the property of the community, and they left all decisions about its use to community councils.

The following study describes the beginning of the process by which federal and state governments in the nineteenth century cooperated to divide community-owned lands among individual Indians, who were then persuaded, sometimes fraudulently, to sell their property to speculators.

In the twentieth century, the federal government has used the same method of individualizing land ownership in pursuit of its policy of "terminating" Indian reservations. Again, the result has been the reduction of the amount of land under Indian ownership.

By the year 1830, the vanguard of the southern frontier had crossed the Mississippi and was pressing through Louisiana, Arkansas, and Missouri. But the line of settlement was by no means as solid as frontier lines were classically supposed to be. East of the Mississippi, white occupancy was limited by Indian tenure of northeastern Georgia, enclaves in western North Carolina and southern Tennessee, eastern Alabama, and the northern two thirds of Mississippi. In this twenty-five-million-acre domain lived nearly 60,000 Cherokees, Creeks, Choctaws, and Chickasaws.

The Jackson administration sought to correct this anomaly by removing the tribes beyond the reach of white settlements, west of the Mississippi. As the President demanded of Congress in December,

"Indian Removal and Land Allotment: The Civilized Tribes and Jacksonian Justice" by Mary E. Young from *The American Historical Review*, October 1958. Reprinted by permission of the author.

1830: "What good man would prefer a country covered with forests and ranged by a few thousand savages to our extensive Republic, studded with cities, towns, and prosperous farms, embellished with all the improvements which art can devise or industry execute, occupied by more than 12,000,000 happy people, and filled with all the blessings of liberty, civilization, and religion?"

The President's justification of Indian removal was the one usually applied to the displacement of the Indians by newer Americans—the superiority of a farming to a hunting culture, and of Anglo-American "liberty, civilization, and religion" to the strange and barbarous way of the red man. The superior capacity of the farmer to exploit the gifts of nature and of nature's God was one of the principal warranties of the triumph of westward-moving "civilization."

Such a rationalization had one serious weakness as an instrument of policy. The farmer's right of eminent domain over the lands of the savage could be asserted consistently only so long as the tribes involved were "savage." The southeastern tribes, however, were agriculturists as well as hunters. For two or three generations prior to 1830, farmers among them fenced their plantations and "mixed their labor with the soil," making it their private property according to accepted definitions of natural law. White traders who settled among the Indians in the mid-eighteenth century gave original impetus to this imitation of Anglo-American agricultural methods. Later, agents of the United States encouraged the traders and mechanics, their half-breed descendants, and their fullblood imitators, who settled out from the tribal villages, fenced their farms, used the plow, and cultivated cotton and corn for the market. In the decade following the War of 1812, missionaries of various Protestant denominations worked among the Cherokees, Choctaws, and Chickasaws, training hundreds of Indian children in the agricultural, mechanical, and household arts and introducing both children and parents to the further blessings of literacy and Christianity.

The "civilization" of a portion of these tribes embarrassed United States policy in more ways than one. Long-term contact between the southeastern tribes and white traders, missionaries, and government officials created and trained numerous half-breeds. The half-breed men acted as intermediaries between the less sophisticated Indians and the white Americans. Acquiring direct or indirect control of tribal politics, they often determined the outcome of treaty negotiations. Since they proved to be skillful bargainers, it became common practice to win their assistance by thinly veiled bribery. The rise of the half-breeds to power, the rewards they received, and their efforts on behalf of tribal reform gave rise to bitter opposition. By the mid-1820's, this opposition made it dangerous for them to sell tribal lands. Furthermore, many of the new leaders had valuable plantations, mills, and trading establishments on these lands. Particularly among the Cherokees and Choctaws, they took pride in their achievements and those of their people in assimilating the trappings of civilization. As "founding Fathers," they prized the political and territorial integrity of the newly organized Indian "nations." These interests and convictions gave birth to a fixed determination, embodied in tribal laws and intertribal agreements, that no more cessions of land should be made. The tribes must be permitted to develop their new way of life in what was left of their ancient domain.

Today it is a commonplace of studies in culture contact that the assimilation of alien habits affects different individuals and social strata in different ways and that their levels of acculturation vary considerably. Among the American Indian tribes, it is most often the families with white or half-breed models who most readily adopt the Anglo-American way of life. It is not surprising that half-breeds and whites living among the Indians should use their position as go-betweens to improve their status and power among the natives. Their access to influence and their efforts toward reform combine with pressures from outside to disturb old life ways, old securities, and established prerogatives. Resistance to their leadership and to the cultural alternatives they espouse is a fertile source of intratribal factions.

To Jacksonian officials, however, the tactics of the half-breeds and the struggles among tribal factions seemed to reflect a diabolical plot. Treaty negotiators saw the poverty and "depravity" of the common Indian, who suffered from the scarcity of game, the missionary attacks on his accustomed habits and ceremonies, and the ravages of "demon rum" and who failed to find solace in the values of Christian and commercial civilization. Not unreasonably, they concluded that it was to the interest of the tribesman to move west of the Mississippi. There, sheltered from the intruder and the whisky merchant, he could lose his savagery while improving his nobility. Since this seemed so obviously to the Indian's interest, the negotiators conveniently concluded that it was also his desire. What, then, deterred emigration? Only the rapacity of the half-breeds, who were unwilling to give up their extensive properties and their exalted position.

These observers recognized that the government's difficulties were in part of its own making. The United States had pursued an essentially contradictory policy toward the Indians, encouraging both segregation and assimilation. Since Jefferson's administration, the government had tried periodically to secure the emigration of the eastern tribes across the Mississippi. At the same time, it had paid agents and subsidized missionaries who encouraged the Indian to follow the white man's way. Thus it had helped create the class of tribesmen skilled in agriculture, pecuniary accumulation, and political leadership. Furthermore, by encouraging the southeastern Indians to become cultivators and Christians, the government had undermined its own moral claim to eminent domain over tribal lands. The people it now hoped to displace could by no stretch of dialectic be classed as mere wandering savages.

By the time Jackson became President, then, the situation of the United States vis-à-vis the southeastern tribes was superficially that of irresistible force and immovable object. But the President, together with such close advisers as Secretary of War John H. Eaton and General John Coffee, viewed the problem in a more encouraging perspective. They believed that the government faced not the intent of whole tribes to remain near the bones of their ancestors but the selfish determination of a few quasi-Indian leaders to retain their riches and their ill-used power. Besides, the moral right of the civilized tribes to their lands was a claim not on their whole domain but rather on the part cultivated by individuals. Both the Indian's natural right to his land and his political capacity for keeping it were products of his imitation of white "civilization." Both might be eliminated by a rigorous application of the principle that to treat an Indian fairly was to treat him like a white man. Treaty negotiations by the tried methods of purchase and selective bribery had failed. The use of naked force without the form of voluntary agreement was forbidden by custom, by conscience, and by fear that the administration's opponents would exploit religious sentiment which cherished the rights of the red man. But within the confines of legality and the formulas of voluntarism it was still possible to acquire the much coveted domain of the civilized tribes.

The technique used to effect this object was simple: the entire population of the tribes was forced to deal with white men on terms familiar only to the most acculturated portion of them. If the Indian is civilized, he can behave like a white man. Then let him take for his own as much land as he can cultivate, become a citizen of the state where he lives, and accept the burdens which citizenship entails. If he is not capable of living like this, he should be liberated from the tyranny of his chiefs and allowed to follow his own best interest by emigrating beyond the farthest frontiers of white settlement. By the restriction of the civilized to the lands they cultivate and by the emigration of the savages millions of acres will be opened to white settlement.

The first step dictated by this line of reasoning was the extension of state laws over the Indian tribes. Beginning soon after Jackson's election, Georgia, Alabama, Mississippi, and Tennessee gradually brought the Indians inside their borders under their jurisdiction. Thus an Indian could be sued for trespass or debt, though only in Mississippi and Tennessee was his testimony invariably acceptable in a court of law. In Mississippi, the tribesmen were further harassed by subjection —or the threat of subjection—to such duties as mustering with the militia, working on roads, and paying taxes. State laws establishing country governments within the tribal domains and, in some cases, giving legal protection to purchasers of Indian improvements encouraged the intrusion of white settlers on Indian lands. The laws nullified the legal force of Indian customs, except those relating to marriage. They provided heavy penalties for anyone who might enact or enforce tribal law. Finally, they threatened punishment to any person who might attempt to deter another from signing a removal treaty or enrolling for emigration. The object of these laws was to destroy the tribal governments and to thrust upon individual Indians the uncongenial alternative of adjusting to the burdens of citizenship or removing beyond state jurisdiction.

The alternative was not offered on the unenlightened supposition that the Indians generally were capable of managing their affairs unaided in a white man's world. Governor Gayle of Alabama, addressing the "former chiefs and headmen of the Creek Indians" in June of 1834, urged them to remove from the state on the grounds that

> you speak a different language from ours. You do not understand our laws and from your habits, cannot be brought to understand them. You are ignorant of the arts of civilized life. You have not like your white neighbors been raised in habits of industry and economy, the only means by which anyone can live, in settled countries, in even tolerable comfort. You know nothing of the skill of the white man in trading and making bargains, and cannot be guarded against the artful contrivances which dishonest men will resort to, to obtain your property under forms of contracts. In all

these respects you are unequal to the white men, and if your people remain where they are, you will soon behold them in a miserable, degraded, and destitute condition.

The intentions of federal officials who favored the extension of state laws are revealed in a letter written to Jackson by General Coffee. Referring to the Cherokees, Coffee remarked:

> Deprive the chiefs of the power they now possess, take from them their own code of laws, and reduce them to plain citizenship . . . and they will soon determine to move, and then there will be no difficulty in getting the poor Indians to give their consent. All this will be done by the State of Georgia if the U. States do not interfere with her law. . . . This will of course silence those in our country who constantly seek for causes to complain—It may indeed turn them loose upon Georgia, but that matters not, it is Georgia who clamors for the Indian lands, and she alone is entitled to the blame if any there be.

Even before the laws were extended, the threat of state jurisdiction was used in confidential "talks" to the chiefs. After the states had acted, the secretary of war instructed each Indian agent to explain to his charges the meaning of state jurisdiction and to inform them that the President could not protect them against the enforcement of the laws. Although the Supreme Court, in *Worcester* vs. *Georgia,* decided that the state had no right to extend its laws over the Cherokee nation, the Indian tribes being "domestic dependent nations" with limits defined by treaty, the President refused to enforce this decision. There was only one means by which the government might have made "John Marshall's decision" effective—directing federal troops to exclude state officials and other intruders from the Indian domain. In January, 1832, the President informed an Alabama congressman that the United States government no longer assumed the right to remove citizens of Alabama from the Indian country. By this time, the soldiers who had protected the territory of the southeastern tribes against intruders had been withdrawn. In their unwearying efforts to pressure the Indians into ceding their lands, federal negotiators emphasized the terrors of state jurisdiction.

Congress in May, 1830, complemented the efforts of the states by appropriating $500,000 and authorizing the President to negotiate removal treaties with all the tribes east of the Mississippi. The vote on this bill was close in both houses. By skillful use of pamphlets, petitions, and lobbyists, missionary organizations had enlisted leading congressmen in their campaign against the administration's attempt to force the tribes to emigrate. In the congressional debates, opponents of the bill agreed that savage tribes were duty-bound to relinquish their hunting grounds to the agriculturist, but they argued that the southeastern tribes were no longer savage. In any case, such relinquishment must be made in a freely contracted treaty. The extension of state laws over the Indian country was coercion; this made the negotiation of a free contract impossible. Both supporters and opponents of the bill agreed on one cardinal point—the Indian's moral right to keep his land depended on his actual cultivation of it.

A logical corollary of vesting rights in land in proportion to cultivation was the reservation to individuals of as much land as they had improved at the time a treaty was signed. In 1816, Secretary of War William H. Crawford had proposed such reservations, or allotments, as a means of accommodating the removal policy to the program of assimilation. According to Crawford's plan, individual Indians who had demonstrated their capacity for civilization by establishing farms and who were willing to become citizens should be given the option of keeping their cultivated lands, by fee simple title, rather than emigrating. This offer was expected to reconcile the property-loving half-breeds to the policy of emigration. It also recognized their superior claim, as cultivators, on the regard and generosity of the government. The proposal was based on the assumption that few of the Indians were sufficiently civilized to want to become full-time farmers or state citizens.

The Crawford policy was applied in the Cherokee treaties of 1817 and 1819 and the Choctaw treaty of 1820. These agreements offered fee simple allotments to heads of Indian families having improved lands within the areas ceded to the government. Only 311 Cherokees and eight Choctaws took advantage of the offer. This seemed to bear out the assumption that only a minority of the tribesmen would care to take allotments. Actually, these experiments were not reliable. In both cases, the tribes ceded only a fraction of their holdings. Comparatively few took allotments; but on the other hand, few emigrated. The majority simply remained within the diminished tribal territories east of the Mississippi.

The offer of fee simple allotments was an important feature of the negotiations with the tribes in the 1820's. When the extension of state laws made removal of the tribes imperative, it was to be expected that allotments would comprise part of the consideration offered for the ceded lands. Both the ideology which rationalized the removal policy and the conclusions erroneously drawn from experience with the earlier allotment treaties led government negotiators to assume that a few hundred allotments at most would be required.

The Choctaws were the first to cede their eastern lands. The treaty of Dancing Rabbit Creek, signed in September, 1830, provided for several types of allotment. Special reservations were given to the chiefs and their numerous family connections; a possible 1,600 allotments of 80 to 480 acres, in proportion to the size of the beneficiary's farm, were offered others who intended to emigrate. These were intended for sale to private persons or to the government, so that the Indian might get the maximum price for his improvements. The fourteenth article of the treaty offered any head of an Indian family who did not plan to emigrate the right to take up a quantity of land proportional to the number of his dependents. At the end of five years' residence those who received these allotments were to have fee simple title to their lands and become citizens. It was expected that approximately two hundred persons would take land under this article.

❖   ❖   ❖

Widespread intrusion on Indian lands began with the extension of state laws over the tribal domains. In the treaties of cession, the government promised to remove intruders, but its policy in this respect was vacillating and ineffective. Indians whose allotments covered valuable plantations proved anxious to promote the sale of their property by allowing buyers to enter the ceded territory as soon as possible. Once this group of whites was admitted, it became difficult to discriminate against others. Thus a large number of intruders settled among the Indians with the passive connivance of the War Department and the tribal leaders. The task of removing them was so formidable that after making a few gestures the government generally evaded its obligation. The misery of the common Indians, surrounded by intruders and confused by the disruption of tribal authority, was so acute that any method for securing their removal seemed worth trying. Furthermore, their emigration would serve the interest of white settlers, land speculators, and their representatives in Washington. The government therefore chose to facilitate the sale of allotments even before the Indians received fee simple title to them.

The Plains Indians

PETER FARB

After the appearance of the white man in the Western Hemisphere, different Indian groups went through various cultural changes as they struggled to preserve their identity and their lands. Perhaps the most impressive product of the Indians' adaptations to the white presence on the American continent was the elaborate culture that evolved among the nomadic tribes of the Great Plains once they acquired the white man's animal—the horse.

The Spaniards introduced horses in Mexico in the sixteenth century, and herds of the animals spread northward over the plains. Late in the seventeenth century, North American Indians began to breed Spanish horses. When white settlers reached the Great Plains over a century later, they met the first mounted Indians ever to be seen—the prototypes of the fierce, proud Indians encountered today in Western movies.

By the time of their first real contacts with whites, the Indians were well on their way to developing a complex culture that centered on the horse and the buffalo, the great native of the plains on which they relied for food, shelter, and clothing. The horse had literally transformed their lives by dramatically increasing their mobility and giving them greater effectiveness in waging war and in hunting the all-important buffalo. By the time of the Civil War, more than two-thirds of the Indians that remained in the United States belonged to the Great Plains civilization.

The tragic end of the Plains Indian culture at the close of the nineteenth century was marked by the massacre of Indians at Wounded Knee, South Dakota. Wovoka, the last of the great

Indian messiahs, had dreamed of a resurgence of the declining Indian culture, but the greater powers of the United States government held sway.

To many people, the typical Indian was the Plains Indian, a painted brave in full regalia, trailing a war bonnet, astride a horse which he rode bareback, sweeping down upon a wagon train, in glorious technicolor. In actual fact, the picturesque culture of the Plains Indian was artificial, not aboriginal, and it did not last very long. The amalgam known as the Plains culture was not fully accomplished until the early 1800's—and like the spring grass of the high plains, it withered quickly.

This culture emerged almost inconspicuously in the middle of the eighteenth century as its catalytic agent, the horse, spread northward from Spanish settlements in New Mexico. Within only a few generations, the horse was found throughout the central heartland of the continent, and Indians from all directions spilled onto the plains. They originally spoke many different languages and had various customs, but they all found in the horse a new tool to kill greater numbers of bison than they had ever believed possible. They became inconceivably rich in material goods, far beyond their wildest dreams, and like a dream it all faded. By about 1850, the Plains culture was already on the wane as the "manifest destiny" of a vigorous United States to push westward shoved them aside. The fate of the Plains Indians had been sealed with the arrival of the first miners and the first prairie schooner. The battles of extermination between Plains Indians and United States cavalry represent America's own great epic—its *Iliad*, its *Aeneid*, its Norse saga— but this epic was no more true than any other.

Despite the surrounded forts, the saving of the last bullet for oneself, the occasional acts of heroism, and the frequent acts of bestiality on both sides—despite this picture portrayed in the Great American Epic, there was remarkably little formal combat. Deaths and hardship there were in plenty as the Plains Indians met their catastrophic end,

From the book *Man's Rise to Civilization as Shown by the Indians of North America from Primeval Times to the Coming of the Industrial State* by Peter Farb, copyright © 1968 by Peter Farb. Reprinted by permission of E. P. Dutton & Co., Inc., and Martin Secker & Warburg Ltd.

but most deaths were due to starvation, exposure, disease, brutality, and alcoholism, and not to bullets. In all the actual battles between White soldiers and Indian braves, only several thousand deaths on both sides were due to bullets and arrows. The wars of the plains were not epics but mopping-up operations. In the process, the millions of bison very nearly vanished without leaving any survivors, the plains were turned into a dust bowl, and the once-proud Indian horsemen were broken in body and spirit.

The famed Plains Indian culture did not exist in all its glory when Coronado first explored the plains. Lured on by tales of rich lands, where kings were supposed to be lulled to sleep by the chimes of golden bells, Coronado eventually reached Kansas in 1541. Here the Spaniards saw the beast they had been hearing so much about: the remarkable "cow," actually a bison, as large as a Spanish bull, but with an enormous mane and small curved horns. They also met some impoverished Indians who lived in conical tipis "built like pavilions," according to the chronicler of the expedition. He was particularly impressed by the way the bison seemed to provide most of the materials needed by the Indians:

> With the skins they build their houses; with the skins they clothe and show themselves; from the skins they make ropes and also obtain wool. With the sinews they make threads, with which they sew their clothes and also their tents. From the bones they shape awls. The dung they use for firewood, since there is no other fuel in that land. The bladders they use as jugs and drinking containers.

Hunting bison on foot was not productive, and it certainly could not support large numbers of Indians. Such hunting was practiced largely by the wretched nomads who moved around in small groups and who lived off the occasional weakened bison they could kill or those they could stampede over bluffs. Most of the aboriginal cultures on the plains and prairies were based on the cultivation of maize, beans, and squash. Agriculture had spread westward from the eastern Woodlands, and it followed the fingerlike extensions of rivers throughout the arid Dakotas, Texas, and virtually to the foothills of the Rockies. Hunting bison, for these people, was only incidental to the primary subsistence based on agriculture. They went on a hunt about once a year to supplement their vegetable diet and to obtain hides, sinew, bone, and other raw materials.

Once the horse arrived on the plains, that way of life changed. The nomadic bison hunters became ascendant over the farmers, who either were driven off their lands or abandoned agriculture to become bison hunters themselves. Indians had never seen the horse until the Spaniards brought it to the New World, for sometime during the great glacial melt it had become extinct in North America. The Indians obtained the first horses after the Spaniards settled New Mexico in 1598. (Contrary to previous belief, the Indians captured no horses from de Soto, Coronado, or other early explorers, for these horses either died or were taken home again.) The Spaniards prohibited the sale of horses to Indians, but the revolt of the Pueblo Indians between 1680 and 1692 threw some of the animals on the Indian markets of North America. The Spaniards restocked their herds, which proliferated, but they were unable to prevent further horse stealing by Indians. Horses were bartered—or stolen—from Indian group to group. Soon a whole new Indian profession of horse merchant grew up, and the animals—as well as the knowledge of how to break and train them—spread northward from New Mexico. In addition, some Spanish horses had gone wild and roamed the plains in herds. The Spaniards called them *mesteños* ("wild"), from which the English word "mustangs" is derived.

By the first half of the eighteenth century, enterprising Indian merchants had already sold the horse to Indians as far north as the Northern Shoshone of Wyoming and taught them its management. The Shoshone slowly built up their herds and learned to ride as if they had been born to the saddle. No longer did they have to remain impoverished and secretive inhabitants of the Rocky Mountains, at the mercy of more powerful Indian groups. They swooped down the eastern flanks of the mountains and onto the high plains, where they found a bonanza in bison and a way to even the score with their traditional persecutors, the Blackfoot. From all over, other Indian groups converged on the plains and quickly adapted themselves to an economy based on the bison. The lands of the agriculturists were usurped, and the plains became a maelstrom of varied and often conflicting cultures.

A LIVING EXPERIMENT IN CULTURE CHANGE

The stolen, bartered, bought, or captured horse was a new cultural element in the heartland of North America, and it changed the entire way of life there. The whole of the plains, from Alberta to Texas, became peopled by groups of great diversity who had come from all directions and often from great distances. There were Athabaskans from the north (Kiowa-Apache), Algonkians (Cree, Cheyenne, Blackfoot) and Siouans (Mandan, Crow, Dakota) from the east, Uto-Aztecans (Comanche, Ute) from the west, Caddoans (Pawnee, Arikara) from the south. The plains became a melting pot for more than thirty different peoples, belonging to at least five language stocks. It has given anthropologists a living laboratory of culture change. Culture change is the way in which a group alters because of new circumstances, or the way it borrows traits from other cultures and fits them into the configurations of its own.

By about 1800 the gross differences in culture among all these peoples had disappeared; the Sun Dance ceremony, for example, was eventually observed by virtually every tribe. Of course differences apparent to the trained eye of the anthropologist still existed; yet it is remarkable that a people from the eastern forests and another from the Great Basin of the West, two thousand miles away, should within only a few generations have become so nearly identical. Even more remarkable, this homogeneity was achieved with great speed, was not imposed on unwilling people by a more powerful group, and was done in the absence of a common tongue—save for "sign language," the lingua franca of the Plains tribes.

The Plains Cree demonstrate how a people originally distant from the plains in both culture and geography eventually could become so typical of it. The Cree were first recorded in the *Jesuit Relations* of 1640, but at that time they had nothing to do with the plains at all. They inhabited the forests between Hudson Bay and Lake Superior, and they were roving hunters and gatherers of wild rice. Their culture was typical of the Northern Algonkian bands, and after the Hudson's Bay Company was founded they turned to trapping. The demand by Whites for more beaver pelts led them to push westward; because they had obtained guns from White traders, they were able to dispossess the previous inhabitants. By about the middle of the eighteenth century, some of the Cree had already penetrated to the west of Lake Winnipeg. Their culture had changed considerably. It was now parasitic on the White trader for weapons, clothing, and cooking utensils—and sometimes even food, because the Cree spent his time trapping rather than hunting. Then the Cree living farthest west discovered the resource of the bison. Historical records reveal that as early as 1772 they had developed primitive ways of hunting bison, although they still did not possess the horse. Within only a generation, though, the Plains Cree had emerged—a typical equestrian Plains tribe, very different in customs and outlook from the Cree that still inhabited the forests, although both groups continued to speak the same language.

And all this was due to the horse. No longer were just stray or stampeded bison taken, but the herds were pursued on swift horses and the choicest animals killed. No longer was the whole animal utilized for raw materials, which had so impressed the chronicler of the Coronado expedition, but the Indians could now afford the luxury of waste. They stocked the tipi with supplies for the future: meat dried in the sun (jerkee), or else pounded and mixed with fat and berries to become pemmican. Even though most of the Plains Indians never saw a White close up until their swift decline, his influence was felt profoundly as his goods and trade articles flowed westward across the plains by barter from one tribe to another. Tipis almost twenty-five feet in diameter were filled to overflowing with new-found riches. An economic revolution, for which the Indians' tradition had not prepared them, took place. The women no longer toiled in the fields—for gardening was not as profitable as hunting, nor could it be practiced in the presence of nomadic horsemen—and they stopped making pottery because brass kettles were obtained from Whites. Permanent villages disappeared, and with them went the elaborate customs and crafts, rules for marriage and residence.

After the Indians discovered the effectiveness of rifles, an armaments race began on the plains. Just as Indians earlier had realized the value of horses, and those lacking them were driven to obtain them by any means, the acquisition of rifles upset the entire balance of power. As soon as one tribe acquired firepower, the competition for others to obtain equal armaments became fierce. Not only the rifles had to be acquired, but there was also a continuing need for powder and for lead. The Indians were driven to take ever greater chances in raids to steal horses which they might barter for guns and ammunition. For a period of nearly fifty years, the plains became an arena of turmoil in which the status quo changed from year to year, as successive groups became supreme in supplies of horses or guns, or in the powerful allies they could muster.

The Plains Indians in their heyday were a study in hyperbole, and as make-believe as the set for a western movie. They sprang from greatly differing traditions, from farmers and from hunters and from collectors of wild plants. Each contributed something of its own that created almost overnight a flamboyant culture whose vigor was for a time unequaled. In this world of hyperbole, many traditions that existed in non-Plains Indian societies became wildly exaggerated. Other Indians also possessed clubs and associations, but none were so extravagant in ritual and insignia as the Plains warrior societies. Indians elsewhere also believed in the reality of visions, but none so relentlessly pursued the vision quest and were so caught up in the emotional excesses of religion as the Plains tribes. Other Indians tortured captives, but none evoked pain so exquisitely in their own bodies.

❊   ❊   ❊

VISION QUESTS

Most North American Indians greatly respected visions, but few immersed themselves so deeply in them as did the Plains tribes. Sometimes a spirit might come of its own accord in a vision, just to befriend a mortal, but usually the Plains Indian had to go in active pursuit of his vision. He did this by isolating himself, fasting and thirsting, and practicing self-torture, at the same time imploring the spirits to take pity on his suffering. The youth gashed his arms and legs, and among the Crow it was the custom to cut off a joint from a finger of the left hand. Cheyenne vision-seekers thrust skewers of wood under pinches of skin in the breast, these skewers were attached to ropes, which in turn were tied to a pole. All day the youth leaned his full weight away from the pole, pulling and tugging at his own flesh while he implored the spirits to give him a vision.

Mortification of the flesh has always held a fascination for religious fanatics everywhere, for it is the most obvious way that this too, too human flesh can break its link with the world of men and approach the threshold of the gods. Among those who have groped toward deities in this way are the Jewish Essenes around the Dead Sea, the many ascetic orders of Christian monks, the Whirling Dervishes of Islam, and the hermits of Buddhism.

The spirit might at last take pity on the Plains Indian youth—actually it was dehydration, pain, and delirium taking their effects—and give him supernatural guidance. A successful vision supported the youth for the rest of his life. He always had a guardian spirit on whom he could call for help and guidance, although from time to time he had to repeat the self-torture to renew his familiarity with the spirit. During his vision, the youth usually learned what items—such as feathers, a stone pipe, a piece of skin, maize kernels—he should collect for a sacred medicine bundle and put in a small pouch. A particularly lucky youth might also receive his own songs, which when sung served as a call to supernatural aid; that they sounded like gibberish to everyone else only reinforced the belief that he had received a unique vision. A few youths failed to receive any visions at all, even though they tried repeatedly. Those who could not obtain a vision on their own could sometimes purchase one, as well as a replica of the successful visionary's sacred medicine bundle.

What is remarkable about such visions is that they were not invariably experienced, since the entire Plains culture worked toward producing them. Every Plains youth grew up believing firmly in the reality of the vision, so no resistance to the idea had to be overcome. Secondly, the youth worked himself into an intense emotional state by starvation, thirst, self-torture, exposure to the sun, and isolation—all of which are known to produce hallucinations. Thirdly, the shape in which the vision came to him was predetermined by the structure of the myths and visions he had heard about since childhood. Finally, in retelling his vision, he unconsciously reconstructed it and filled in gaps, adapting it to the norms of behavior of his culture—much as we do in reporting an incoherent dream, no matter how sincerely we believe we are not distorting it.

Plains Indian visions were clearly recognized as differing from person to person and from tribe to tribe. Some of the individual differences were biological and psychological. An Indian with an auditory personality might hear loud calls of birds or gibberish songs, whereas a visual type would be apt to see a horse with strange markings. Probably some individual fears and anxieties went into the vision. Despite the Plains warrior's attitude of fearlessness, a common vision was the sudden transformation of rocks and trees into enemies; but the youth was made invulnerable to their arrows by his guardian spirit. Often the vision involved the visit of some animal. An eagle might fly by, the flapping of its wings sounding like crashes of thunder; and bison, elk, bears, and hawks appeared quite often among the nobler beasts. Among the Pawnee (who, alone of the Plains tribes, had worked out an orderly system of religious beliefs, including a supreme being), the stars and other heavenly bodies entered quite freely into visions.

The desire for a vision existed among most of the Indians of North America, and it seems to have developed in two different directions. Among some Indians, it led directly to shamanism, for shamans were believed to be recipients of particularly intense visions and to have the power to summon up new visions at will. The other line of development led to visions of more limited power that had to be sought after. In this second category, there was a great range of variation, from the Plains youth, who suffered ordeals, to the Great Basin Shoshone, who passively waited for the spirit to find him.

Before the contrasting attitudes of the Plains tribes and the Great Basin Shoshone can be explained, the vision must first be recognized for what it is: a resort to supernatural aid in a dangerous undertaking, in which individual skill alone is not enough to guarantee success. The Plains culture provided numerous such dangerous undertakings, such as riding among a herd of stampeding bison or stealthily entering an enemy camp. For the Plains warrior, the rewards of such undertakings were certainly great enough to compensate for the few days of self-torture and fasting required to obtain a guardian spirit. The arid country of the Great Basin Shoshone, however, provided no such rewards. There the land yielded a bare minimum, and the rewards went not to the man who showed courage and daring, but to the one who simply exerted industry in collecting seeds or grasshoppers. Any yearning for visions that existed among the Great Basin Shoshone was not for protection in the dangers of the hunt or in warfare, but for the cure of snake bites or sickness.

The various responses of different cultures toward visions partly explains why some Indians took enthusiastically to the White man's alcohol and others did not. The use of firewater was particularly intense among the Plains, as well as among the nearby forest Indians, who were the ancestors of many Plains Indians. Alcohol was promptly recognized by the Plains Indians as a short-cut method of producing derangement of the senses and hallucinations. In primeval North America the Plains tribes had been remarkably free from the use of hallucinogenic plants such as peyote and mushrooms. The Plains vision-seekers were not even fortunate enough to have *Datura* or Jimsonweed, for its original range in the West was probably in only portions of the Southwest and southern California. Nor had the Plains tribes learned that tobacco, which they smoked in a few ritual puffs, could be swallowed to produce considerable discomfort and emotional upset, the way many Central and South American Indians used it.

Only when the Plains culture was disintergrating rapidly after about 1850 did a hallucinogenic cactus known as peyote take hold. Peyote is native to northern Mexico, but it spread like a grass fire from tribe to tribe as far north as the Canadian plains. Although peyote is used elsewhere in North America to a limited extent, it was most widely and promptly accepted by the Plains tribes. Peyote afforded a way to seek visions; it also provided an escape from the humiliation of the complete defeat by Whites in the latter part of the last century.

THE END OF A CULTURE

After the Civil War, a tide of White settlers streamed westward, and they sealed the fate of the Plains tribes. Treaty after treaty was broken by Whites as the Indian lands were crisscrossed by easterners covetous of acreage and precious metals. At first the Whites tried to restrict the Plains Indians to valueless territories, but that policy soon changed to a war of extermination. Said General William Tecumseh Sherman in 1867: "The more I see of these Indians, the more convinced I am that they all have to be killed or be maintained as a species of paupers." To help clear the Indians from the plains, the Whites struck at their food base, the bison. They themselves not only destroyed the animals, but they also contrived to get the Indians to collaborate with them by offering to buy vast quantities of such delicacies as bison tongue.

Tensions between the Whites and the Plains Indians increased during the 1870's. On July 5, 1876, newspapers reporting celebrations of the young nation's Centennial reported also the news of a humiliating defeat. The elite Seventh Cavalry, a tough outfit of 260 men, which was organized specifically for killing Plains Indians—and led by Lieutenant Colonel Custer—had been annihilated on June 25 by a combined force of Sioux and Cheyenne in the battle of Little Bighorn. But for Sitting Bull and Crazy Horse, the victory over Custer had been empty, and only marked the beginning of the end for the Plains Indians. From that time on troops pursued them mercilessly from waterhole to waterhole; their women and children were slaughtered before their eyes, their encampments and their riches burned. The glory and the poetry had gone out of the Plains Indians. Mighty chiefs emerged from hiding as miserable fugitives, hungry and without bullets for their guns. The survivors, like so many cattle, were herded onto reservations, where rough handling, cheap whiskey, starvation, exposure, and disease severely depleted their numbers.

The very end of the Plains culture can be dated exactly. In 1890 the surviving Plains Indians enthusiastically listened to a native messiah who foretold the return of dead Indians and the magical disappearance of the Whites. Alarmed, the United States government sent out cavalry to suppress this Ghost Dance, as it was called. While being placed under arrest, Sitting Bull was accidentally killed; and some three hundred Sioux, mostly women and children waiting to surrender at Wounded Knee Creek, South Dakota, were massacred by trigger-happy troops. Wounded Knee marked the end of any hopes the Plains Indians still cherished. The Ghost Dance had proven as make-believe as the rest of their improbable culture.

The Red Man's Burden

PETER COLLIER

After the Plains Indians were defeated late in the nineteenth century, the United States government undertook a program of breaking up the Indian reservations that remained and thus forcing the nation's Indians to disperse and to adapt to white ways of life. For the purpose of dismantling the reservations, the government revived the policy of land allotment developed during the presidency of Andrew Jackson to remove the Five Civilized Tribes from the Southeast. Under the Jacksonian removal program, land that had been granted by treaty to the entire Indian nation was divided among individual Indians, who were then persuaded—often fraudulently—to sell to white speculators. Theoretically, individual land holdings would lead the Indians to work harder and would thus help them to conform to the white American ideal of individual achievement. But economic individualism is foreign to Indian culture, and the land-allotment program only worked to divest the Indians of the little land that still belonged to them.

In the late nineteenth century, government policies struck hard at the Indian way of life, forbidding the practice of Indian religions and seeking to undermine tribal organization. Typical of the Indian legislation passed during this period was the Dawes Severalty Act of 1887, which empowered the President to allot one hundred and sixty acres of reservation land to individual Indian families and lesser amounts to single Indians. The leftover reservation land—often the choice portions—was then sold by the government. Under this program, the Indians lost about 86,000,000 acres from a total of 138,000,000 between 1887 and 1934.

With the New Deal and President Roosevelt's appointment

of John Collier as Commissioner of Indian Affairs, the government's devastating Indian policy was temporarily reversed. Collier was a scholarly and sensitive friend of the Indians and recognized the destruction wrought by past measures. At Collier's urging, Congress passed the Wheeler-Howard Act (known as the Indian Reorganization Act) in 1934, which ended the allotment program and called for the use of public funds to purchase new lands for certain Indian nations victimized by the old policy. Under Collier's leadership, the New Deal government also gave a boost to Indian culture. The constitutional right of the Indians to practice their own religions was asserted despite complaints from various missionary organizations, and Indian crafts were revived even though the Indians had forgotten many of the traditional skills. Government relief policies and public health measures contributed to a slight improvement in the standard of living and a decrease in the death rate among Indians. For the first time since their conquest by white America, the Indian population began to increase.

Unfortunately, the beneficial effects of the Indian Reorganization Act began to be undone in the 1950's when the Eisenhower administration adopted the policy of "terminating" all Indian reservations in order to "get the government out of the Indian business." Currently, however, the outlook for the Indian is somewhat brighter. Various Indian groups are working hard to develop a viable movement for the preservation of a distinctive Indian life and culture, and the Nixon administration has gone on record as opposing the policy of termination and advocating Indian control of Indian affairs.

The following passage discusses the plight of the Indians today as a result of past and present federal action, focusing on the temporary takeover of Alcatraz Island by Indians in 1969.

When fourteen Indian college students invaded Alcatraz on a cold, foggy morning in the first part of November—claiming ownership "by right of discovery," and citing an 1868 treaty allowing the Sioux possession of unused federal lands—they seemed in a light-hearted

From "The Red Man's Burden," by Peter Collier, © Ramparts Magazine, Inc., 1970. Reprinted by permission of the author.

mood. After establishing their beachhead, they told the press that they had come there because Alcatraz already had all the necessary features of a reservation: dangerously uninhabitable buildings; no fresh water; inadequate sanitation; and the certainty of total unemployment. They said they were planning to make the five full-time caretakers wards of a Bureau of Caucasian Affairs, and offered to take this troublesome real estate off the white man's hands for $24, payment to be made in glass beads. The newspapers played it up big, calling the Indians a "raiding party." When, after a 19-hour stay, the Indians were persuaded to leave the island, everyone agreed that it had been a good publicity stunt.

If the Indians had ever been joking about Alcatraz, however, it was with the bitter irony that fills colonial subjects' discourse with the mother-country. When they returned to the mainland, they didn't fall back into the cigar-store stoicism that is supposedly the red man's prime virtue. In fact, their first invasion ignited a series of meetings and strategy-sessions; two weeks later they returned to the Rock, this time with a force of nearly 100 persons, a supply network, and the clear intention of staying. What had begun as a way of drawing attention to the position of the contemporary Indian developed into a plan for doing something about it. And when the government, acting through the General Services Administration, gave them a deadline for leaving, the Indians replied with demands of their own: Alcatraz was theirs, they said, and it would take U.S. Marshals to remove them and their families; they planned to turn the island into a major cultural center and research facility; they would negotiate only the mechanics of deeding over the land, and that only with Interior Secretary Walter Hickel during a face to face meeting. The Secretary never showed up, but the government's deadlines were withdrawn.

> *On this island, I saw not whether the people had personal property, for it seemed to me that whatever one had, they all took share of, especially of eatable things.*
>
> CRISTOPHER COLUMBUS

Alcatraz is Indian territory: The old warning to "Keep Off U.S. Property" now reads "Keep Off Indian Property"; security guards with red armbands stand near the docks to make sure it is obeyed. Women tend fires beneath huge iron cauldrons filled with food, while their kids play frisbee in what was once a convicts' exercise yard. Some of the men work on the prison's wiring system or try to get more cellblocks cleared out for the Indian people who are arriving daily from all over the country; others sit fishing on the wharf with hand-lines, watching quietly as the rip-tides churn in the Bay. During the day, rock music plays over portable radios and a series of soap operas flit across a TV; at night, the prison is filled with the soft sounds of ceremonial drums and eerie songs in Sioux, Kiowa and Navajo.

In the few weeks of its occupation, Alcatraz had become a mecca, a sort of red man's Selma. Indian people come, stay a few days, and then leave, taking with them a sense of wonderment that it has happened. Middle-aged "establishment" Indians are there. They mix with younger insurgents like Lehman Brightman (the militant Sioux who heads a red power organization called the United Native Americans), Mad-Bear Anderson (the Iroquois traditionalist from upstate New York who fought to get the United Nations to stop the U.S. Army Corps of Engineers' flooding of precious Seneca Indian lands), Sid Mills (the young Yakima who demanded a discharge from the Army after returning from Vietnam so that he could fight his real war—against the state of Washington's denial of his people's fishing rights), and Al Bridges (one of the leaders of the first Washington fish-ins in 1964, who now faces a possible ten-year prison sentence for defying the state Fish and Game Commission). The composition of the ad hoc Indian community changes constantly, but the purpose remains the same: to make Alcatraz a powerful symbol of liberation springing out of the long American imprisonment.

The people enjoy themselves, spending a lot of time sitting around the campfire talking and gossiping. But there is a sense of urgency beneath the apparent lassitude. Richard Oakes, a 27-year-old Mohawk who worked in high steel construction before coming West to go to college, is one of the elected spokesmen. Sitting at a desk in the old Warden's Office, he talks about the hope of beginning a new organization, the Confederacy of American Indian Nations, to weld Indian groups all over the country into one body capable of taking power away from the white bureaucracy. He acknowledges that the pan-Indian movements which have sprung up before have always been crushed. "But time is running out for us," he says. "We have everything at stake. And if we don't make it now, then we'll get trapped at the bottom of that white world out there, and wind up as some kind of Jack Jones with a social security number and that's all. Not just on Alcatraz, but every place else, the Indian is in his last stand for cultural survival."

This sentiment is reflected in the slogans lettered on walls all over the prison, the red paint bleeding down onto the concrete. One of them declares: "Better Red than Dead."

> *I also heard of numerous instances in which our men had cut out the private parts of females and wore them in their hats while riding in the ranks.*
>
> A U.S. ARMY LIEUTENANT, TESTIFYING
> ABOUT THE SAND CREEK MASSACRE OF 1864

The Alcatraz occupation is still popularly regarded as the engaging fun and games of Indian college kids. In its news coverage of the U.S. Coast Guard's feeble attempt to blockade ships running supplies to the island, one local television station found amusement in showing their films to the musical accompaniment of U.S. cavalry bugle calls. It was not so amusing to the occupiers, however. The California Indians now on the Rock know that their people were decimated from a population of 100,000 in 1850 when the gold rush settlers arrived, to about 15,000 thirty years later, and that whole tribes, languages and cultures were erased from the face of the earth. There are South Dakota Indians there whose grandparents were alive in 1890 when several hundred Sioux, mostly women and children leaving the reservation to find food, were caught at Wounded Knee, killed, and buried in a common grave—the old daguerreotypes still showing heavily-mustachioed soldiers standing stiffly over the frozen bodies like hunters with their trophies. Cowboys and Indians is not a pleasant game for the Alcatraz Indians and some must wonder whether, in another 150 years, German children will be gaily playing Nazis and Jews.

But the past is not really at issue. What is at stake today, as Richard Oakes says, is cultural survival. Some of the occupiers have known Indian culture all their lives; some have been partially assimilated away from it and are now trying to return. All understand that it is in jeopardy, and they want some assurance that Indian-ness will be available to their children. It sounds like a fair request, but fairness has never ruled the destiny of the Indian in America. In fighting for survival, the Indians of Alcatraz are challenging the lies perpetuated by anthropologists and bureaucrats alike, who insist that the red man is two things: an incompetent "ward" addicted to the paternalism of government, and an anachronism whose past is imprisoned in white history and whose only future is as an invisible swimmer in the American mainstream. The people on Alcatraz have entered a struggle on a large scale that parallels the smaller, individual struggles for survival that many of them have known themselves; it is the will to exist as individuals that brought them together in determination to exist as a people.

When Robert Kennedy came, that was the only day they ever showed any respect for the Indian, just on that one day, and after that, they could care less.

A FRESHMAN STUDENT AT BLACKFOOT, IDAHO, HIGH SCHOOL

One of the original 14 on Alcatraz was a pretty 22-year-old Shoshone-Bannock girl named La Nada Means. Her hair is long and reddish-black; her nose arches slightly and prominent cheekbones square out her face. Her walk is slightly pigeon-toed, the result of a childhood disease for which she never received treatment. If you tell her that she looks very Indian, she will thank you, but with a searching look that suggests she has heard the same comment before, and not as a compliment.

"When I was little," she says, "I remember my family as being very poor. There were 12 of us kids, and we were always hungry. I remember sometimes getting to the point where I'd eat anything I could get my hands on—leaves, small pieces of wood, anything. The other thing I remember is the meanness of the small towns around the reservation. Blackfoot, Pocatello—they all had signs in the store windows to keep Indians out. One of them I'll never forget; it said, 'No Indians or Dogs Allowed.' There were Indian stalls in the public bathrooms; Indians weren't served in a lot of the restaurants; and we just naturally all sat in the balcony of the theaters. You learn early what all that means. It becomes part of the way you look at yourself."

She grew up on the Fort Hall reservation in Southern Idaho. The Jim Crow atmosphere of the surrounding small towns has lessened somewhat with the passage of time and the coming of the civil-rights bills, but it is still very much present in the attitude of white townsfolk towards Indians. And while there are no longer the small outbreaks of famine that occurred on the reservation when La Nada was growing up in the '50's, Fort Hall is still one of the bleakest areas in the country, and the people there are among the poorest.

Like most Indian children of her generation (and like a great many today), La Nada Means was sent away to school. Her youth became a series of separations from home and family, each more traumatic than the one before. The first school she attended was St. Mary's School for Indian Girls in Springfield, South Dakota. "I took a lot of classes in subjects like 'Laundry,'" she remembers, "where the classwork was washing the headmaster's clothes. All Indian people are supposed to be good with their hands, you know, and also hard workers, so we didn't do too much regular schoolwork at St. Mary's. They also had what they called a Summer Home Program where you're sent out during the summer break to live with a white family. It was supposed to teach you white etiquette and things like that, and make you forget your savage Indian ways. When I was 13, I was sent up to Minnesota, where I became a sort of housekeeper for the summer. I don't remember too much about it, except that the wages I got, about $5 a week, were sent back to St. Mary's and I never saw them. After being at that school a little while, I got all upset. They said I was 'too outspoken,' and expelled me. After I got back to Fort Hall, I had my first breakdown."

For awhile she attended public school in Blackfoot, the small town bordering the reservation. She was suspended because she objected to the racial slurs against Indians which were built into the curriculum. She was 15 when the Bureau of Indian Affairs (BIA) sent her to its boarding school in Chilocco, Oklahoma. On her first day there, the matrons ordered her to lower the hems on the two dresses she owned. She refused and was immediately classified as a troublemaker. "At Chilocco, you're either a 'good girl' or a 'bad girl,'" she says. "They put me in the bad girls' dormitory right away with Indians mainly from the Northwest. The Oklahoma Indians were in the good girls' dorm, and the matrons constantly tried to keep us agitated by setting the tribes to fighting with each other. Everything was like the Army. There were bells, drills and set hours for everything. The food was called 'GI Chow.' There was a lot of brutality, but it was used mainly on the boys, who lived in another wing. Occasionally they'd let the boys and girls get together. You all stood in this big square; you could hold hands, but if the matrons saw you getting too close, they'd blow a whistle and then you'd have to march back to the dorm."

La Nada made the honor roll, but was expelled from Chilocco after a two-month stay for being involved in a fight. "The matrons just had it in for me, I guess. They got about 100 other Indian girls against me and a few other 'bad girls.' They put us in a small room and when the fight was ready to begin, they turned out the lights and walked out, locking the doors behind them. We had a 'riot,' and I got beat up. The next day, the head of the school called me into his office and said that I didn't fit in."

She was sent off with one dollar, a sack lunch, and a one-way bus ticket from Chilocco back to Idaho. She lived with her family for a few months, helping her father collect data about conditions at Fort Hall, and then was sent by the BIA to another of its boarding schools, Stewart Institute, in Carson City, Nevada. Her reputation as a "difficult Indian" followed her, and she was again sent home after being at Stewart for less than a day. The BIA threatened to send her to "reform" school; then it forgot about her. "I stayed around the reservation for awhile," she says, "and when I got to be to 17, I took GED [high school equivalent] exams. I only had about nine real years of schooling, but I scored pretty well and got into Idaho State College. I lasted there for a semester, and then quit. I didn't really know what to do. At Fort Hall, you either work in some kind of menial job with the BIA agency there, or you go off the reservation to find a job in one of the towns. If you choose the BIA, you know that they'll try to drill a subservient mentality into you; and in the towns, the discrimination is pretty bad."

La Nada again spent time working with her father, a former tribal chairman. They sent out letters to congressmen and senators describing conditions on the reservations, and tried to get the Bureau of Indian Affairs office to respond. As a result, her father was harassed by local law enforcement officials. La Nada drifted for a time and then asked the BIA for "relocation" off the reservation. Many of the Fort Hall Indians have taken this route and 80 per cent of them return to the reservation, because as La Nada says, "things in the slums where you wind up are even worse than on the reservation, and you don't have your people to support you."

The BIA gave her a one-way ticket to San Francisco, one of eight major relocation centers in the country. When she first arrived, she sat in the local BIA office from 8 to 5 for a few days, waiting for them to help her find a job. They didn't, and she found a series of temporary clerk jobs by herself. As soon as she found work, the BIA cut off her $140 a month relocation payment. She wound up spending a lot of time in the "Indian bars" which are found in San Francisco and every other relocation town. She worked as a housekeeper in the private home for Indian girls where the BIA had first sent her, and as a barmaid in a beer parlor. She was "drunk most of the time," and she became pregnant. She was 17 years old.

"After I had the baby," she says, "my mother came out from the reservation and got him. She said they'd take care of him back home until I got on my feet. I really didn't know what to do. The only programs the BIA has are vocational training for menial jobs, and I didn't especially want to be a beautician. Actually, I wanted to try college again, but when I told this to a BIA counselor, he said they didn't have any money for that and told me I was being 'irrational and unrealistic.'

"All types of problems develop when you're on relocation. The Indian who has come to the city is like a man without a country. Whose jurisdiction are you under, the BIA's or the state's? You go to a county hospital when you're sick and they say, 'Aren't you taken care of by the Indian Affairs people?' It's very confusing. You hang around with other Indians, but they are as bad off as you are. Anyway, I started sinking lower and lower. I married this Sioux and lived with his family awhile. I got pregnant again. But things didn't work out in the marriage, and I left. After I had the baby, I ended up in the San Francisco General psychiatric ward for a few weeks. I was at the bottom, really at the bottom. Indian people get to this point all the time, especially when they're relocated into the big city and are living in the slums. At that point, you've got two choices: either kill yourself and get it all over with —a lot of Indians do this—or try to go all the way up, and this is almost impossible."

As she looks at it now, La Nada feels she was "lucky." She tried to get admitted to the local colleges, but was refused because of her school record. Finally, because the University of California "needed a token Indian in its Economic Opportunity Program for minority students," she was admitted in the fall of 1968. She did well in her classes and became increasingly active, helping to found the United Native Americans organization and working to get more Indian students admitted into the EOP program. "After my first year there," she says, "everything was going along all right. I liked school and everything, and I felt I was doing some good. But I felt myself getting swallowed up by something that was bigger than me. The thing was that I didn't want to stop being an Indian, and there were all these pressures, very hidden ones, that were trying to make me white." At the summer break she went back to the reservation and spent some time with her family. The next quarter she became involved in the Third World Liberation Front strike at Berkeley, fighting for a School of Ethnic Studies, including a Native American program. She was suspended by the University.

La Nada's experiences, far from being extreme cases, are like those of most young Indians. If she is unique at all, it is because she learned the value of fighting back.

We need fewer and fewer "experts" on Indians. What we need is a cultural leave-us-alone agreement, in spirit and in fact.

VINE DELORIA, JR.

Each generation of Americans rediscovers for itself what is fashionably called the "plight" of the Indian. The American Indian today has a life expectancy of approximately 44 years, more than 25 years below the national average. He has the highest infant mortality rate in the country (among the more than 50,000 Alaskan natives, one of every four babies dies before reaching his first birthday). He suffers from epidemics of diseases which were supposed to have disappeared from America long ago.

A recent Department of Public Health report states that among California Indians, "water from contaminated sources is used in 38 to 42 per cent of the homes, and water must be hauled under unsanitary conditions by 40 to 50 per cent of all Indian families." Conditions are similar in other states. A high proportion of reservation housing throughout the country is officially classified as "substandard," an antiseptic term which fails to conjure up a tiny, two-room log cabin holding a family of 13 at Fort Hall; a crumbling Navajo hogan surrounded by broken plumbing fixtures hauled in to serve as woodbins; or a gutted automobile body in which a Pine Ridge Sioux family huddles against the South Dakota winter.

On most reservations, a 50 per cent unemployment rate is not considered high. Income per family among Indian people is just over $1,500 per year—the lowest of any group in the country. But this, like the other figures, is deceptive. It does not suggest, for instance, the quality of the daily life of families on the Navajo reservation who live on $600 per year (exchanging sheep's wool and hand-woven rugs with white traders for beans and flour), who never have real money and who are perpetually sinking a little further into credit debt.

To most Americans, the conditions under which the Indian is forced to live are a perennial revelation. On one level, the symptoms are always being tinkered with half-heartedly and the causes ignored; on another level, the whole thrust of the government's Indian policy appears calculated to perpetuate the Indians' "plight." This is why La Nada Means and the other Indians have joined what Janet McCloud, a leader of the Washington fishing protests, calls "the last, continuing Indian War." The enemies are legion, and they press in from every side: the studiously ignorant politicians, the continuously negligent Department of the Interior, and the white business interests who are allowed to prey upon the reservations' manpower and resources. But as the Indian has struggled to free himself from the suffocating embrace of white history, no enemy has held the death grip more tightly than has his supposed guardian, in effect his "keeper": the Bureau of Indian Affairs.

The Bureau came into being in 1834 as a division of the War Department. Fifteen years later it was shifted to the Department of the Interior, the transition symbolizing the fact that the Indian was beginning to be seen not as a member of a sovereign, independent nation, but as a "ward," his land and life requiring constant management. This is the view that has informed the BIA for over a century. With its 16,000 employees and its outposts all over the country, the Bureau has become what Cherokee anthropologist Robert Thomas calls "the most complete colonial system in the world."

It is also a classic bureaucratic miasma. A recent book on Indian Affairs, *Our Brother's Keeper*, notes that on the large Pine Ridge reservation, "$8,040 a year is spent per family to help the Oglala Sioux Indians out of poverty. Yet median income among these Indians is $1,910 per family. At last count there was nearly one bureaucrat for each and every family on the reservation."

The paternalism of the BIA, endless and debilitating, is calculated to keep the Indian in a state of perpetual juvenilization, without rights, dependent upon the meager and capricious beneficence of power. The Bureau's power over its "wards," whom it defines and treats as children, seems limitless. The BIA takes care of the Indian's money, doling it out to him when it considers his requests worthy; it determines the use of the Indian's land; it is in charge of the development of his natural resources; it relocates him from the reservation to the big city ghetto; it educates his children. It relinquishes its hold over him only reluctantly, even deciding whether or not his will is valid after he dies.

This bureaucratic paternalism hems the Indian in with an incomprehensible maze of procedures and regulations, never allowing him to know quite where he stands or what he can demand and how. Over 5,000 laws, statutes and court decisions apply to the Indians alone. As one Indian student says, "Our people have to go to law school just to live a daily life."

The BIA is the Indian's point of contact with the white world, the concrete expression of this society's attitude towards him. The BIA manifests both stupidity and malice; but it is purely neither. It is guided by something more elusive, a whole world view regarding the Indian and what is good for him. Thus the BIA's overseership of human devastation begins by teaching bright-eyed youngsters the first formative lessons in what it is to be an Indian.

Suggestions for Further Reading

Two good general introductions to American Indian life are Alvin M. Josephy, Jr., *The Indian Heritage of America* ° (Knopf, 1968), and Peter Farb, *Man's Rise to Civilization as Shown by the Indians of North America from Primeval Times to the Coming of the Industrial State* ° (Dutton, 1968). Relations between Indians and whites throughout American history are treated in William T. Hagan, *American Indians* ° (University of Chicago Press, 1961); Roy Harvey Pearce, *The Savages of America: A Study of the Indian and the Idea of Civilization* ° (Johns Hopkins Press, 1953); and a collection of documents edited by Wilcomb E. Washburn, *The Indian and the White Man* ° (Doubleday, 1964). Indian wars of the colonial period are dealt with in Alden Vaughan, *New England Frontier: Puritans and Indians, 1620–1675* ° (Little, Brown, 1965), and Douglas Leach, *Flintlock and Tomahawk: New England in King Philip's War* ° (Norton, 1958). Nancy Oestreich Lurie considers the cultural impact of the colonists on the Indians in "Indian Cultural Adjustment to European Civilization," in James Morton Smith (ed.), *Seventeenth-Century America: Essays on Colonial History* ° (University of North Carolina Press, 1959).

For the Indian policy of the federal government in the early years of the new nation, see Reginald Horsman, *Expansion and American Indian Policy, 1783–1812* (Michigan State University Press, 1967), and F. P. Prucha, *American Indian Policy in the Formative Years* ° (Harvard University Press, 1962). An excellent study of the impact of white settlement on a specific Indian nation is Anthony F. C. Wallace, *The Death and Rebirth of the Seneca* ° (Knopf, 1970). The best available biography of Tecumseh is Glenn Tucker, *Tecumseh, Vision of Glory* (Bobbs-Merrill, 1956).

The literature on Indian removal from the Southeast is voluminous. Good starting points are Dale Van Every's *Disinherited: The Lost Birthright of the American Indian* ° (Morrow, 1966) and the collection of documents edited by Louis Filler and Allan Guttman, *Removal of the Cherokee Nation: Manifest Destiny or National Dishonor* ° (Heath, 1962). Robert S. Cotterill discusses the life of the Indians before their dispossession in *The Southern Indians: The Story of the Civilized Tribes Before Removal* (University of Oklahoma Press, 1954); and Grant Foreman tells the sad tale of removal in *Indian Removal: The Emigration of the Five Civilized Tribes of Indians* (2d ed.; University of Oklahoma Press, 1953). Angie Debo takes a close look at two of the Five Civilized Tribes in *The Road to Disappearance: A History of the Creek Indians* (University of Oklahoma Press, 1941) and *The Rise and Fall of the Choctaw Republic* (University of Oklahoma Press, 1961).

° Available in paperback edition.

Two basic anthropological studies of the Plains Indians are E. A. Hoebel, *The Cheyennes: Indians of the Great Plains* ° (Holt, Rinehart and Winston, 1960), and R. H. Lowie, *Indians of the Plains* ° (McGraw-Hill, 1954). For the impact of the horse on Indian culture, see F. G. Roe, *The Indian and the Horse* (University of Oklahoma Press, 1955). Mari Sandoz movingly recounts the breakup of the Plains Indian culture in *Cheyenne Autumn* ° (Hastings House, 1953). The defeat of the Sioux is described in Robert Utley, *Last Days of the Sioux Nation* ° (Yale University Press, 1963). Thomas Berger's novel *Little Big Man* ° (Dial, 1964), presents an authentic picture of elements of Plains Indian culture. The story of the white man's conquest of the Western Indians in the late nineteenth century is told by Dee Brown in *Bury My Heart at Wounded Knee: An Indian History of the American West* ° (Holt, Rinehart and Winston, 1971).

The current revolt among young Indians is described by Stan Steiner in *The New Indians* ° (Harper and Row, 1968). Vine Deloria, Jr., a Standing Rock Sioux, has challenged American history in *Custer Died for Your Sins: An Indian Manifesto* ° (Macmillan, 1969). A stimulating symposium on the contemporary Indian is Stuart Levine and Nancy O. Lurie (eds.), *The American Indian Today* ° (Everett-Edwards, 1968), originally published in the fall 1965 issue of *Mid-Continent American Studies Journal*. Three novels that offer perhaps the best means of understanding the cultural conflict faced by American Indians today are Frank Waters, *The Man Who Killed the Deer* ° (Holt, Rinehart and Winston, 1942); Hal Borland, *When the Legends Die* ° (Lippincott, 1963); and N. Scott Momaday, *House Made of Dawn* ° (Harper and Row, 1968).

Blacks

The Beginnings
of Slavery in America

WINTHROP D. JORDAN

By the end of the seventeenth century the English colonies in America had turned to the African slave and his descendants to solve the problems arising from a chronic shortage of unskilled labor. The English adapted for their own use the Spanish system of African enslavement, which had begun early in the sixteenth century in the Caribbean. Indian slavery, too, had been widely practiced in Latin America, to the point of bringing the native Indian populations close to extinction. But in North American colonies, though Indian captives were frequently enslaved in the early years of colonization, it appears that Indian slavery was never economically profitable. As a result, the African became the slave in the English colonies.

Slavery, in the sense of lifetime bondage, is an institution as old as human history. Almost every past civilization has had some system of involuntary service that may with some accuracy be called slavery. Throughout history, military conquest has been the most common means of enslavement. What distinguished North American slavery, however, was its racial character. By the beginning of the eighteenth century, any African in the English colonies was assumed to be a slave unless he could prove otherwise. Except in exceptional circumstances, not only the original African but his descendants forever were confined to slave status.

From the earliest days of settlement in North America, the historical record clearly shows that some blacks were free. What it does not show is the process by which African slavery became the widespread institution that it was by 1700. In fact, historians have argued as to whether slavery produced racial prejudice or racial prejudice produced slavery—a question that could have vital significance for easing racial tensions in America today. If, for instance, slavery, as an absolute form of economic inequality, led to racial prejudice, then the elimination of economic inequality in the United States might contribute tremendously to the elimination of racial prejudice. If, on the other hand, prejudice preceded slavery, then equal economic opportunity might not be expected for blacks until the roots of racial prejudice have been identified and removed.

The following selection, a study of early racial attitudes among the English in the New World, indicates that neither of the above positions can be demonstrated on the basis of historical evidence, though either is possible. It explores possible reasons for the development of a slavery system based on race.

In scanning the problem of *why* Negroes were enslaved in America, certain constant elements in a complex situation can be readily, if roughly, identified. It may be taken as given that there would have been no enslavement without economic need, that is, without persistent demand for labor in underpopulated colonies. Of crucial importance, too, was the fact that for cultural reasons Negroes were relatively helpless in the face of European aggressiveness and technology. In themselves, however, these two elements will not explain the enslavement of Indians and Negroes. The pressing exigency in America was labor, and Irish and English servants were available. Most of them would have been helpless to ward off outright enslavement if their masters had thought themselves privileged and able to enslave them. As a group, though, masters did not think themselves so empowered. Only with Indians and Negroes did Englishmen attempt so radical a deprivation of liberty—which brings the matter abruptly to the most difficult and imponderable question of all: what was it about Indians and Negroes which set them apart, which rendered them *different* from Englishmen, which made them special candidates for degradation?

To ask such questions is to inquire into the *content* of English at-

"The Beginnings of Slavery in America" from *White Over Black: American Attitudes Toward the Negro, 1550–1812* by Winthrop D. Jordan. Reprinted by permission of The University of North Carolina Press and the Institute of Early American History and Culture.

titudes, and unfortunately there is little evidence with which to build an answer. It may be said, however, that the heathen condition of the Negroes seemed of considerable importance to English settlers in America—more so than to English voyagers upon the coasts of Africa—and that heathenism was associated in some settlers' minds with the condition of slavery. This is not to say that the colonists enslaved Negroes because they were heathens. The most clear-cut positive trace of such reasoning was probably unique and certainly far from being a forceful statement: in 1660 John Hathorne declared, before a Massachusetts court in partial support of his contention that an Indian girl should not be compelled to return to her master, that "first the law is undeniable that the indian may have the same distribusion of Justice with our selves, ther is as I humbly conceive not the same argument as amongst the negroes[,] for the light of the gospell is begining to appeare amongst them—that is the indians."

The importance and persistence of the tradition which attached slavery to heathenism did not become evident in any positive assertions that heathens might be enslaved. It was not until the period of legal establishment of slavery after 1660 that the tradition became manifest at all, and even then there was no effort to place heathenism and slavery on a one-for-one relationship. Virginia's second statutory definition of a slave (1682), for example, awkwardly attempted to rest enslavement on religious difference while excluding from possible enslavement all heathens who were not Indian or Negro. Despite such logical difficulties, the old European equation of slavery and religious difference did not rapidly vanish in America, for it cropped up repeatedly after 1660 in assertions that slaves by becoming Christian did not automatically become free. By about the end of the seventeenth century, Maryland, New York, Virginia, North and South Carolina, and New Jersey had all passed laws reassuring masters that conversion of their slaves did not necessitate manumission [emancipation]. These acts were passed in response to occasional pleas that Christianity created a claim to freedom and to much more frequent assertions by men interested in converting Negroes that nothing could be accomplished if masters thought their slaves were about to be snatched from them by meddling missionaries. This decision that the slave's religious condition had no relevance to his status as a slave (the only one possible if an already valuable economic institution was to be retained) strongly suggests that heathenism was an important component in the colonists' initial reaction to Negroes early in the century.

Yet its importance can easily be overstressed. For one thing, some of the first Negroes in Virginia had been baptized before arrival. In the early years others were baptized in various colonies and became more than nominally Christian; a Negro woman joined the church in Dorchester, Massachusetts, as a full member in 1641. With some Negroes becoming Christian and others not, there might have developed a caste differentiation along religious lines, yet there is no evidence to suggest that the colonists distinguished consistently between the Negroes they converted and those they did not. It was racial, not religious, slavery which developed in America.

Still, in the early years, the English settlers most frequently contrasted themselves with Negroes by the term *Christian,* though they also sometimes described themselves as *English;* here the explicit religious distinction would seem to have lain at the core of English reaction. Yet the concept embodied by the term *Christian* embraced so much more meaning than was contained in specific doctrinal affirmations that it is scarcely possible to assume on the basis of this linguistic contrast that the colonists set Negroes apart because they were heathen. The historical experience of the English people in the sixteenth century had made for fusion of religion and nationality; the qualities of being English and Christian had become so inseparably blended that it seemed perfectly consistent to the Virginia Assembly in 1670 to declare that "noe negroe or Indian though baptised and enjoyned their owne Freedome shall be capable of any such purchase of christians, but yet not debarred from buying any of their owne nation." Similarly, an order of the Virginia Assembly in 1662 revealed a well-knit sense of self-identity of which Englishness and Christianity were interrelated parts: "METAPPEN a Powhatan Indian being sold for life time to one Elizabeth Short by the king of Wainoake Indians who had no power to sell him being of another nation, *it is ordered* that the said Indian be free, he speaking perfectly the English tongue and desiring baptism."

From the first, then, vis-à-vis the Negro the concept embedded in the term *Christian* seems to have conveyed much of the idea and feeling of *we* as against *they:* to be Christian was to be civilized rather than barbarous, English rather than African, white rather than black. The term *Christian* itself proved to have remarkable elasticity, for by the end of the seventeenth century it was being used to define a species of slavery which had altogether lost any connection with explicit religious difference. In the Virginia code of 1705, for example, the term sounded much more like a definition of race than of religion:

And for a further christian care and usage of all christian servants, *Be it also enacted, by the authority aforesaid, and it is hereby enacted,* That no negroes, mulattos, or Indians, although christians, or Jews, Moors, Mahometans, or other infidels, shall, at any time, purchase any christian servant, nor any other, except of their own complexion, or such as are declared slaves by this act.

By this time "Christianity" had somehow become intimately and explicitly linked with "complexion." The 1705 statute declared

that all servants imported and brought into this country, by sea or land, who were not christians in their native country (except Turks and Moors in amity with her majesty, and others that can make due proof of their being free in England, or any other christian country, before they were shipped, in order to transportation hither) shall be accounted and be slaves, and as such be here bought and sold notwithstanding a conversion to christianity afterwards.

As late as 1753 the Virginia slave code anachronistically defined slavery in terms of religion when everyone knew that slavery had for generations been based on the racial and not the religious difference.

It is worth making still closer scrutiny of the terminology which Englishmen employed when referring both to themselves and to the two peoples they enslaved, for this terminology affords the best single means of probing the content of their sense of difference. The terms *Indian* and *Negro* were both borrowed from the Hispanic languages, the one originally deriving from (mistaken) geographical locality and the other from human complexion. When referring to the Indians the English colonists either used that proper name or called them *savages*, a term which reflected primarily their view of Indians as uncivilized, or occasionally (in Maryland especially) *pagans*, which gave more explicit expression to the missionary urge. When they had reference to Indians the colonists occasionally spoke of themselves as *Christians* but after the early years almost always as *English*.

In significant contrast, the colonists referred to *Negroes* and by the eighteenth century to *blacks* and to *Africans*, but almost never to Negro *heathens* or *pagans* or *savages*. Most suggestive of all, there seems to have been something of a shift during the seventeenth century in the terminology which Englishmen in the colonies applied to themselves. From the initially most common term *Christian*, at mid-century there was a marked drift toward *English* and *free*. After about 1680, taking the colonies as a whole, a new term appeared—*white*.

So far as the weight of analysis may be imposed upon such terms, diminishing reliance upon *Christian* suggests a gradual muting of the specifically religious element in the Christian-Negro disjunction in favor of secular nationality: Negroes were, in 1667, "not in all respects to be admitted to a full fruition of the exemptions and impunities of the English." As time went on, as some Negroes became assimilated to the English colonial culture, as more "raw Africans" arrived, and as increasing numbers of non-English Europeans were attracted to the colonies, the colonists turned increasingly to the striking physiognomic difference. By 1676 it was possible in Virginia to assail a man for "eclipsing" himself in the "darke imbraces of a Blackamoore" as if "Buty consisted all together in the Antiphety of Complections." In Maryland a revised law prohibiting miscegenation (1692) retained *white* and *English* but dropped the term *Christian*—a symptomatic modification. As early as 1664 a Bermuda statute (aimed, ironically, at protecting Negroes from brutal abandonment) required that the "last Master" of senile Negroes "provide for them such accommodations as shall be convenient for Creatures of that hue and colour untill their death." By the end of the seventeenth century dark complexion had become an independent rationale for enslavement: in 1709 Samuel Sewall noted in his diary that a "Spaniard" had petitioned the Massachusetts Council for freedom but that "Capt. Teat alledg'd that all of that Color were Slaves." Here was a barrier between *we* and *they* which was visible and permanent: the Negro could not become a white man. Not, at least, as yet.

What had occurred was not a change in the justification of slavery from religion to race. No such justifications were made. There seems to have been, within the unarticulated concept of the Negro as a different sort of person, a subtle but highly significant shift in emphasis. Consciousness of the Negro's heathenism remained through the eighteenth and into the nineteenth and even the twentieth century, and an awareness, at very least, of his different appearance was present from the beginning. The shift was an alteration in emphasis within a single concept of difference rather than a development of a novel conceptualization. The amorphousness and subtlety of such a change is evident, for instance, in the famous tract, *The Negro's and Indian's Advocate,* published in 1680 by the Reverend Morgan Godwyn. Baffled and frustrated by the disinterest of planters in converting their slaves, Godwyn declared at one point that "their *Complexion,* which being most obvious to the sight, by which the *Notion* of things doth seem to be most certainly conveyed to the Understanding, is apt to make no *slight* impressions upon rude Minds, already prepared to admit of any thing for *Truth* which shall make for Interest." Altering his emphasis a few pages later, Godwyn complained that "these two words, *Negro* and *Slave*," are "by custom grown Homogeneous and Convertible; even as *Negro* and *Christian, Englishman* and *Heathen,* are by the like corrupt Custom and Partiality made Opposites." Most arresting of all, throughout the colonies the terms *Christian, free, English* and *white* were for many years employed indiscriminately as metonyms. A Maryland law of 1681 used all four terms in one short paragraph!

Whatever the limitations of terminology as an index to thought and feeling, it seems likely that the colonists' initial sense of difference from the Negro was founded not on a single characteristic but on a congeries of qualities which, taken as a whole, seemed to set the Negro apart. Virtually every quality in the Negro invited pejorative feelings. What may have been his two most striking characteristics, his heathenism and his appearance, were probably prerequisite to his complete debasement. His heathenism alone could never have led to permanent enslavement since conversion easily wiped out that failing. If his appearance, his racial characteristics, meant nothing to the English settlers, it is difficult to see how slavery based on race ever emerged, how the concept of complexion as the mark of slavery ever entered the colonists' minds. Even if the colonists were most unfavorably struck by the Negro's color, though, blackness itself did not urge the complete debasement of slavery. Other qualities—the utter strangeness of his language, gestures, eating habits, and so on—certainly must have contributed to the colonists' sense that he was very different, perhaps disturbingly so. In Africa these qualities had for Englishmen added up to *savagery;* they were major components in that sense of *difference* which provided the mental margin absolutely requisite for placing the European on the deck of the slave ship and the Negro in the hold.

The available evidence (what little there is) suggests that for Englishmen settling in America, the specific religious difference was initially of greater importance than color, certainly of much greater relative importance than for the Englishmen who confronted Negroes in their African homeland. Perhaps Englishmen in Virginia, living uncomfortably close to nature under a hot sun and in almost daily contact with tawny Indians, found the Negro's color less arresting than they might have in other circumstances. Perhaps, too, these first Virginians sensed how inadequately they had reconstructed the institutions and practices of Christian piety in the wilderness; they would perhaps appear less as failures to themselves in this respect if compared to persons who as Christians were *totally* defective. In this connection they may be compared to their brethren in New England, where godliness appeared (at first) triumphantly to hold full sway; in New England there was distinctly less contrasting of Negroes on the basis of the religious disjunction and much more militant discussion of just wars. Perhaps, though, the Jamestown settlers were told in 1619 by the Dutch shipmaster that these "negars" were heathens and could be treated as such. We do not know. The available data will not bear all the weight that the really crucial questions impose.

Of course once the cycle of degradation was fully under way, once slavery and racial discrimination were completely linked together, once the engine of oppression was in full operation, then there is no need to plead *ignoramus.* By the end of the seventeenth century in all the colonies of the English empire there was chattel racial slavery of a kind which would have seemed familiar to men living in the nineteenth century. No Elizabethan Englishman would have found it familiar, though certain strands of thought and feeling in Elizabethan England had intertwined with reports about the Spanish and Portuguese to engender a willingness on the part of English settlers in the New World to treat some men as suitable for private exploitation. During the seventeenth century New World conditions had exploited this predisposition and vastly enlarged it, so much so that English colonials of the eighteenth century were faced with full-blown slavery—something they thought of not as an institution but as a host of ever present problems, dangers, and opportunities.

The Black Ethos
in Slavery

STERLING STUCKEY

When African slaves were first brought to the New World, the circumstances of their new life worked powerfully to destroy their cultural heritage. Members of the same political groups were separated, use of an African language was forbidden, and blacks were discouraged from continuing their religious practices. Since most African religions were linked with a specific land area where the ancestors of the people were buried, these religions would not have traveled well in any case. Unlike blacks in the Caribbean and in Brazil, who were able to preserve certain aspects of African culture because of enormous concentrations of slaves from the same African regions, blacks in the United States were effectively cut off from most of their past.

It does not necessarily follow, however, that American blacks were left with no cultural and intellectual resources with which to form a new culture. Nor does the fact that they left few written records of their past imply that their inner lives suffered from lack of substance. In recent years, historians and anthropologists have strongly disagreed over the extent to which Africanisms survived among American blacks and over the impact of African culture on the United States, especially the South. In addition, the emphasis of some historians on the passivity and the childlike qualities often attributed to the slaves has given rise to an impassioned controversy over the slave personality. These and other debates centering on the experience of slavery have aroused a greater interest than ever before in exploring the cultural and intellectual life of the slaves. Apart from the descriptions of slave life provided by white observers, both sympathetic and hostile, the slaves themselves left a mass of illuminating material, including several hundred narratives composed by fugitive slaves, the religious and secular slave songs (primary spirituals and work songs), and a large body of folktales.

The spirituals, particularly, provide significant insights into the developing intellectual life of the American bondsmen. After the beginning of the Second Great Awakening at the turn of the nineteenth century, revivalist churches, chiefly Baptist and Methodist, began to seek actively the conversion of the slaves. In this they sometimes had the support of slaveowners who were genuinely concerned for the spiritual welfare of their slaves or who were convinced that Christianity would increase the slaves' passivity. Other, perhaps more perceptive, masters recognized the revolutionary potential of a religion that proclaimed all men equal before God, and they prohibited their slaves from participating in religious services of any kind. During the nineteenth century, what has been called the "invisible church" grew up among the slaves, who were taking the ideas of Christianity but altering them in subtle ways to make them their own. It was this church that produced many of the spirituals and inspired such rebels as Nat Turner, who drew his imagery of wrath and judgment from the Bible.

The essay that follows provides a sensitive introduction to the "ethos"—the fundamental character and beliefs—of the black slaves in America, as shown by the songs that they sang. It also gives a clear indication of the richness of the life to be uncovered through the use of this kind of source material.

Frederick Douglass, commenting on slave songs, remarked his utter astonishment, on coming to the North, "to find persons who could speak of the singing among slaves as evidence of their contentment and happiness." The young Du Bois, among the first knowledgeable critics of the spirituals, found white Americans as late as 1903 still telling Afro-Americans that "life was joyous to the black slave, careless and happy." "I can easily believe this of some," he wrote, "of many. But not all the past South, though it rose from the dead, can gainsay the heart-touching witness of these songs."

From "Through the Prism of Folklore: The Black Ethos in Slavery" by Sterling Stuckey from *The Massachusetts Review*, IX, Summer 1968, © 1969 The Massachusetts Review, Inc. Reprinted by permission of The Massachusetts Review, Inc.

They are the music of an unhappy people, of the children of disappointment; they tell of death and suffering and unvoiced longing toward a truer world, of misty wanderings and hidden ways.

Though few historians have been interested in such wanderings and ways, Frederick Douglass, probably referring to the spirituals, said the songs of slaves represented the sorrows of the slave's heart, serving to relieve the slave "only as an aching heart is relieved by its tears." "I have often sung," he continued, "to drown my sorrow, but seldom to express my happiness. Crying for joy, and singing for joy, were alike uncommon to me in the jaws of slavery."

Sterling Brown, who has much to tell us about the poetry and meaning of these songs, has observed: "As the best expression of the slave's deepest thoughts and yearnings, they [the spirituals] speak with convincing finality against the legend of contented slavery." Rejecting the formulation that the spirituals are mainly otherworldly, Brown states that though the creators of the spirituals looked toward heaven and "found their triumphs there, they did not blink their eyes to trouble here." The spirituals, in his view, "never tell of joy in the 'good old days.' . . . The only joy in the spirituals is in dreams of escape."

Rather than being essentially otherworldly, these songs, in Brown's opinion, "tell of this life, or 'rollin' through an unfriendly world!" To substantiate this view, he points to numerous lines from spirituals: "Oh, bye and bye, bye and bye, I'm going to lay down this heavy load"; "My way is cloudy"; "Oh, stand the storm, it won't be long, we'll anchor by and by"; "Lord help me from sinking down"; and "Don't know what my mother wants to stay here fuh, Dis ole world ain't been no friend to huh." To those scholars who "would have us believe that when the Negro sang of freedom, he meant only what the whites meant, namely freedom from sin," Brown rejoins:

> Free individualistic whites on the make in a prospering civilization, nursing the American dream, could well have felt their only bondage to be that of sin, and freedom to be religious salvation. But with the drudgery, the hardships, the auction block, the slave-mart, the shackles, and the lash so literally present in the Negro's experience, it is hard to imagine why for the Negro they would remain figurative. The scholars certainly did not make this clear, but rather take refuge in such dicta as "the slave never contemplated his low condition." [1]

[1] From "Negro Folk Expression" by Sterling Brown from *Phylon*, October 1953. Reprinted by permission of Phylon.

"Are we to believe," asks Brown, "that the slave singing 'I been rebuked, I been scorned, done had a hard time sho's you bawn,' referred to his being outside the true religion?" A reading of additional spirituals indicates that they contained distinctions in meaning which placed them outside the confines of the "true religion." Sometimes, in these songs, we hear slaves relating to divinities on terms more West African than American. The easy intimacy and argumentation, which come out of a West African frame of reference, can be heard in "Hold the Wind."

> When I get to heaven, gwine be at ease,
> Me and my God *gonna do as we please.*
>
> Gonna chatter with the Father, argue with the Son,
> *Tell um 'bout the world I just come from.* (Italics added.)

If there is a tie with heaven in those lines from "Hold the Wind," there is also a clear indication of dislike for the restrictions imposed by slavery. And at least one high heavenly authority might have a few questions to answer. *Tell um 'bout the world I just come from* makes it abundantly clear that some slaves—even when released from the burdens of the world—would keep alive painful memories of their oppression.

If slaves could argue with the son of God, then surely, when on their knees in prayer, they would not hesitate to speak to God of the treatment being received at the hands of their oppressors.

> Talk about me much as you please, (2)
> Chillun, talk about me much as you please,
> Gonna talk about you when I get on my knees.[2]

That slaves could spend time complaining about treatment received from other slaves is conceivable, but that this was their only complaint, or even the principal one, is hardly conceivable. To be sure, there is certain ambiguity in the use of the word "chillun" in this context. The reference appears to apply to slaveholders.

The spiritual "Samson," as Vincent Harding has pointed out, probably contained much more (for some slaves) than mere biblical implications. Some who sang these lines from "Samson," Harding suggests, might well have meant tearing down the edifice of slavery. If so, it was the ante-bellum equivalent of today's "burn baby burn."

[2] From *The Negro Caravan* by Brown, Lee and Davis, Arno Press Inc. 1969. Reprinted by permission of Arno Press Inc.

He said, "An' if I had-'n my way,"
He said, "An' if I had-'n my way,"
He said, "An' if I had-'n my way,
I'd tear the buildin' down!"

He said, "And now I got my way, (3)
And I'll tear this buildin' down."

Both Harriet Tubman and Frederick Douglass have reported that some of the spirituals carried double meanings. Whether most of the slaves who sang those spirituals could decode them is another matter. Harold Courlander has made a persuasive case against widespread understanding of any given "loaded" song, but it seems to me that he fails to recognize sufficiently a further aspect of the subject: slaves, as their folktales make eminently clear, used irony repeatedly, especially with animal stories. Their symbolic world was rich. Indeed, the various masks which many put on were not unrelated to this symbolic process. It seems logical to infer that it would occur to more than a few to seize upon some songs, even though created originally for religious purposes, assign another meaning to certain words, and use these songs for a variety of purposes and situations.

At times slave bards created great poetry as well as great music. One genius among the slaves couched his (and their) desire for freedom in a magnificent line of verse. After God's powerful voice had "Rung through Heaven and down in Hell," he sang, "My dungeon shook and my chains, they fell."

In some spirituals, Alan Lomax has written, Afro-Americans turned sharp irony and "healing laughter" toward heaven, again like their West African ancestors, relating on terms of intimacy with God. In one, the slaves have God engaged in a dialogue with Adam:

"Stole my apples, I believe."
"No, marse Lord, I spec it was Eve."
Of this tale there is no mo'
Eve et the apple and Adam de co'.[3]

Douglass informs us that slaves also sang ironic seculars about the institution of slavery. He reports having heard them sing: "We raise de wheat, dey gib us de corn; We sift de meal, dey gib us de huss; We

[3] From *Folk Songs of North America* by Alan Lomax, copyright © 1960 by Alan Lomax; © 1960 by Cassell and Company, Ltd. Reprinted by permission of Doubleday & Company, Inc. and Cassell and Company, Ltd.

peel de meat, dey gib us de skin; An dat's de way dey take us in." [4]
Slaves would often stand back and see the tragicomic aspects of their
situation, sometimes admiring the swiftness of blacks:

> Run, nigger, run, de patrollers will ketch you,
> Run, nigger, run, it's almost day.
> Dat nigger run, dat nigger flew;
> Dat nigger tore his shirt in two. [5]

And there is:

> My ole mistiss promise me
> W'en she died, she'd set me free,
> She lived so long dat 'er head got bal'
> An' she give out'n de notion a-dyin' at all. [6]

In the ante-bellum days, work songs were of crucial import to
slaves. As they cleared and cultivated land, piled levees along rivers,
piled loads on steamboats, stowed cotton bales into the holds of ships,
and cut roads and railroads through forest, mountain, and flat, slaves
sang while the white man, armed and standing in the shade, shouted
his orders. Through the sense of timing and coordination which characterized work songs well sung, especially by the leaders, slaves sometimes quite literally created works of art. These songs not only militated
against injuries but enabled the bondsmen to get difficult jobs done
more easily by not having to concentrate on the dead level of their
work. "In a very real sense the chants of Negro labor," writes Alan
Lomax, "may be considered the most profoundly American of all our
folk songs, for they were created by our people as they tore at American rock and earth and reshaped it with their bare hands, while rivers
of sweat ran down and darkened the dust."

> Long summer day makes a white man lazy,
> Long summer day.
> Long summer day makes a nigger run away, sir,
> Long summer day. [7]

Other slaves sang lines indicating their distaste for slave labor:

[4] From *Life and Times* by Frederick Douglass (Collier Books edition, 1962). Reprinted
by permission of The Macmillan Company.
[5] From "Negro Folk Expression" by Sterling Brown.
[6] From *The Negro Caravan* by Brown, Lee and Davis.
[7] From *Folk Songs of North America* by Alan Lomax.

Ol' massa an' ol' missis,
Sittin' in the parlour,
Jus' fig'in' an' a-plannin'
How to work a nigger harder.[8]

And there are these bitter lines, the meaning of which is clear:

Missus in the big house,
Mammy in the yard,
Missus holdin' her white hands,
Mammy workin' hard, (3)
Missus holdin' her white hands,
Mammy workin' hard.

Old Marse ridin' all time,
Niggers workin' round,
Marse sleepin' day time,
Niggers diggin' in the ground, (3)
Marse sleepin' day time,
Niggers diggin' in the ground.[9]

Courlander tells us that the substance of the work songs "ranges from the humorous to the sad, from the gentle to the biting, and from the tolerant to the unforgiving." The statement in a given song can be metaphoric, tangent or direct, the meaning personal or impersonal. "As throughout Negro singing generally, there is an incidence of social criticism, ridicule, gossip, and protest." Pride in their strength rang with the downward thrust of axe—

When I was young and in my prime, (hah!)
Sunk my axe deep every time, (hah!)

Blacks later found their greatest symbol of manhood in John Henry, descendant of Trickster John of slave folk tales:

A man ain't nothing but a man,
But before I'll let that steam driver beat me down
I'll die with my hammer in my hand.

Though Frances Kemble, an appreciative and sensitive listener to work songs, felt that "one or two barbaric chants would make the

[8] *Ibid.*
[9] From *Negro Folk Music, U.S.A.* by Harold Courlander, New York: Columbia University Press, 1963. Reprinted by permission of Columbia University Press.

fortune of an opera," she was on one occasion "displeased not a little" by a self-deprecating song, one which "embodied the opinion that 'twenty-six black girls not make mulatto yellow girl,' and as I told them I did not like it, they have since omitted it." What is pivotal here is not the presence of self-laceration in folklore, but its extent and meaning. While folklore contained some self-hatred, on balance it gives no indication whatever that blacks, as a group, liked or were indifferent to slavery, which is the issue.

To be sure, only the most fugitive of songs sung by slaves contained direct attacks upon the system. Two of these were associated with slave rebellions. The first, possibly written by ex-slave Denmark Vesey himself, was sung by slaves on at least one island off the coast of Charleston, S.C., and at meetings convened by Vesey in Charleston. Though obviously not a folk song, it was sung by the folk.

> Hail! all hail! ye Afric clan,
> Hail! ye oppressed, ye Afric band,
> Who toil and sweat in slavery bound
> And when your health and strength are gone
> Are left to hunger and to mourn,
> Let independence be your aim,
> Ever mindful what 'tis worth.
> Pledge your bodies for the prize,
> Pile them even to the skies!

The second, a popular song derived from a concrete reality, bears the marks of a conscious authority:

> You mought be rich as cream
> And drive you coach and four-horse team,
> But you can't keep de world from moverin' round
> Nor Nat Turner from gainin' ground.
>
> And your name it mought be Caesar sure,
> And got you cannon can shoot a mile or more,
> But you can't keep de world from moverin' round
> Nor Nat Turner from gainin' ground.

The introduction of Denmark Vesey, class leader in the A.M.E. [African Methodist Episcopal] Church, and Nat Turner, slave preacher, serves to remind us that some slaves and ex-slaves were violent as well as humble, impatient as well as patient.

It is also well to recall that the religious David Walker, who had lived close to slavery in North Carolina, and Henry Highland Garnet, ex-slave and Presbyterian minister, produced two of the most inflammatory, vitriolic and doom-bespeaking polemics America has yet seen. There was theological tension here, loudly proclaimed, a tension which emanated from and was perpetuated by American slavery and race prejudice. This dimension of ambiguity must be kept in mind, if for no other reason than to place in bolder relief the possibility that a great many slaves and free Afro-Americans could have interpreted Christianity in a way quite different from white Christians.

Even those songs which seemed most otherworldly, those which expressed profound weariness of spirit and even faith in death, through their unmistakable sadness, were accusatory, and God was not their object. If one accepts as a given that some of these appear to be almost wholly escapist, the indictment is no less real. Thomas Wentworth Higginson came across one—". . . a flower of poetry in that dark soil," he called it.

> I'll walk in de graveyard, I'll walk through de graveyard,
>   To lay dis body down.
> I'll lie in de grave and stretch out my arms,
>   Lay dis body down.

Reflecting on "I'll lie in de grave and stretch out my arms," Higginson said that "never, it seems to me, since man first lived and suffered, was his infinite longing for peace uttered more plaintively than in that line."

There seems to be small doubt that Christianity contributed in large measure to a spirit of patience which militated against open rebellion among the bondsmen. Yet to overemphasize this point leads one to obscure a no less important reality: Christianity, after being reinterpreted and recast by slave bards, also contributed to that spirit of endurance which powered generations of bondsmen, bringing them to that decisive moment when for the first time a real choice was available to scores of thousands of them.

When that moment came, some slaves who were in a position to decide for themselves did so. W. E. Du Bois re-created their mood and the atmosphere in which they lived.

> There came the slow looming of emancipation. Crowds and armies
> of the unknown, inscrutable, unfathomable Yankees; cruelty behind
> and before; rumors of a new slave trade, but slowly, continuously,
> the wild truth, the bitter truth, the magic truth, came surging
> through. There was to be a new freedom! And a black nation went

tramping after the armies no matter what it suffered; no matter how it was treated, no matter how it died.

The gifted bards, by creating songs with an unmistakable freedom ring, songs which would have been met with swift, brutal repression in the ante-bellum days, probably voiced the sentiments of all but the most degraded and dehumanized. Perhaps not even the incredulous slavemaster could deny the intent of the new lyrics. "In the wake of the Union Army and in the contraband camps," remarked Sterling Brown, "spirituals of freedom sprang up suddenly. . . . Some celebrated the days of Jubilo: 'O Freedom; O Freedom!' and 'Before I'll be a slave, I'll be buried in my grave!' and 'Go home to my lord and be free.'" And there was: "'No more driver's lash for me. . . . Many thousand go.'"

Du Bois brought together the insights of the poet and historian to get inside the slaves:

> There was joy in the South. It rose like perfume—like a prayer. Men stood quivering. Slim dark girls, wild and beautiful with wrinkled hair, wept silently; young women, black, tawny, white and golden, lifted shivering hands, and old and broken mothers, black and gray, raised great voices and shouted to God across the fields, and up to the rocks and the mountains.

Some sang:

> Slavery chain done broke at last, broke at last, broke at last,
> Slavery chain done broke at last,
> Going to praise God till I die.
> I did tell him how I suffer,
> In de dungeon and de chain,
> *And de days I went with head bowed down,*
> And my broken flesh and pain,
> Slavery chain done broke at last, broke at last, broke at last.

Whatever the nature of the shocks generated by the war, among those vibrations felt were some that had come from Afro-American singing ever since the first Africans were forcibly brought to these shores. DuBois was correct when he said that the new freedom song had not come from Africa, but that "the dark throb and beat of that Ancient of Days was in and through it." Thus, the psyches of those who gave rise to and provided widespread support for folk songs had not been reduced to *tabula rasas* on which a slave-holding society could at pleasure sketch out its wish fulfillment fantasies.

We have already seen the acute degree to which some slaves realized they were being exploited. Their sense of the injustice of slavery made it so much easier for them to act out their aggression against whites (by engaging in various forms of "day to day" resistance) without being overcome by a sense of guilt, or a feeling of being ill-mannered. To call this nihilistic thrashing about would be as erroneous as to refer to their use of folklore as esthetic thrashing about. For if they did not regard themselves as the equals of whites in many ways, their folklore indicates that the generality of slaves must have at least felt superior to whites morally. And that, in the context of oppression, could make the difference between a viable human spirit and one crippled by the belief that the interests of the master are those of the slave.

When it is borne in mind that slaves created a large number of extraordinary songs and greatly improved a considerable proportion of the songs of others, it is not at all difficult to believe that they were conscious of the fact that they were leaders in the vital area of art— giving protagonists rather than receiving pawns. And there is some evidence that slaves were aware of the special talent which they brought to music. Higginson has described how reluctantly they sang from hymnals—"even on Sunday"—and how "gladly" they yielded "to the more potent excitement of their own 'spirituals.'" It is highly unlikely that the slaves' preference for their own music went unremarked among them, or that this preference did not affect their estimate of themselves. "They soon found," commented Alan Lomax, "that when they sang, the whites recognized their superiority as singers, and listened with respect." He might have added that those antebellum whites who listened probably seldom understood.

What is of pivotal import, however, is that the esthetic realm was the one area in which slaves knew they were not inferior to whites. Small wonder that they borrowed many songs from the larger community, then quickly invested them with their own economy of statement and power of imagery rather than yield to the temptation of merely repeating what they had heard. Since they were essentially group rather than solo performances, the values inherent in and given affirmation by the music served to strengthen bondsmen in a way that solo music could not have done. In a word, slave singing often provided a form of group therapy, a way in which a slave, in concert with others, could fend off some of the debilitating effects of slavery.

The Washington
Race Riot, 1919

ARTHUR I. WASKOW

The racial division of American society has produced untold misery in this country and has given rise to a pattern of urban racial violence for which the United States has become well-known. Episodes of racially motivated violence have marked American history almost from its beginnings, ranging from lynchings by whites in the South to more recent black ghetto uprisings in the North. There is evidence that genuine "race riots"—a distinct form of racial violence in which members of both races enter into active conflict—took place in New York City as early as 1712.

During the period between the beginning of the First World War and the end of the Second World War, race riots were the characteristic form of racial violence, reaching a peak in the year 1919. Indeed, James Weldon Johnson, the executive director of the NAACP, called the summer of 1919 the "Red Summer" because of the blood that flowed in the streets. At least twenty-two race riots broke out that summer in American cities, both North and South.

Several factors helped to build up the racial hostilities that exploded in 1919. First, the war had spurred a large migration of blacks from rural areas of the South to Northern cities, where many new jobs in commerce and industry were open to blacks for the first time. In addition to opening up new industries, the war mobilization cut off the normal flow of immigrant labor to the North, requiring the active recruitment of black workers. Furthermore, many native whites who might have filled the new positions were drawn into military service, thus permitting blacks to get a foothold in the war industries. When the war ended, demobilization produced a wave of unemployment, and blacks were often the first to be fired. Competition for jobs became acute and led to bitter feeling. Racial tension was increased as returning whites sought to restore the racial patterns that had been altered by the war.

In the forefront of increasingly militant Northern blacks were those who had served in the armed forces during the war. Although the American military discriminated against black troops in a number of ways, and although there had been many racial incidents both at home and abroad during the war, black soldiers felt they had earned a share of the benefits of American society, and they were not inclined to be pushed around without fighting back. Upon their return to this country, several black soldiers, some in army uniform, were lynched by angry mobs. Such atrocities added to the blacks' determination to struggle against their attackers and to hold on to the meager gains they had made during the war.

On May 10, 1919, a riot in Charleston, South Carolina, marked the beginning of the Red Summer, which lasted until the end of September. The major riots of the summer took place in Washington, D.C.; Chicago, Illinois; Longview, Texas; Knoxville, Tennessee; and Omaha, Nebraska. The Chicago riot was the most costly in terms of life, leaving fifteen whites and twenty-three blacks dead and many others wounded. But the Washington riot was particularly startling, because it took place in the nation's capital and because it began, not in some remote sector of the city, but on Pennsylvania Avenue midway between the Capitol and the White House.

The first of the 1919 riots to attract great national attention occurred in Washington, D.C., where a summer of increasing tension between Negroes and whites culminated in an explosion in mid-July.

Relations between the races in the capital had been affected by the accession of the southern-oriented Wilson administration and by the World War. Beginning in 1913, Negroes in the federal service had been segregated at work by their new southern supervisors, where they had never been segregated before; and there had been stirrings of anger among Washington's Negroes over the suddenly more "southern" outlook of their lives.

From *From Race Riot to Sit-In* by Arthur I. Waskow, copyright © 1966 by Doubleday & Company, Inc. Reprinted by permission of the publisher.

Then, with the coming of the war, job prospects changed again. As Emmett Scott, secretary-treasurer of Howard University, described the situation, the war boom in federal employment in Washington gave additional jobs to whites, some of whom left private jobs which Negroes then took over. Negroes were both angered by civil-service discrimination against them and rewarded with a sudden surge in income and self-respect in private employment, where some skilled laborers among them made more money than the white civil servants. Some whites in their turn resented this sudden twist of events. Scott's analysis was confirmed by Louis Brownlow, a commissioner of the District of Columbia, who felt that jealousy among whites at the relatively greater prosperity of Negroes since the war had stirred bitterness between the races.

The fact that Washington's population had been swelled during the war by a major influx of southern whites and a moderate influx of southern Negroes, the one group still intending to "teach any fresh 'nigger' his place" and the other determined to be free or to win revenge, exacerbated the racial tensions within the city. The Negroes' sense of independence was strengthened by their service in France during the war, frequently under officers who had been trained in the Reserve Officers Training Corps (ROTC) at Washington's Howard University.

The existing conflicts were brought to a boil by opportunistic journalism. The *Washington Post*, then published by Ned McLean, was bitterly antagonistic to the District of Columbia government and especially to the top command of the police force. McLean especially objected to tough police enforcement of Prohibition. He began hounding the police through his newspaper, and in the summer of 1919 began to criticize them for not controlling a "crime wave" of assaults and robberies. The *Post* kept the idea of a "crime wave" alive by sensationalizing the usual summer crime statistics and playing up ordinary cases of assault. Prominent among these were alleged instances of attempts by Negroes to rape white women.

On July 9, the Washington branch of the NAACP sent a letter to all four daily newspapers in the city, "calling their attention to the fact that they were sowing the seeds of a race riot by their inflammatory headlines." According to the branch, only one newspaper answered— the *Star*—and that acknowledged the justice of the complaint. The next day, however, the *Times* printed a news story emphasizing the NAACP's interest in bringing to justice all Negroes accused of crime, and leaving out its criticism of the tendency of the press to identify particular Negro criminals with the entire Negro population.

The tension continued to increase. Suspects were arrested in some of the attempted rape cases and then released to the accompaniment of more attacks on police "laxity" by the *Post*. On Saturday, July 19, the *Post* featured another case of alleged assault with the headline, "NEGROES ATTACK GIRL . . . WHITE MEN VAINLY PURSUE." The body of the story described an "attack" in which two Negroes jostled a secretary on her way home, tried to seize her umbrella, and "frightened at her resistance to their insulting actions," fled. The paper also reported that the chief of police, Major Raymond W. Pullman, had ordered all young men "found in isolated or suspicious parts of the city after nightfall" held for questioning.

The incident reported by the *Post* on Saturday morning bore deadly fruit on Saturday night. The girl "attacked" was the wife of a man in the naval aviation department. Two hundred sailors and Marines decided to avenge the slight to his and their honor by lynching two Negroes who had been suspected of the attack but released by the police. The sailors began a march into southwest Washington, stopping every Negro they met and beating several, both men and women. Civilians began to join the march, and when one Negro and his wife fled to their home the mob followed and attempted to break in through hastily set up barricades.

At that point, both District and military police responded to a riot call and dispersed the mob. Ten arrests were made: two of white Navy men, and eight of Negroes who were "held for investigation." When three more Negroes were later stopped on the street by District police patrolling the area, one of them fired at the policemen and wounded one of them. This last event was the first use of violence by Negroes on Saturday night, although the eight-to-two arrest rate might be imagined to have indicated a higher rate of lawbreaking by Negroes. It is hard to avoid concluding that the unneutral behavior of the police had much to do with the Negro attack on them and with the later increase of violence from both Negroes and whites.

On Sunday morning, the Washington branch of the NAACP asked Josephus Daniels, the Secretary of the Navy, to restrain the sailors and Marines who had led the attack. They warned of a more serious clash if no action were taken. But none was taken. Indeed, Daniels' later diary notes on the riot suggested that he blamed most of it on the Negroes and was not greatly interested in protecting them.

On Sunday night the situation exploded. Shortly before 10 P.M., a policeman arrested a young Negro on a minor charge at a heavily trafficked corner on Pennsylvania Avenue, halfway between the Capitol and the White House. While the policeman waited for the patrol wagon, "hundreds of men in khaki and blue and many negroes" crowded around. The Negro under arrest was snatched away from the police by several white men and beaten over the head. The police recovered him and dispersed the crowd, but arrested no whites. Down the street, a few minutes later, another fight broke out between white servicemen and Negro civilians. This time three Negroes were badly injured.

From then on, the violence multiplied. Soldiers and sailors marched up Pennsylvania Avenue, chasing and beating Negroes, yanking them off streetcars, and growing ever more belligerent. The police, few in number and aided only by a handful of soldiers detailed as a provost guard, scarcely interfered, except to arrest about fifteen men, white and Negro, on charges of disorderly conduct. Most Negroes fled, but some fought back. At midnight, the soldiers and sailors had to return to their barracks. But after 1 A.M., even more violent struggles broke out at several corners in the downtown area, with white as well as Negro civilians involved in these clashes.

In reporting the riot on Monday morning, the *Washington Post* gave it the leading place and large black headlines. The paper added a crucial paragraph:

> It was learned that a mobilization of every available service man stationed in or near Washington or on leave here has been ordered for tomorrow evening near the Knights of Columbus hut on Pennsylvania Avenue between Seventh and Eighth Streets. The hour of assembly is 9 o'clock and the purpose is a "clean up" that will cause the events of the last two evenings to pale into insignificance.

No explanation was made of where the "orders" came from, and the publication of this notice brought the strongest condemnation of the *Post* from the Negro community and the District officials.

During the day on Monday, a flurry of meetings were held and statements issued on the violence of Sunday night. The George Washington Post of the American Legion condemned the participation of servicemen or ex-servicemen in the nightly race riots. The NAACP asked the Secretary of War to investigate and punish the guilty soldiers. It also sent a committee to the District commissioners and the chief of police to ask for more effective action by the police to protect Negroes. Herbert J. Seligmann of the NAACP's national office in New York arrived in Washington to get firsthand information on the riot. Pastors of Negro churches, meeting under the sponsorship of the National Race Congress, condemned the police force for taking "no precaution that a competent and efficient police department would have employed," and demanded that the War and Navy departments cancel the leaves of all servicemen in the Washington area.

In Congress, members of the Senate and House committees on the District of Columbia expressed their hope that the riots would cease or be suppressed, but did not recommend any specific action. Congressmen not on these committees were more specific. A Florida congressman demanded a congressional investigation of the failure of the police to apprehend Negro assailants of white women, arguing that this failure had caused the riot. A New York congressman demanded that the Army, Navy, and Marine Corps prevent their men from joining the riots, and received assurances from three high-ranking officers that servicemen would be prevented from participating in any renewal of the riots Monday night. Two other members of the House demanded that the President declare martial law.

District Commissioner Brownlow met with Secretary of War Newton D. Baker and Army Chief of Staff Peyton March in order to plan for the use of troops to quell the rioting. Brownlow told the press that co-operation between the District police and the Army was certain to end the trouble. He said preparations had been made to bring troops in from Army camps in the District and even from Camp Meade, Maryland, if necessary, to police the District. Brownlow also urged Washingtonians to stay out of the downtown area Monday night. No general cancellation of servicemen's leaves was announced, but base commanders were told to detain in barracks all men "without a good excuse for leave."

While this flurry of conferences and statements continued, the first riot cases were being disposed of in police court. Four Negroes who had been arrested Sunday night on charges of disorderly conduct and unlawful assembly were set free. A white sailor was found guilty of disorderly conduct in organizing the original mob march on Saturday night, and was turned over to the Navy for punishment.

During Monday afternoon, Negroes who were alarmed by the *Post*'s "mobilization notice" began to arm themselves. Guns were bought in Washington and Baltimore. "Alley Negroes," some of them soldiers from the Negro regiment recruited in Washington, took out the rifles they had used in France. One story that persisted for decades had it that officers at the Howard University ROTC prepared to give arms and ammunition to the Negro population if it should become necessary. During the day came the first evidence of the new determination of Negroes to "fight back" and even to attack. One mob of twenty-five or thirty boarded a streetcar and beat the motorman and conductors. Others fired from a speeding automobile on sailors in the Naval Hospital grounds. Still others set out in a gang for the Navy Yard, presumably to be on hand when employees finished work; but these were dispersed by the police before they could reach the Yard.

But Monday afternoon was only a faint prelude. That night, despite the precautions and the public statements, the riot was renewed, in a form far worse than before. Four men were killed outright, eleven others mortally or seriously wounded. Of these fifteen, six were white policemen, one a white Marine, three white civilians, and five Negro civilians. Dozens of others sustained injuries that were less serious but required hospitalization. Three hundred men were arrested for riotous behavior or for carrying concealed weapons.

The force that had been set up to cope with the riots was made up of 700 Washington police and 400 soldiers, sailors, and Marines organized as an emergency provost guard. Few servicemen took part in the Monday night disturbances. But a surging mob of 1,000 white civilians made repeated attempts to break through a cavalry cordon in order to attack the Negro residential areas, once almost doing so after massing at the Treasury and marching past the White House. But several cavalry charges broke up these attempts. Whenever the mob found Negroes in the downtown area, the Negroes were savagely beaten. Police were able only to keep the mob moving, not to disperse it. Some Negroes caught in this melee responded to attack by firing pistols at the mob.

Meanwhile, in the Negro areas Negroes were beating white men, and were firing upon passing streetcars and automobiles from houses along the way. Eight or ten automobiles were manned by armed Negroes and were used as armored cavalry in lightning attacks on white residential districts, randomly firing at houses and people. Other automobiles were used by whites in the same fashion, and at least one running dogfight was reported between Negroes and whites in two such cars. Several policemen were wounded or killed while trying to arrest armed Negroes or to raid houses that had been used as sniper centers.

On Tuesday, a startled press was calling for "uncompromising measures," for more military patrols, even for martial law. The District commissioners rejected suggestions that President Wilson be asked to declare martial law, and instead worked out plans for much more forceful military support of the civil government. President Wilson called in Secretary of War Baker, who then arranged with General March, Secretary of the Navy Daniels, and the Washington police chief to order into the District additional troops from Camp Meade, Marines from Quantico, and sailors from two ships lying in the Potomac. In command of these augmented military forces was placed Major General William G. Haan, who ordered troops into every section of the city.

Early in the evening, Baker and Brownlow conferred on the troop dispositions. Haan, accompanied by Police Chief Pullman, drove through the city to inspect the troops. Haan announced publicly that he was satisfied that the situation was well in hand, with one third of his force on actual patrol and two thirds in reserve with speedy transport available to be hurried to any danger point. But privately he talked with military men in New York about the possibility that troops might have to be sent from there. In effect, these arrangements all but supplanted local police, who had become suspect to the Negro community, by the more nearly neutral federal troops.

General Haan also exerted himself to control the city's newspapers, on the theory that much of the riot was "merely a newspaper war." He later wrote a brother officer, "When I got them [the newspapers] to agree to say approximately what I wanted them to say, which was the truth, then soon everything was over."

While these military preparations were being made, the Negro community took steps both to protect its members and to reduce the chance of violence. The NAACP's local legal committee arranged to defend many Negroes who had been arrested for carrying weapons, protesting against the arrests of many such men "while the white men from whom they were attempting to protect themselves were not molested." Another NAACP committee visited Brownlow to report that Negro prisoners after being arrested "were often beaten up and abused by the police officers." They asked to be deputized to visit precinct stations to see that Negro prisoners were treated well, but Brownlow spoke with the police authorities and later said full provision had been made through regular channels for correct treatment of prisoners. Other Negro leaders visited Capitol Hill to ask for a congressional investigation of what they thought was police antagonism to Negroes, exemplified by the failure of the police to hire a single Negro patrolman in four years. Police captains in the heavily Negro precincts met with local Negro leaders and arranged for the early closing of moving-picture theaters, near-beer saloons, and poolrooms in the Negro areas. Leading Negro ministers urged their congregations to keep off the streets.

Minor efforts to prevent another outbreak were made within the federal bureaucracy. The Commerce Department urged all its employees to keep off the street at night and to discuss the subject of race relations "temperately." In the Division of Negro Economics in the Labor Department, the assistant director was asked to get in touch with leading Negro ministers in Washington and try to arrange a meeting with white clergymen that might produce a joint statement to calm the public. The Assistant Secretary of Labor advised against letting even the slightest "tinge" of official sanction be lent to any activity involving the race riot; but he suggested that names of ministers who might be interested could be given as "a personal matter" to an outsider who could then make the contacts himself.

All these efforts at peace-making and order-keeping finally bore fruit on Tuesday night, July 22. Two thousand federal troops, the admonitions for self-control, and an intermittent driving rain together succeeded in preventing crowds from gathering. Only two important incidents marred the night. One Negro tried to escape arrest and was shot, but not seriously hurt, by a Marine on patrol. Two white men on guard duty as officers of the Home Defense League (a police reserve created during the war) were shot, and one of them was killed, when they attempted to halt a Negro for questioning. But aside from these events, a night of rumors and alarms held little violence. "Several times," according to one newspaper, "the cavalry galloped through the streets to answer calls for assistance and found on their arrival that they were not needed." Toward morning, as it became clear that there would be little trouble, and as the wet streets made more and more difficulty for the cavalry detachment, it was withdrawn and put on reserve. At dawn the infantry and naval patrols were withdrawn.

The relaxation allowed Secretary Baker to write the President on Wednesday that the situation was finally in hand. Baker explained that the one death had grown "out of no controversy or excitement but . . .

an unprovoked and impulsive act, perhaps the act of a man of unstable mind, deranged by excitement growing out of the general situation." He reported that the attitude of the Negroes, particularly their leaders, had been helpful. As for Wednesday evening, Baker said he had instructed Haan to keep his troops on duty at points from which they could quickly meet any emergency.

The rest was anticlimax. Several members of the NAACP staff visited Senator Arthur Capper, a Kansas Republican, Wednesday and won his support for a congressional investigation of race riots and lynching. On Thursday, a coroner's jury held one Negro for murder of a white Marine, although the Negro claimed he had drawn his pistol in self-defense against a mob and had hit the Marine accidentally. But by Thursday it was clear that the riot was over, and attention turned to the prevention of future riots.

Summary

of the Kerner Report

on Civil Disorders

THE KERNER COMMISSION

In the years since the Second World War, black Americans have developed a variety of programs aimed at freeing themselves from white oppression and discrimination. They scored a major legal victory with the Supreme Court ruling of May 1954, which declared laws requiring racially segregated schools unconstitutional and set a precedent that led to the abolition of almost all legally enforced segregation in this country. The lawyers of the NAACP's Legal Defense and Education Fund were responsible for the preparation of this court case, and it was argued before the Supreme Court by Thurgood Marshall, who later became the first black man appointed to that court. Also during the 1950's, several changes in the customary racial patterns of life in the South were brought about as a result of the nonviolent direct-action campaigns organized by followers of Martin Luther King, Jr., and by the young members of the Student Nonviolent Coordinating Committee (since renamed the Student National Coordinating Committee). Using sit-ins, freedom rides, and boycotts, the nonviolent civil rights movement successfully drew the nation's attention to the South's continued denial of basic rights to its black citizens.

It was clear even in the early years of the civil rights movement that neither legal action nor nonviolent protest could be of much service to blacks in the North and the West, where discriminatory laws rarely existed and where the patterns of racial discrimination were far more subtle and erratic. Yet Northern society was almost as segregated as Southern, and the frustrations of Northern blacks—particularly in the urban ghettos—were rapidly mounting. By the mid-1960's, Northern ghetto-dwellers had found their own form of protest. Variously termed "riots," "revolts," and "civil disorders," literally hundreds of violent protests erupted in both Northern and Southern cities between 1964 and 1967. These outbursts were spontaneous, unorganized expressions of hostility aimed at the symbols of authority and oppression. Because of their clearly political nature, they are perhaps best described as "uprisings."

Unlike the race riots of the past, the new outbreaks of racial violence did not involve aggressive action by opposing groups of whites and blacks. Rather, the whites involved in the disturbances were usually only those who represented white authority and oppression to the ghetto-dwellers—policemen, firemen, and national guardsmen. In the great majority of the uprisings, the violence of the blacks was directed only against property—typically, against slum buildings and exploitative ghetto stores and shops. In fact, looting was the most widely noted activity of the protesters, leading one study to characterize the uprisings as "consumer revolts." Only when police and guardsmen invaded the ghettos—presumably to restore order—did violence against people break out.

Anxious to quiet an alarmed public, President Lyndon Johnson appointed a commission under the chairmanship of Governor Otto Kerner of Illinois to study the background and the causes of the disorders in the cities and to recommend policies to prevent their recurrence. This commission came to the unexpected yet obvious conclusion that "white racism is essentially responsible for the explosive mixture which has been accumulating in our cities since the end of World War II."

The summary of the Kerner Commission's report on why the riots took place is printed in the following pages. Certainly, the commission's analysis of the conditions of ghetto life was serious and thorough. However, it may have proceeded from a mistaken assumption: that "the major goal is the creation of a true union—a single society and a single American identity." In reality, the creation of a truly plural society and a truly plural American identity may be the only solution to the race problems of America today.

WHY DID IT HAPPEN?

Chapter 4
The Basic Causes

In addressing the question "Why did it happen?" we shift our focus from the local to the national scene, from the particular events of the summer of 1967 to the factors within the society at large that created a mood of violence among many urban Negroes.

These factors are complex and interacting; they vary significantly in their effect from city to city and from year to year; and the consequences of one disorder, generating new grievances and new demands, become the causes of the next. Thus was created the "thicket of tension, conflicting evidence and extreme opinions" cited by the President.

Despite these complexities, certain fundamental matters are clear. Of these, the most fundamental is the racial attitude and behavior of white Americans toward black Americans.

Race prejudice has shaped our history decisively; it now threatens to affect our future.

White racism is essentially responsible for the explosive mixture which has been accumulating in our cities since the end of World War II. Among the ingredients of this mixture are:

> *Pervasive discrimination and segregation* in employment, education and housing, which have resulted in the continuing exclusion of great numbers of Negroes from the benefits of economic progress.
>
> *Black in-migration and white exodus,* which have produced the massive and growing concentrations of impoverished Negroes in our major cities, creating a growing crisis of deteriorating facilities and services and unmet human needs.
>
> *The black ghettos,* where segregation and poverty converge on the young to destroy opportunity and enforce failure. Crime, drug addiction, dependency on welfare, and bitterness and resentment against society in general and white society in particular are the result.

At the same time, most whites and some Negroes outside the ghetto have prospered to a degree unparalleled in the history of civilization. Through television and other media, this affluence has been

"Summary of the Kerner Report on Civil Disorders" from the Kerner Commission, *The Report of the National Advisory Commission on Civil Disorders,* U.S. Government Printing Office, 1968.

flaunted before the eyes of the Negro poor and the jobless ghetto youth.

Yet these facts alone cannot be said to have caused the disorders. Recently, other powerful ingredients have begun to catalyze the mixture:

Frustrated hopes are the residue of the unfulfilled expectations aroused by the great judicial and legislative victories of the Civil Rights Movement and the dramatic struggle for equal rights in the South.

A climate that tends toward approval and encouragement of violence as a form of protest has been created by white terrorism directed against nonviolent protest; by the open defiance of law and federal authority by state and local officials resisting desegregation; and by some protest groups engaging in civil disobedience who turn their backs on nonviolence, go beyond the constitutionally protected rights of petition and free assembly, and resort to violence to attempt to compel alteration of laws and policies with which they disagree.

The frustrations of powerlessness have led some Negroes to the conviction that there is no effective alternative to violence as a means of achieving redress of grievances, and of "moving the system." These frustrations are reflected in alienation and hostility toward the institutions of law and government and the white society which controls them, and in the reach toward racial consciousness and solidarity reflected in the slogan "Black Power."

A new mood has sprung up among Negroes, particularly among the young, in which self-esteem and enhanced racial pride are replacing apathy and submission to "the system."

The police are not merely a "spark" factor. To some Negroes police have come to symbolize white power, white racism and white repression. And the fact is that many police do reflect and express these white attitudes. The atmosphere of hostility and cynicism is reinforced by a widespread belief among Negroes in the existence of police brutality and in a "double standard" of justice and protection—one for Negroes and one for whites.

To this point, we have attempted to identify the prime components of the "explosive mixture." In the chapters that follow we seek to analyze them in the perspective of history. Their meaning, however, is clear:

In the summer of 1967, we have seen in our cities a chain reaction of racial violence. If we are heedless, none of us shall escape the consequences.

Chapter 5
Rejection and Protest: An Historical Sketch

The causes of recent racial disorders are embedded in a tangle of issues and circumstances—social, economic, political and psychological —which arise out of the historic pattern of Negro-white relations in America.

In this chapter we trace the pattern, identify the recurrent themes of Negro protest and, most importantly, provide a perspective on the protest activities of the present era.

We describe the Negro's experience in America and the development of slavery as an institution. We show his persistent striving for equality in the face of rigidly maintained social, economic and educational barriers, and repeated mob violence. We portray the ebb and flow of the doctrinal tides—accommodation, separatism, and self-help —and their relationship to the current theme of Black Power. We conclude:

> The Black Power advocates of today consciously feel that they are the most militant group in the Negro protest movement. Yet they have retreated from a direct confrontation with American society on the issue of integration and, by preaching separatism, unconsciously function as an accommodation to white racism. Much of their economic program, as well as their interest in Negro history, self-help, racial solidarity and separation, is reminiscent of Booker T. Washington. The rhetoric is different, but the ideas are remarkably similar.

Chapter 6
The Formation of the Racial Ghettos [1]

Throughout the twentieth century the Negro population of the United States has been moving steadily from rural areas to urban and from South to North and West. In 1910, 91 percent of the nation's 9.8 million Negroes lived in the South and only 27 percent of American Negroes lived in cities of 2,500 persons or more. Between 1910 and 1966 the total Negro population more than doubled, reaching 21.5 million, and the number living in metropolitan areas rose more than

[1] The term "ghetto" as used in this report refers to an area within a city characterized by poverty and acute social disorganization, and inhabited by members of a racial or ethnic group under conditions of involuntary segregation.

five-fold (from 2.6 million to 14.8 million). The number outside the South rose eleven-fold (from 880,000 to 9.7 million).

Negro migration from the South has resulted from the expectation of thousands of new and highly paid jobs for unskilled workers in the North and the shift to mechanized farming in the South. However, the Negro migration is small when compared to earlier waves of European immigrants. Even between 1960 and 1966, there were 1.8 million immigrants from abroad compared to the 613,000 Negroes who arrived in the North and West from the South.

As a result of the growing number of Negroes in urban areas, natural increase has replaced migration as the primary source of Negro population increase in the cities. Nevertheless, Negro migration from the South will continue unless economic conditions there change dramatically.

Basic data concerning Negro urbanization trends indicate that:

> Almost all Negro population growth (98 percent from 1950 to 1966) is occurring within metropolitan areas, primarily within central cities.[2]
> The vast majority of white population growth (78 percent from 1960 to 1966) is occurring in suburban portions of metropolitan areas. Since 1960, white central-city population has declined by 1.3 million.
> As a result, central cities are becoming more heavily Negro while the suburban fringes around them remain almost entirely white.
> The twelve largest central cities now contain over two-thirds of the Negro population outside the South, and one-third of the Negro total in the United States.

Within the cities, Negroes have been excluded from white residential areas through discriminatory practices. Just as significant is the withdrawal of white families from, or their refusal to enter, neighborhoods where Negroes are moving or already residing. About 20 percent of the urban population of the United States changes residence every year. The refusal of whites to move into "changing" areas when vacancies occur means that most vacancies eventually are occupied by Negroes.

The result, according to a recent study, is that in 1960 the average

---

- [2] A "central city" is the largest city of a standard metropolitan statistical area, that is, a metropolitan area containing at least one city of 50,000 or more inhabitants.

segregation index for 207 of the largest United States cities was 86.2. In other words, to create an unsegregated population distribution, an average of over 86 percent of all Negroes would have to change their place of residence within the city.

Chapter 7
Unemployment, Family Structure, and Social Disorganization

Although there have been gains in Negro income nationally, and a decline in the number of Negroes below the "poverty level," the condition of Negroes in the central city remains in a state of crisis. Between 2 and 2.5 million Negroes—16 to 20 percent of the total Negro population of all central cities—live in squalor and deprivation in ghetto neighborhoods.

Employment is a key problem. It not only controls the present for the Negro American but, in a most profound way, it is creating the future as well. Yet, despite continuing economic growth and declining national unemployment rates, the unemployment rate for Negroes in 1967 was more than double that for whites.

Equally important is the undesirable nature of many jobs open to Negroes and other minorities. Negro men are more than three times as likely as white men to be in low-paying, unskilled or service jobs. This concentration of male Negro employment at the lowest end of the occupational scale is the single most important cause of poverty among Negroes.

In one study of low-income neighborhoods, the "subemployment rate," including both unemployment and underemployment, was about 33 percent, or 8.8 times greater than the overall unemployment rate for all United States workers.

Employment problems, aggravated by the constant arrival of new unemployed migrants, many of them from depressed rural areas, create persistent poverty in the ghetto. In 1966, about 11.9 percent of the nation's whites and 40.6 percent of its nonwhites were below the "poverty level" defined by the Social Security Administration (currently $3,335 per year for an urban family of four). Over 40 percent of the nonwhites below the poverty level live in the central cities.

Employment problems have drastic social impact in the ghetto. Men who are chronically unemployed or employed in the lowest status jobs are often unable or unwilling to remain with their families. The handicap imposed on children growing up without fathers in an atmosphere of poverty and deprivation is increased as mothers are forced to work to provide support.

The culture of poverty that results from unemployment and family breakup generates a system of ruthless, exploitative relationships within the ghetto. Prostitution, dope addiction and crime create an environmental "jungle" characterized by personal insecurity and tension. Children growing up under such conditions are likely participants in civil disorder.

Chapter 8
Conditions of Life in the Racial Ghetto

A striking difference in environment from that of white, middle-class Americans profoundly influences the lives of residents of the ghetto.

Crime rates, consistently higher than in other areas, create a pronounced sense of insecurity. For example, in one city one low-income Negro district had 35 times as many serious crimes against persons as a high-income white district. Unless drastic steps are taken, the crime problems in poverty areas are likely to continue to multiply as the growing youth and rapid urbanization of the population outstrip police resources.

Poor health and sanitation conditions in the ghetto result in higher mortality rates, a higher incidence of major diseases, and lower availability and utilization of medical services. The infant mortality rate for nonwhite babies under the age of one month is 58 percent higher than for whites; for one to 12 months it is almost three times as high. The level of sanitation in the ghetto is far below that in high-income areas. Garbage collection is often inadequate. Of an estimated 14,000 cases of rat bite in the United States in 1965, most were in ghetto neighborhoods.

Ghetto residents believe they are "exploited" by local merchants; and evidence substantiates some of these beliefs. A study conducted in one city by the Federal Trade Commission showed that distinctly higher prices were charged for goods sold in ghetto stores than in other areas.

Lack of knowledge regarding credit purchasing creates special pitfalls for the disadvantaged. In many states garnishment practices compound these difficulties by allowing creditors to deprive individuals of their wages without hearing or trial.

Chapter 9
Comparing the Immigrant and Negro Experience

In this chapter, we address ourselves to a fundamental question that many white Americans are asking: Why have so many Negroes, unlike the European immigrants, been unable to escape from the ghetto and from poverty? We believe the following factors play a part:

The Maturing Economy: When the European immigrants arrived, they gained an economic foothold by providing the unskilled labor needed by industry. Unlike the immigrant, the Negro migrant found little opportunity in the city. The economy, by then matured, had little use for the unskilled labor he had to offer.

The Disability of Race: The structure of discrimination has stringently narrowed opportunities for the Negro and restricted his prospects. European immigrants suffered from discrimination, but never so pervasively.

Entry into the Political System: The immigrants usually settled in rapidly growing cities with powerful and expanding political machines, which traded economic advantages for political support. Ward-level grievance machinery, as well as personal representation, enabled the immigrant to make his voice heard and his power felt.

By the time the Negro arrived, these political machines were no longer so powerful or so well equipped to provide jobs or other favors, and in many cases were unwilling to share their influence with Negroes.

Cultural Factors: Coming from societies with a low standard of living and at a time when job aspirations were low, the immigrants sensed little deprivation in being forced to take the less desirable and poorer-paying jobs. Their large and cohesive families contributed to total income. Their vision of the future—one that led to a life outside the ghetto—provided the incentive necessary to endure the present.

Although Negro men worked as hard as the immigrants, they were unable to support their families. The entrepreneurial opportunities had vanished. As a result of slavery and long periods of unemployment, the Negro family structure had become matriarchal; the males played a secondary and marginal family role—one which offered little compensation for their hard and unrewarding labor. Above all, segregation denied Negroes access to good jobs and the opportunity to leave the ghetto. For them, the future seemed to lead only to a dead end.

Today, whites tend to exaggerate how well and quickly they escaped from poverty. The fact is that immigrants who came from rural backgrounds, as many Negroes do, are only now, after three generations, finally beginning to move into the middle class.

By contrast, Negroes began concentrating in the city less than two generations ago, and under much less favorable conditions. Although some Negroes have escaped poverty, few have been able to escape the urban ghetto.

Suggestions for Further Reading

An excellent study of American slavery in the context of world history is David B. Davis, *The Problem of Slavery in Western Culture* ° (Cornell University Press, 1966). On the question of whether slavery led to prejudice or prejudice led to slavery, see Oscar and Mary Handlin, "Origins of the Southern Labor System," *William and Mary Quarterly,* 3d Ser., Vol. 7 (April, 1950), 199–222, reprinted as Chapter 1 of Oscar Handlin, *Race and Nationality in American Life* ° (Little, Brown, 1957); Carl Degler, "Slavery and the Genesis of American Race Prejudice," *Comparative Studies in Society and History,* Vol. 2 (October, 1959), 49–66, enlarged, revised, and reprinted in Degler's *Out of Our Past* ° (Harper and Row, 1959), 26–39; and Winthrop D. Jordan, "Modern Tensions and the Origins of American Slavery," *Journal of Southern History,* Vol. 28 (February, 1962), 18–30. Two excellent collections of essays on the development of slavery in the New World are Allen Weinstein and Frank O. Gatell (eds.), *American Negro Slavery: A Modern Reader* ° (Oxford University Press, 1968), and Laura Foner and Eugene Genovese (eds.), *Slavery in the New World: A Reader in Comparative History* ° (Prentice-Hall, 1969).

Of particular interest are works pertaining to the slaves' formulations of their own experience—the folktales, songs, and narratives that make up the distinctive oral tradition of black America. A brief presentation of the variety of primary source materials available to historians is William F. Cheek (ed.), *Black Resistance Before the Civil War* ° (Glencoe, 1970). Spirituals are collected in James Weldon Johnson and J. Rosamond Johnson (eds.), *The Books of American Negro Spirituals* ° (Viking, 1925, 1926). See also Harold Courlander, *Negro Folk Music U.S.A.* ° (Columbia University Press, 1963). Folktales are collected in Langston Hughes and Arna Bontemps (eds.), *The Book of Negro Folklore* ° (Dodd, Mead, 1958); Richard Dorson (ed.), *American Negro Folktales* ° (Fawcett, 1967); and J. Mason Brewer (ed.), *American Negro Folklore* (Quadrangle, 1968). Charles H. Nichols has surveyed and analyzed narratives composed by fugitive slaves in *Many Thousand Gone: The Ex-Slaves' Account of Their Bondage and Freedom* ° (Brill, 1963). Perhaps the most important of these narratives is the *Narrative of the Life of Frederick Douglass, an American Slave, Written by Himself* ° (Anti-Slavery Office, 1845). Readily available collections of narratives by former slaves are Gilbert Osofsky (ed.), *Puttin' On Ole Massa: The Slave Narratives of Henry Bibb, William Wells Brown, and Solomon Northrup* ° (Harper and Row, 1969); Arna Bontemps (ed.), *Great Slave Narratives* ° (Beacon, 1969), which presents the narratives of Olaudah Equiano, W. C. Pennington, and William and Ellen Craft; and Norman R.

° Available in paperback edition.

Yetman (ed.), *Life Under the Peculiar Institution: Selections from the Slave Narrative Collection* ° (Holt, Rinehart and Winston, 1970).

Several of C. Vann Woodward's essays on the post-bellum South have been collected under the title *The Burden of Southern History* ° (Louisiana State University Press, 1960). Woodward describes the development of segregation in the South in *The Strange Career of Jim Crow* ° (2d rev. ed.; Oxford University Press, 1966). The problems faced by Southern blacks after the Civil War are considered in Charles E. Wynes (ed.), *The Negro in the South since 1865* ° (University of Alabama Press, 1965). Rayford W. Logan provides a survey of attitudes toward Afro-Americans during the Gilded Age in *The Negro in American Life and Thought: The Nadir, 1877–1901* (Dial, 1954), published in paperback under the title *The Betrayal of the Negro.* ° Postwar attitudes and political activities of Southern whites are considered in Lawrence J. Friedman, *The White Savage: Racial Fantasies in the Postbellum South* ° (Prentice-Hall, 1970).

Racial strife is the subject of Allen Grimshaw (ed.), *Racial Violence in the United States* (Aldine, 1969). For studies of specific race riots, see the report of the Chicago Commission on Race Relations, *The Negro in Chicago: A Study of Race Relations and a Race Riot* (University of Chicago Press, 1922); William M. Tuttle, Jr., *Race Riot: Chicago in the Red Summer of 1919* (Atheneum, 1970); and Elliott M. Rudwick, *Race Riot at East St. Louis, July 2, 1917* ° (Southern Illinois University Press, 1964). Organized antiblack agitation is described in David Chalmers, *Hooded Americanism* ° (Doubleday, 1965), and in Kenneth Jackson, *The Ku Klux Klan in the City, 1915–1930* ° (Oxford University Press, 1968).

The revolt of the victims of American history reached early milestones with the 1954 Supreme Court decision against the racial segregation of schools, the Montgomery, Alabama, bus boycott of 1955, and the black student sit-ins of 1960. On the Supreme Court decision and the nation's subsequent failure to implement it, see the book by Anthony Lewis and *The New York Times,* entitled *Portrait of a Decade: The Second American Revolution* ° (Random House, 1964). Martin Luther King, Jr., tells the story of the bus boycott in *Stride Toward Freedom: The Montgomery Story* ° (Harper and Row, 1958). The sit-ins are described by Howard Zinn in *SNCC: The New Abolitionists* ° (Beacon, 1964). In *The Negro Revolt* ° (Harper and Row, 1962), Louis Lomax describes the background of the revolt that broke out in the late 1950's and early 1960's.

The changes in the mood of the black revolt as it moved from nonviolence to self-defense are described in two excellent articles: Allen J. Matusow, "From Civil Rights to Black Power: The Case of SNCC, 1960–1966," in Barton J. Bernstein and Allen J. Matusow (eds.), *Twentieth-Century America: Recent Interpretations* ° (Harcourt Brace Jovanovich, 1969), pp. 531–57, and Vincent Harding, "Black Radicalism: The Road from Montgomery," in Alfred F. Young (ed.), *Dissent: Explorations in the History of American Radicalism* ° (Northern Illinois University Press, 1968), pp. 321–54. See Julius Lester, *Look Out Whitey! Black Power's Gon' Get Your Mama* ° (Dial, 1968), for another treatment of the same topic.

Charles E. Silberman, in *Crisis in Black and White* ° (Random House, 1964), provides an excellent study of the background to the racial explosions that took place in Northern cities in the mid-1960's. In *Dark Ghetto: Dilemmas of Social Power* ° (Harper and Row, 1965), Kenneth Clark explores the psychological aspects of life in a black ghetto. Novelist and essayist James Baldwin describes the mood of black people on the eve of the urban insurrections in *The Fire Next Time* ° (Dial, 1963). Robert Conot's excellent *Rivers of Blood, Years of Darkness* ° (Bantam, 1967) describes the background and the foreground of the Watts rebellion of 1965. The conditions of urban ghetto life that lead to violent outbreaks are explored in Paul Jacobs, *Prelude to Riot: A View of Urban America from the Bottom* ° (Random House, 1966).

The ideas and impact of Malcolm X, whose legacy inspires several strands of contemporary black protest, are explored in *The Autobiography of Malcolm X* ° (Grove, 1964); George Breitman (ed.), *Malcolm X Speaks* ° (Merit, 1965); and John Henrik Clarke (ed.), *Malcolm X: The Man and His Times* ° (Macmillan, 1969).

Bobby Seale, a founder of the Black Panther party, tells the story of this organization in *Seize the Time: The Story of the Black Panther Party and Huey P. Newton* ° (Random House, 1970). A useful collection of statements by Panther leaders is Philip F. Foner (ed.), *The Black Panthers Speak* ° (Lippincott, 1970).

On white racism, see Gary B. Nash and Richard Weiss (eds.), *The Great Fear: Race in the Mind of America* ° (Holt, Rinehart and Winston, 1970); Thomas F. Gossett, *Race: The History of an Idea in America* ° (Southern Methodist University Press, 1963); and Joel Kovel, *White Racism: A Psychohistory* ° (Pantheon, 1970).

Poor Whites

The Indentured Servant

MARCUS W. JERNEGAN

During the first hundred years of English colonization the labor force was made up primarily of indentured servants from England—men, women, and children who sold themselves into temporary bondage in return for passage to the New World. It has been recently estimated that from one-half to three-fourths of the immigrants to the English colonies in the seventeenth century fit into this category.

Considering the many hazards faced by New World settlers, the reluctance of prosperous English tradesmen or craftsmen to journey to North America is understandable. The three thousand miles that separated it from England, the strangeness of the land, and the danger of conflict with the Indians made the attraction of the New World slight for those with any degree of comfort in the old. Apart from a few daring speculators, most of the prosperous immigrants were men seeking the freedom to practice Puritan or other non-Anglican religions. Most of these immigrants settled in New England and in Pennsylvania.

There was, however, a great demand for new population in the New World. Laborers were needed to grow food for the colonists and thus to allow the development of ordinary commerce. Moreover, additional manpower was needed to defend the settlements against increasingly hostile Indians as well as against the French and the Spanish.

Fortunately for the development of the colonies, several sources of labor were available. First, there was a growing surplus of population in England. Farmland, which had been divided into individually owned strips and farmed communally, was increasingly consolidated into large tracts of land, thereby forcing the peasants either to become tenant farmers or to look for new means of livelihood. Industrialization, which might have absorbed these landless peasants, was more than a century away, and city life held little promise for them. Many turned to indentured servitude as a solution to their problems, to the relief of both England and the colonies. Other servants came to the colonies as the result of the civil wars in the British Isles during the seventeenth century. James I, Oliver Cromwell, and the later Stuart kings sent Scottish and Irish prisoners to the colonies— chiefly to the West Indies but also to the North American mainland.

The following essay describes still other sources of the dependent labor class that grew up in the New World. It also compares the living conditions of the immigrants before they left England with those that awaited them in the New World.

Could we draw the curtain which conceals the life of prehistoric people, we should see that the servant problem is as old as the human race. Indeed, if it were possible for extremes to meet, cave-dwellers and denizens of twentieth-century skyscrapers would doubtless converse sympathetically on this never-ending problem. Its existence is due to the universal desire of man to use the strength of others for his own profit and pleasure—an unchangeable trait of human nature.

During the colonial period of our history, service was performed in the main by two classes—the Negro slave and the indentured white servant. The white servant, a semi-slave, was more important in the seventeenth century than even the Negro slave, in respect to both numbers and economic significance. Perhaps the most pressing of the early needs of the colonists was for a certain and adequate supply of labor. It was the white servants who supplied this demand and made possible a rapid economic development, particularly of the middle and southern colonies. In 1683 there were twelve thousand of these semi-slaves in Virginia, composing about one-sixth of the population, while nearly two-thirds of the immigrants to Pennsylvania during the eighteenth century were white servants. Every other colony made greater or less use of them, and it is likely that more than a quarter of a million persons were of this class during the colonial period.

From "A Forgotten Slavery of Colonial Days" by Marcus W. Jernegan from *Harper's Magazine*, October 1913, copyright 1913, by Minneapolis Star and Tribune Co., Inc. Reprinted from the October, 1913 issue of Harper's Magazine.

Such a widespread and important institution has great significance for the social and economic history of Europe and America in the seventeenth and eighteenth centuries. Moreover, the story is full of human interest because of methods used to supply the demand, similar to methods in the slave-trade: the classes of people from which some servants were drawn—convicts, paupers, and dissolute persons of every type; the stormy life of many servants and the troublesome moral and social problems which their presence engendered, such as intermarriage with Negro slaves; the runaway criminal servants, and their influence on moral standards and on other phases of life in the colonies.

White servitude developed rapidly because of favorable conditions—a large demand for servants coupled with a large supply. The economic theory of European states in the seventeenth century called for a large population in their colonies, in order that trade and commerce might develop rapidly. The colonists were to supply food and raw materials, and the home country was to develop manufactures. Means, therefore, must be devised, first, to attract settlers who would develop the economic resources of the colonies, and, second, to provide them with an adequate supply of labor. There were vast areas of rich virgin lands, which, in the southern and middle colonies, were usually granted in a manner to promote rapid increase of population and extension of cultivated tracts. This method was known as the "headright" system. Anyone emigrating was rewarded with a gift of land— about a hundred and fifty acres. Since labor was needed to clear and work this land, anyone importing a servant was entitled to an additional allotment, a "head right." To induce laborers to emigrate, a similar allotment was promised to them after each had served a term of years as a servant. Thus free land solved the two most pressing problems mentioned above.

Fortunately, the enormous demand for white servants came when economic conditions had created a large supply. In the sixteenth century, English agriculture was giving way to sheep-raising, so that a few herders often took the place of many farm laborers. As a result, the unemployed, the poor, and the criminal classes increased rapidly. Justices, who were landowners, had the power to fix the maximum wages of farm laborers. Sometimes they made them very low, hardly a shilling a day; for the lower the wage the greater the profits of the tenant farmer, and, therefore, the greater his ability to pay higher rents demanded by the landowner. Thus, while wages remained practically stationary, wheat multiplied in price nearly four times in this period,

1500–1600. In other words, a man worked forty weeks in 1600 for as much food as he received in 1500 by working ten weeks. To prevent scarcity of farm laborers, the statute of apprentices (1562) forbade anyone below the rank of a yeoman to withdraw from agricultural pursuits to be apprenticed to a trade. Moreover, the poor laws passed in this period compelled each parish to support its poor, and provided penalties for vagrancy. Thus the farm laborer had no chance to better himself. Conditions were almost beyond description, and in lean years people perished from famine. Sheffield in 1615, with a population of 2,207, had 725 relying on charity, 37.8 per cent of the population. As a result, the colonies were regarded as a convenient dumping ground for undesirable citizens. Velasco, the Spanish minister in England, wrote his sovereign, 1611, "Their principal reason for colonizing these parts is to give an outlet to so many idle, wretched people as they have in England, and thus prevent the dangers that might be feared of them."

It is evident that if this surplus population could be transferred to the American colonies, both the mother country and the colonists would profit. One of the earliest proposals was made by Sir George Peckham, 1582. He declared that there were such great numbers living in penury and want that they might be willing to "hazard their lives and serve one year for meat, drinke, and apparell only without wages, in hope thereby to amend their estates." It was natural for men and women, in order to secure free transportation to America, to bind themselves by written contract, called an indenture, to serve some individual for a term of years.

There were three main classes of servants. One who entered into such a contract with an agent, often the shipmaster, was called an indentured servant. The shipmaster reimbursed himself, on arrival in America, by selling the time of the servant to the highest bidder. The second class included the "redemptioners," or "free-willers." They signed no contract beforehand, but were given transportation by the shipmaster with the understanding that on arrival they were to have a few days to indenture themselves to someone to pay for their passage. Failing this, the shipmaster could sell them himself. The free-willer then was at a great disadvantage. He had to bargain in competition with many others, and was so much at the mercy of the buyer or shipmaster that laws were passed by several colonies limiting his time of service and defining his rights.

The third class consisted of those forced into servitude, such as convicts, felons, vagrants, and dissolute persons, and those kidnaped or "spirited" away by the so-called "spirits" or "crimps." Convicts were often granted royal pardon on condition of being transported. For example, Charles I, in 1635, gave orders to the sheriff of London to deliver to Captain Thomas Hill or Captain Richard Carleton nine female convicts for removal to Virginia, to be sold as servants. At an early date judges imposed penalties of transportation on convicted criminals and others. Thus Narcissus Luttrell notes in his diary, November 17, 1692, that the magistrates had ordered on board a ship lying at Leith, bound for Virginia, fifty lewd women out of the house of correction and thirty others who walked the streets at night. An act of Parliament in 1717 gave judges still greater power by allowing them to order the transportation of convicts for seven years, known as "His Majesty's seven-year passengers," and, in case the penalty for the crime was death, for fourteen years. Those agreeing to transport convicts could sell them as servants. From London prisons, especially Newgate and the Old Bailey, large numbers were sent forth, the latter alone supplying not far from 10,000 between 1717 and 1775. Scharf, the historian of Maryland, declares that 20,000 felons were imported into that colony before the Revolution. At least nine of the colonies are known to have received felons as servants, so that the total number sent was not far from 50,000. Lists of felons ordered transported were often printed in the *Gentleman's Magazine;* one of May, 1747, numbering 887. Remembering this, perhaps, Dr. Johnson said in 1769, "Sir, they are a race of convicts, and ought to be content with anything we may allow them short of hanging."

❈   ❈   ❈

The main work of the servant was to clear the land and cultivate the crop, though artisans, of course, worked at their trades. Boucher asserts that two-thirds of the persons employed as schoolmasters in Maryland just before the Revolution were either indentured servants or convicts. A letter from Washington's overseer complains of the fact that his servants were difficult to manage because of a liking for liquor. "The Sot Weed Factor" makes one of the female servants "who passed for a chambermaid" speak thus:

> In better Times, e'er to this Land
> I was unhappily Trapann'd;
> Perchance as well I did appear,
> As any Lord or Lady here,
> Not then a Slave for twice two Year.

My cloaths were fashioned new,
Nor were my Shifts of Linnen Blue;
But things are changed, now at the Hoe,
I daily work, and Barefoot go,
In weeding Corn or feeding Swine,
I spend my melancholy Time.
Kidnap'd and Fool'd, I thither fled,
To Shun a hated Nuptial Bed,
And to my cost already find,
Worse Plagues than those I left behind.

Interesting phases of the institution of white servitude appear in the laws regulating their status. Unlike the slave, the white servant could bring suit for justice. The court could order his freedom or lessen his term of service. It could require the master to provide the servant with medical attendance, see that freedom dues were paid and that he had sufficient food and clothing. On the other hand, his time belonged to his master, and severe work could be exacted. His privileges and freedom of movement were restricted. He could not absent himself from his master without permission. He could be whipped for disobedience. He was not allowed to buy or sell anything without leave. Tavern-keepers could not entertain him or sell him liquor. He could neither marry without his master's consent, nor could he vote or hold office, but he could be sold or seized to satisfy an outstanding debt.

The treatment and condition of servants varied widely in different colonies and at different periods, depending on the nature of the work and the character of the servant and the master. In general, their treatment was better in New England and the middle colonies than in the southern. Harrowing tales of cruelty and abuse of white servants are common, but the same kind of treatment was meted out to servants in England during this period. In the court records of Middlesex County, England, 1673, we find that Thomas Tooner was cited to answer to the charge of inhumanly beating his female servant with knotted whipcords, so that "the poor servant is a lamentable spectacle to behold." The lash was likewise the usual mode of correction in the colonies. Eddis, writing in 1769–77, declares that servants in Maryland groaned beneath a worse than Egyptian bondage. Runaway servants were severely punished, and elaborate laws were passed to secure their arrest and punish all who aided them to freedom.

Some perplexing moral problems were caused by white servants. The question of intermarriage between servant and slave arose, as well as that of restraining looser relations between these classes. Nearly all the colonies were forced to pass laws to prevent such relations between servants, between free men and servants, and between Negro slaves and servants. A great increase of illegitimate mulatto children in the eighteenth century is one evidence of low moral standards. In Virginia, the parish vestry books record large sums expended for the support of such children. Laws were passed to prevent intermarriage of black and white. For example, the preamble of the Virginia Act of 1691 states that it was enacted "for the prevention of that abominable and spurious mixture which hereafter may increase in his dominion as well by negroes intermarrying with English or other white women as by their unlawful intercourse with one another." A Maryland act provided that the children of a servant-woman resulting from intermarriage with a Negro slave should be slaves to her master for life. But since unprincipled masters urged the marriage of their servant-women to slaves, the law was repealed. Nevertheless, miscegenation continued.

It is obvious that the economic significance of the white servant was very important. Benjamin Franklin said in 1759, "The labor of the plantations is performed chiefly by indentured servants brought from Great Britain, Ireland, and Germany, because the high price it bears cannot be performed in any other way." Free labor on a wage system was impossible because of both high wages and scarcity of labor. Few would work for hire when land could be had for almost nothing. The certainty of supply, the power of control, its economy, and the large profits resulting made the system superior to other forms until the Negro slave was imported on a large scale. John Pory, of Virginia, wrote in 1619 that "one man by the means of six servants hath cleared at one crop [tobacco] a thousand pounds English. . . . Our principal wealth consisteth of servants."

Socially, the white servant was an important factor in helping to build up a landed aristocracy in the South, because he made possible the cultivation of extensive areas of land. But in the course of a few years he became a free citizen and owner of a small estate. Thus was developed a yeoman class, a much-needed democratic element in the southern colonies, while at the same time settlers were secured for the back lands, where they were needed to protect the frontier. Nevertheless, they did not form a distinct class after becoming freedmen. Some were doubtless the progenitors of the "poor white trash" of the South, but it is likely that environment rather than birth was the main factor in producing this class. While comparatively few rose to prominence, yet there are some notable examples to the contrary. Two signers of the Declaration of Independence—George Taylor and Mathew Thornton—and Charles Thompson, the Secretary of the Continental Congress, had all been white servants. It is certain also that many became successful planters, and perhaps the majority, respectable and desirable citizens.

On the whole, the effects of the institution were beneficial. Great Britain was relieved of her undesirable citizens; many German peasants were given the opportunity to better their condition; the colonies were supplied with laborers for the rougher work, and servant-artisans supplied wants impossible to meet in any other way. That the white servant was useful, even after the Revolution, is seen by the fact that large numbers continued to come to Pennsylvania, where the institution existed until 1831. By that time various causes were leading to its abolition. Opposition developed in Europe because of the drain of the labor supply to America. In the South the Negro slave had tended to supplant the white servant, while in the North labor-saving machinery was doing so much of his work that he was no longer needed.

Poor Whites
in the South

C. VANN WOODWARD

After the Civil War, agriculture went into a slump through-out the nation, particularly in the war-ruined South. Poor whites in the South—most of them rural laborers—were left with little basis for self-respect aside from their feelings of superiority to blacks. Thus it became increasingly important to them to keep blacks in a subordinate position. While the black man had been a slave, the distinction in status was clear. But now that he was free, the competition for status became acute. Since both whites and blacks were in a depressed financial condition, simple economic distinctions could not be made. Insecure whites found the solution to their status problems in segregation—an insti-tution that had hardly been necessary before the Civil War—and they encouraged the willing legislatures to enact laws severely restricting the activities of blacks. By the end of the nineteenth century, aided by several decisions of the Supreme Court, the segregationists had constructed a dual society in the South such that the least distinguished white was able to convince himself that he was better than the most distinguished black.

Also in the postwar years, poor whites began to drift from the fields and hills of the South into the newly developed mill towns. But industry offered them merely a new type of misery, for owners kept wages at a minimum and responded to signs of labor unrest by threatening to replace white laborers with blacks.

It is one of the tragedies of American history that poor whites and blacks were never able to join together in order to force Southern capitalism to institute some form of industrial democracy. The Populist movement in the 1890's did briefly stimulate cooperation between blacks and whites, but by early in the twentieth century even Populist leaders were emphasizing racial hatred rather than interracial cooperation. Indeed, with few exceptions, poor whites through the years have not only refused to work with blacks for common goals but have sought the blacks' subordination, with the result of depriving both labor groups of important allies in their struggle against management.

The following selection describes the beginnings of industrialization in the post-Reconstruction South, explaining the process by which masses of whites were trapped in poverty.

The appeal that the proslavery argument had for the poorer class of whites had been grounded on the fear of being leveled, economically as well as socially, with a mass of liberated Negroes. Social leveling after emancipation was scotched by sundry expedients, but the menace of economic leveling still remained. The rituals and laws that exempted the white worker from the penalties of caste did not exempt him from competition with black labor, nor did they carry assurance that the penalties of black labor might not be extended to white.

The propagandists of the New-South order, in advertising the famed cheap labor of their region, were not meticulous in distinguishing between the color of their wares. If they stressed the "large body of strong, hearty, active, docile and easily contented negro laborers" who conformed to "the apostolic maxim of being 'contented with their wages,' and [having] no disposition to 'strike,' " they claimed the same virtues for the "hardy native Anglo-Saxon stock." The pledge of the *Manufacturers' Record,* for example, that "long hours of labor and moderate wages will continue to be the rule for many years to come," amounted almost to a clause of security in the promissory note by which the New South got capital to set up business. Additional security was not lacking. "The white laboring classes here," wrote an Alabama booster, "are separated from the Negroes, working all day side by side with them, by an innate consciousness of race superiority. This sentiment dignifies the character of white labor. It excites a sentiment of sympathy and equality on their part with the classes above them, and in this way becomes a wholesome social leaven."

"Poor Whites in the South" from *Origins of the New South, 1877–1913* by C. Vann Woodward. Reprinted by permission of Louisiana State University Press.

It was an entirely safe assumption that for a long time to come race consciousness would divide, more than class consciousness would unite, Southern labor. Fifty strikes against the employment of Negro labor in the period from 1882 to 1900 testify to white labor's determination to draw a color line of its own. It is clear that in its effort to relegate to the Negro the less desirable, unskilled jobs, and to exclude him entirely from some industries, white labor did not always have the co-operation of white employers.

In the cotton mills, at least, racial solidarity between employer and employee held fairly firm. By a combination of pressures and prejudices, a tacit understanding was reached that the cotton-mill villages were reserved for whites only. Probably no class of Southerners responded to the vision of the New South more hopefully than those who almost overnight left the old farm for the new factory. The cotton-mill millennium had been proclaimed as the salvation of "the necessitous masses of the poor whites." One enthusiastic promoter promised that "for the operative it would be Elysium itself." Historians have placed the "philanthropic incentive," undoubtedly present in some cases, high in the list of motives behind the whole mill campaign.

The transition from cotton field to cotton mill was not nearly so drastic as that which accompanied the change from primitive agriculture to modern factory in England and New England. For one thing, the mill families usually moved directly from farm to factory, and usually came from the vicinity of the mill. For another, the ex-farmer mill hand found himself in a mill community made up almost entirely of ex-farmers, where a foreigner, a Northerner, or even a city-bred Southerner was a curiosity. As late as 1907 a study revealed that 75.8 per cent of the women and children in Southern cotton mills had spent their childhood on the farm, and the 20.2 per cent who came from villages usually came from mill villages.

The company-owned shanties into which they moved differed little from the planter- or merchant-owned shanties they had evacuated, except that the arrangement of the houses was a reversion to the "quarters" of the ante-bellum plantation instead of the dispersed cropper system. As pictured by an investigator in Georgia in 1890, "rows of loosely built, weather-stained frame houses, all of the same ugly pattern and buttressed by clumsy chimneys," lined a dusty road. "No porch, no doorstep even, admits to these barrack-like quarters." Outside in the bald, hard-packed earth was planted, like some forlorn standard, the inevitable martin pole with its pendant gourds. Inside were heaped the miserable belongings that had furnished the cropper's cabin: "a shackling bed, tricked out in gaudy patchwork, a few defunct 'split-bottom' chairs, a rickety table, and a jumble of battered crockery," and on the walls the same string of red peppers, gourd dipper, and bellows. In certain mill villages of Georgia in 1890 not a watch or clock was to be found. "Life is regulated by the sun and the factory bell"—just as it had once been by the sun and farm bell. The seasons in the vocabulary of the cracker proletariat were still "hog-killin'," "cotton-choppin'," and " 'tween crops." The church was still the focus of social life, and the mill family was almost as migratory as the cropper family. The whole of this rustic industrialism moved to a rural rhythm.

Mill-village paternalism was cut from the same pattern of poverty and makeshift necessity that had served for plantation and crop-lien paternalism. In place of the country supply store that advanced goods against a crop lien there was the company store that advanced them against wages, and since the weaver was as rarely able to add and multiply as was the plowman, accounts were highly informal. Mill-village workers were sometimes little further advanced toward a money economy than were cotton croppers, and payday might bring word from the company store that the family had not "paid out" that week. Pay was often scrip, good only at the company store, or redeemable in cash at intervals. Company-owned houses were usually provided at low rent and sometimes rent free. "Lint-head" fealty often carried with it certain feudal privileges like those of gathering wood from company lands and pasturing cows on company fields. The unincorporated company town, in which everything was owned by the mill corporation, was the most completely paternalistic. Here company schools and company churches were frequently subsidized by the corporation, which of course controlled employment of preacher and teacher. In the smaller mills the relationship between owner and employees was highly personal and intimate, with a large degree of dependency on the part of the workers. "Not only are relations more friendly and intimate than at the North," found a Northern writer, "but there is conspicuous freedom from the spirit of drive and despotism. Even New England superintendents and overseers in their Southern mills soon glide into prevailing *laissez-faire* or else leave in despair."

After all allowance has been made for the manna of paternalism, the "family wage," and the greater purchasing power of money in the South, the wages of Southern textile workers remained miserably low. The very fact that the wages of the head of a family combined with those of the other adult members were inadequate to support dependents makes the "family wage" a curious apology for the system. Wages of adult male workers of North Carolina in the nineties were 40 to 50 cents a day. Men constituted a minority of the workers, about 35 per cent in the four leading textile states in 1890; women, 40 per cent; and children between the ages of ten and fifteen years, 25 per cent. The wages of children, who entered into degrading competition with their parents, varied considerably, but there is record of mills in North Carolina that paid 10 and 12 cents a day for child labor. The work week averaged about seventy hours for men, women, and children. Wages were slow to improve, and did not keep pace with mounting capitalization and profits. Adult male spinners in representative mills of North Carolina who had received $2.53 a week in 1885 were getting $2.52 in 1895, and adult female spinners in Alabama got $2.76 a week in the former and $2.38 in the latter year. Hourly wages for adult male spinners in the South Atlantic states were not quite 3 cents in 1890, only 2.3 cents in 1895, and a little over 3 cents in 1900; for female spinners in the same section the rate declined from about 4.5 cents an hour in 1890 to 4 cents in 1900. Yet with these wages and conditions, there seems to have been no trouble in filling the company houses to overflowing. Few workers ever returned to farming permanently, and strikes were almost unheard of.

The glimpses one gets of life among this sunbonneted, wool-hatted proletariat raise doubts about the sense of *noblesse oblige* and the "philanthropic incentives" with which their employers have been credited. If paternalism sheltered them from the most ruthless winds of industrial conflict, it was a paternalism that could send its ten-year-old children off to the mills at dawn and see them come home with a lantern at night. It could watch its daughters come to marriageable age with "a dull heavy eye, yellow, blotched complexion, dead-looking hair," its "unmarried women of thirty . . . wrinkled, bent, and haggard," while the lot of them approached old age as illiterate as Negro field hands. If white solidarity between employees and employer was to save the white worker from the living standard of the Negro, the results in the cotton mills were not very reassuring.

The extent to which labor in other industries shared in the prosperity of the New South is indicated by the level of wages maintained. In few industries or crafts did wages rise appreciably, and in many they were actually reduced. In the tobacco industry of the South Atlantic states, for example, cigar makers got 26 cents an hour in 1890 and 25 cents in 1900, while stemmers' wages remained at about 10 cents; in representative leather industries of the same states tanners remained on 11-cent wages, while in the South Central states their wages fell from 12.75 cents in 1890 to 11.5 cents in 1900; compositors' wages in the printing industry advanced from about 24 cents to nearly 26 cents in the South Atlantic states over the decade, from 23 cents to 29 cents in the South Central states; machinists did little better than hold their own in this period; bricklayers' wages declined from 45 cents to 43 cents in the South Central states and rose from 35 cents to about 37 cents in the South Atlantic states; carpenters in the former section got nearly 26 cents in 1890 and over 27 cents in 1900, while in the latter section their wages were raised from about 24 cents to about 26 cents; and wages of unskilled labor in the building trades varied from 8 cents to 12 cents an hour in the nineties.

To a large extent the expanding industrialization of the New South was based upon the labor of women and children who were driven into the mills and shops to supplement the low wages earned by their men. In several states they were being drawn into industry much more rapidly than men. In representative establishments studied in Alabama the number of men increased 31 per cent between 1885 and 1895; that of women increased 75 per cent; girls under eighteen, 158 per cent; and boys under eighteen, 81 per cent. The increases over the same period in Kentucky were 3 per cent for men, 70 per cent for women, 65 per cent for girls, and 76 per cent for boys. Of the 400,586 male children between the ages of ten and fourteen gainfully employed in the United States in 1890, the two census divisions of the Southern states accounted for 256,502, and of the 202,427 girls of that age at work they listed 130,546. The great majority in each case were employed in agriculture, fisheries, and mining. Thousands of women who went to work in the cities lived on subsistence wages. In Charleston shops, where the average weekly earnings for women were $4.22, were "well-born, well-educated girl[s] side by side in the least attractive pursuits with the 'cracker.'" In Richmond, where women's wages averaged $3.93 a week, there was an "almost universal pallor and sallowness of countenance" among working women. In Atlanta "great illiteracy exists among the working girls. Their moral condition also leaves much to be desired. The cost of living is comparatively high."

In spite of the contributions of women and children, the working family in the South seemed less able to own a house than that of any other section. Of the eighteen cities in the whole country with a percentage of home tenancy above 80, eleven were in the South. Birmingham, with 89.84 per cent of tenancy, had the highest rate in the United States; the percentage in Norfolk was 85.62, and in Macon, 84.66. In the South Atlantic states as a whole, over 75 per cent of home dwellers were tenants. Interlarded with the long, shady boulevards of the "best sections" of Nashville, Norfolk, Macon, Memphis, and Montgomery were alleys lined with one- and two-room shanties of colored domestics. In the "worst sections" of every city sprawled the jungle of a dark-town with its own business streets and uproarious, crime-infested "amusement" streets. Beyond, in suburban squalor and isolation, were the gaunt barracks of white industrial workers, huddled around the factories.

Conditions of public health and sanitation under which the urban working classes lived cannot be grasped from general descriptions, since health improvements and safeguards were highly discriminatory within the cities. Richmond justly boasted in 1887 of her relatively high expenditures for municipal improvements, of being "the best-paved city of her population in the Union," and of the splendor of Broad, Main, and Cary streets, "yearly improved by elegant houses built for merchants and manufacturers." Yet in 1888, the United States Commissioner of Labor blamed "bad drainage of the city, bad drinking water, and unsanitary homes" for the appalling conditions of health among the working girls of Richmond. New Orleans, with a long start over her sisters, easily achieved pre-eminence among unsanitary cities by the filth and squalor of her slums. The president of the State Board of Health of Louisiana reported in 1881 that "the gutters of the 472 miles of dirt streets are in foul condition, being at various points choked up with garbage, filth and mud, and consequently may be regarded simply as receptacles for putrid matters and stagnant waters. The street crossings are in like manner more or less obstructed with filth and black, stinking mud."

"We have awakened, or are fast awakening, from our dream," commented a Southern editor. "We have pauperism, crime, ignorance, discontent in as large a measure as a people need. Every question that has knocked at European doors for solution will in turn knock at ours." When work relief was offered at twenty cents a week by private charity in Alexandria, Virginia, "poor women were more than glad to get the work, and came from far and near, and many had to be sent away disappointed every week." In New Orleans "a multitude of people, white and black alike," lived on a dole of thirteen cents a day in the nineties.

Labor in the Southern textile mills, largely unorganized, has claimed a disproportionate share of the attention of scholars. The result has been a neglect of the history of labor in other industries and in the crafts, as well as an encouragement of the impression that no labor movement existed in the region at this period.

A study of the labor movement in the largest Southern city concludes that "the South, to judge by New Orleans, had craft labor movements smaller but similar to those in Northern cities," and that they were growing in power and influence in the eighties and nineties. It was a period of testing unknown strength and challenging tentatively the Old-South labor philosophy of the New-South doctrinaires and their pledge to Northern investors that long hours, low wages, and docile labor were assured.

However appealing white Southern labor found the doctrine of White Supremacy, it realized pretty early that "in nearly all the trades, the rates of compensation for the whites is [sic] governed more or less by the rates at which the blacks can be hired," and that the final appeal in a strike was "the Southern employer's ability to hold the great mass of negro mechanics *in terrorem* over the heads of the white." Agreement upon the nature of their central problem did not bring agreement upon the proper means of dealing with it. Two possible but contradictory policies could be used: eliminate the Negro as a competitor by excluding him from the skilled trades either as an apprentice or a worker, or take him in as an organized worker committed to the defense of a common standard of wages. Southern labor wavered between these antithetical policies from the seventies into the nineties, sometimes adopting one, sometimes the other.

Death in Kentucky

DAVID WELSH

America, as a rule, has kept its poverty out of sight. Traditionally, the poor people in the countryside have been isolated in "pockets of poverty," and in cities and towns they have lived "across the tracks." By formal or informal zoning regulations, most American towns and cities have successfully walled off areas of affluent living, blocking the poor from entering the communities of the rich, except, of course, as domestic workers or service personnel.

One of the most powerful and persistent myths in American life has been that of social and economic mobility. The pattern of economic growth in nineteenth-century America, along with the traditional Puritan emphasis on hard work, sobriety, and thrift, suggested to most Americans that any man who was willing to work hard and to save his money could get ahead in this society. This idea found popular expression in the rags-to-riches tales of Horatio Alger, and it found powerful spokesmen in industrialists such as Andrew Carnegie and clergymen such as Henry Ward Beecher. In the last quarter of the nineteenth century, a veritable "Gospel of Wealth" was elaborated, taking its cues from the laissez-faire mood of the times and from the doctrine of social Darwinism. According to the new gospel, economic success would inevitably come to those who worked hard and were blessed by God's favor. Thus the rich were the natural aristocracy of the state and should be its leaders. The poor were lazy, dissolute, and clearly not in God's good graces. Though their plight was unfortunate, the deprivation of some individuals was natural within the total scheme of things and ought not to be meddled with by the state.

The historical evidence on the causes of poverty in America tells quite a different story. Indeed, even in periods of rapid economic growth and general prosperity, there have always been barriers to the achievement of economic success in this country. Ethnic, religious, and sex discrimination have undermined the efforts of large groups of Americans to attain a reasonable degree of economic security. Taxation has favored the well-to-do and further oppressed the poor. Government aid and protection for certain industries have prevented masses of workers from gaining economic independence. The rural poor have been consistently neglected by the state. Yet the myth persists, sustained by rich and poor alike.

At the conclusion of the Second World War, the American economy was in relatively good shape. Demobilization took place rapidly and with a minimum of economic displacement. The G.I. Bill of Rights offered the advantage of higher education to many servicemen who would otherwise have returned to a lower- or lower-middle-class workingman's life. The 1950's were years of continued prosperity for the nation as a whole, prompting John Kenneth Galbraith, a leading economist, to describe the United States as "the affluent society." Galbraith pointed out that chronic poverty still existed in certain segments of the population, but for all practical purposes the public failed to take notice.

Then, in the early 1960's, poverty in America was rediscovered, and for the first time Americans registered alarm. In 1962, Michael Harrington, a socialist writer and editor, published a small book entitled *The Other America: Poverty in the United States,* in which he pointed out that an appalling number of Americans lived in poverty—some forty or fifty million people, or about one-fourth of the population. In addition, he pointed out that most of the poor were whites—not blacks, Puerto Ricans, or Mexican-Americans, as had previously been assumed. The white poor were concentrated in rural areas, and huge numbers of them lived in the mountainous region of the Eastern states, known as Appalachia. There, in the hollows and on the hillsides of the mountains that stretch from Pennsylvania to Georgia, tens of thousands of native-born whites of English, Scottish, and Scots-Irish ancestry lived in poverty and despair, passed over and forgotten by the so-called affluent society. The realization of the extent of poverty among whites in this country shocked the mass media of the nation as well as the federal government and led to the Kennedy and Johnson administrations' programs for a concerted war on poverty.

Ironically, the war on poverty has produced publicity centering on the plight of America's nonwhite poor, once again drawing attention away from poor whites. The following article deals with one aspect of the poor whites' continuing struggle in certain regions of Appalachia, as they attempt to wrest even a meager existence from the few resources left to them in the mountains.

ACT ONE
SLAUGHTER ON CLEAR CREEK

Scene One

[*where the land is Laid Waste by the Strip Mines and the Little People are chased from their Modest Homes*]

The people who live along Clear Creek, Knott County, piled into their old cars and pickups and drove to Hazard in the next county one muggy evening last June. They were going to "get organized," as one man put it, and their talk was full of extravagant threats, complaints and morbid aphorisms. They were schoolteachers, stonecutters, ex-miners, carpenters, small farmers, storekeepers—poor, but better off than most of the mountain people, who have no means of livelihood but public charity.

Something else distinguished the 150 men and women who gathered that night at the meeting hall of the Pet Milk Co. in Hazard: they owned their own land, and had deeds to prove it. Yet there seemed to be nothing they could do to stop a strip mining company from tearing up their land beyond reclamation, except perhaps, to get organized. One after another they stood up and aired their personal grievances against "the company." There was Herman Ritchie, who used to live on Rattlesnake Branch, Clear Creek—until the bulldozers began shaving off the mountain top to get at the coal:

"My wife was in there with the kids when the rocks began to roll. She got out fast and went to the neighbors. Then the landslide started and the dirt and boulders came down on the house. After that some uprooted trees fell down and knocked in the roof." Ritchie said he applied to the company for compensation but was told there would be none for the present. His in-laws, who own the land, still pay the surface taxes.

His furniture is trapped inside the house; neighbors insist that dogs slip in there at night and sleep in the beds.

Burley Combs, Jr. went away to work at a foundry in Indiana, but he came back home, like a lot of others, and tried to scratch out a living in the hills. He owns a piece of land and an unpainted log house, vacant now. Two days before the meeting, a stump rolled down the mountain and struck the house. Combs and family moved out. The only sign of life there now is a handful of scrawny chickens, pecking diffidently in the coal dust. Like the others, Burley Combs must continue to pay taxes on his land, and if he has any recourse against the company, he doesn't know what it is.

But if the coal operator, as the immediate, visible enemy, bears the brunt of their anger, they are also aware of his distant and powerful allies; even—one hesitates to say it—His Beneficence, the Federal Government.

"All this coal they're mining, do you know where it is going? To TVA, that's where it's going." It was the next day, and over the noise of a wheezing bulldozer, Andy Tomlin was talking. "TVA money is being used to tear up these hills, and they talk about reforestation. I ask you, how can you reforest that?"

He pointed to a hillside stripped of vegetation, the rocky soil freshly turned and ready to roll at the slightest provocation, uprooted trees stuck like darts at right angles to the mountain. One look at that grotesque relic of a mountain and one could only nod in agreement. How can you reforest that, indeed.

"And the TVA is just as responsible as anyone," he added. "I call this political death, hell and destruction on these hill people."

"It seems like they don't have any pity's sake on anybody," said an old man, leaning on his walking stick. "I don't know, but it all points to that. It seems like all we own here is the air we breathe."

A small group of Clear Creek people stood on the access road and talked, to no one in particular, their gaze magnetized by the bulldozers working at the hilltop.

"We love these hills. We grew up here. We don't want to be pushed out of here. This is our surroundings, our living area."

"The company cut an access road right through our cemetery. They've got no respect for the dead, let alone the living."

"Our officials, you can hear them hollering, 'Let's beautify these hills.' They give you a $300 fine for throwing a paper on the highway, and then they let them strip and strip and strip."

"The sheriff and his gang, and the state people up at Frankfort: they're all in with them. One of those overloaded coal trucks caved in a county bridge a few months ago and the company didn't have to pay a cent for it."

"They keep pushing dirt down . . . ain't nowhere it can go except in the hollows and valleys. And just wait till the rains come next spring."

Or Venyard Breeding: "They think they have a right to come in and move your house, do anything they want to. They stick up signs, 'Private Property—No Trespassing,' like they own the place. You can't even walk on your own land, and the state police are out there to make sure you don't."

Or the youngest member of the group, between his teeth: "I wonder if someone shouldn't turn a good rifle loose on them." Then he let out a good laugh, the passivity of his situation momentarily exorcised by the violent thought.

This, certainly, is not a comedy of manners of America in the mid-twentieth century. It is an old Western, one would think, perhaps a pre-war soap opera, or a melodrama of the 1890's. A big corporation, with a government contract, with friends in the State house and friends in court, vs. the "little people," with access to none of the levers of power. Only it is not the nice, nonviolent kind of political struggle most Americans are familiar with. In our Appalachian colony, where power is used in its most naked form, people get killed playing politics every year.

Scene Two

[where the Mellons and other Prominent Magnates count their Gold, thanking the Good Lord for the Boundless Charity of the President-of-All-the-People]

It all started around the turn of the century, when speculators from New York began buying up mineral rights in the Appalachian hills for 25 and 50 cents an acre. Deeds to the land gave them the right, with stipulations, to extract all minerals below the ground. These "land companies," as they were called, would in turn lease portions of a coal seam to the operators, receiving a royalty on each ton of coal mined. Today their holdings in the area are worth an estimated $7,200 an acre in coal royalties alone. One land company, the Virginia Iron & Coal Co., with offices in Philadelphia and extensive holdings in the Appalachian coalfields, is the most profitable large corporation in the United States according to Dun's Review of Modern Industry (April 1965). Its net profit is 61 cents on the dollar, compared with 10 cents for General Motors.

Land companies, which because of depletion allowances, operate virtually tax-free (they are taxed at roughly the same rate as an auto worker), have built up reservoirs of capital enabling them to acquire huge interests in industry, railroads and power companies. Pittsburgh-Consolidation Coal Corp., the nation's largest bituminous coal producer and a land company in its own right, recently became a major stockholder in both Chrysler and U.S. Steel. Controlled by the Mellon family of Pittsburgh, through the Mellon National Bank and Trust, it also acquired more than 100,000 shares of American Electric Power, a holding company for six Appalachian utilities. The president of American Electric is Donald Cook, a close friend of President Johnson. Through Pittsburgh-Consolidation, the Mellons are major stockholders in the merged Norfolk & Western—Virginian railways, which recently carried 76 per cent of total domestic bituminous coal shipped from the mines. Moreover, they benefit from a tax break tantamount to a government subsidy.

Coal, rails, utilities—the biggest defenders of the status quo in Appalachia, and those incorrigible Mellons, have their fingers in them all. But the Mellons are not the whole story. Within 50 miles of Clear Creek are holdings of U.S. Steel, Midland Steel, Bethlehem Steel, International Harvester, Virginia Iron & Coal: some of the most prosperous companies and some of the poorest people, statistically, in the nation.

Most residents of Clear Creek own strips of land running from their houses in the valley to the hill crest. But the coal beneath is owned by the Kentucky River Coal Co., a land company that recently declared dividends of 45 cents on each dollar of sales volume (Dun's Review). It leases the coal rights to Kentucky Oak Mining Co., a nonunion strip and auger operation and the creation of the biggest operators in the Hazard coalfield, William B. Sturgill and Dick Kelly.

In strip mining, bulldozers literally lop off the top of a mountain, trees and all, to get at the coal seam. Machines then strip off the coal and load it into trucks. In auger mining, a huge drill, or auger, bores into the side of a seam and sends the coal shooting back out for loading. Stripping and augering are much cheaper ways of extracting coal than deep mining, and a sharp drop in the price of coal in recent years did much to encourage their spread. The work is almost invariably nonunion, paying $1.25 an hour or less. Markets, too, have stimulated company growth: Detroit Edison, Consumers Power and other utilities in

Michigan, Indiana, Ohio and Illinois are the Hazard strippers' best customers.

But much of their coal goes South, where the Tennessee Valley Authority is in continual quest of cheaper sources of power. When the Sturgill-Kelly combine puts to work its $1 million worth of equipment to despoil the mountain, poison the stream and throw a family out of its meager cabin, it is to fulfill a more than $50 million coal contract with TVA. The price per ton paid by TVA is so low that in general, only a strip or auger mine (and a scab one at that) could fulfill the contract and still make the healthy profit to which the operators are accustomed. The Tennessee Valley, once itself an exploited region, has indeed joined Detroit, Cincinnati and Cleveland in the ranks of the exploiters. With their ready supply of cheap electric power, the prosperous cities of the Tennessee Valley grow even more prosperous while the Kentucky mountain poor get poorer. One can hardly escape the conclusion that TVA, that great government agency, has become an accomplice in the destruction of eastern Kentucky.

Scene Three

[where we learn of a Noble Project to reclaim the land Laid Waste by the Strip Mines]

William Caperton, a husky man in his 30's, runs the Caperton Coal Co., one of the small "dummy" operations set up by the parent company, Kentucky Oak Mining, to avoid paying union wages to the miners.

"How would you like to see our land reclamation project?" he asked, and led us cheerfully to the site, as MacIntosh, taking no pains to conceal his bitterness, grumbled.

"For every acre we tear up, there's $100 bond we put up with the state for land reclaiming," said Caperton.

"$100! Are you kidding?" It was Donald MacIntosh, a gaunt Clear Creek resident. "After what you've done to this mountain you couldn't reclaim ten square feet for that price."

"My friend, you know that's not true. Now just look at these apple trees we've planted. They didn't cost $100, and once they take hold, this part of the mountain will be as good as new."

He pointed to a row of twelve seedlings, already wilting, twelve spindly signs of life on a wasteland of red dirt, and here and there a sprig of new grass.

MacIntosh: "What about that sawdust you're put around your apple trees? You threw all the good topsoil and trees on top of our houses and now nothing grows up here, isn't that right? So you put sawdust around the trees and you still can't make them grow."

Caperton: "Well now, as to that sawdust, I'm not sure but what some truck driver didn't dump it here by mistake. And you see those young apple trees, they're doing all right. And we have been planting elderberry bushes. . . ."

MacIntosh: "I'd like to know how a man can pick apples from a landslide."

Caperton: "We are seeding whole areas with fescue and lespedeza. Those are special varieties of grass. In five years' time we hope to have it all grassed in. We seeded this area two years ago."

MacIntosh: "You need a magnifying glass to find a blade of grass around here."

Caperton: "Why, just last year the governor himself was up here, and they had a big ceremony, planting pine trees and all. I think it was during Conservation Week."

MacIntosh: "You know damn well those pine trees the governor planted didn't live over a week. It's like trying to put makeup on a cadaver and making believe it's alive."

Caperton: "Come on now, you know they lived longer than that. The thing is, they used the wrong fertilizer. . . ."

MacIntosh: "Look at that pool, that red, old, acid mine water. That's what's killed every fish and tadpole on Clear Creek."

Caperton: "There's minnows in that pool."

MacIntosh: "How'd they get there: fall from the sky? Swim upstream? Or did somebody bring them in here yesterday?"

Caperton: "Well now, I was told there was minnows in there. But they might have been talking about some other place. . . ."

Scene Four

[where Deeds mean more than Words]

In Hindman, the Knott County Seat, a group of 19 Clear Creek homeowners trooped up to the mine site with the intention of stopping the work there, if necessary by force. State policemen with shotguns headed them off. Almost immediately, Kentucky Oak Mining sought, and got, an injunction against them. The Knott County Circuit Court issued an order enjoining the 19 from interfering with operations at the strip mine. State police and sheriff's men doubled their guard at the mine.

County Judge Morgan Slone, who was not involved in the incident, says the original deeds signed by Clear Creek residents authorized deep mining of the coal beneath their land, and deep mining only. Slone contends the deeds were altered, in the Knott County Courthouse, to authorize the companies to surface mine as well.

"The companies come in to Hindman from all over this country and get things fixed up the way they want it," he said. "Suddenly they are waving a new deed, and you don't know where they got it from. The companies claim they have on record the right to strip and auger. I don't think they have any right to change the deed from the way it was originally signed. But they just go ahead and run over the people. This day and time, a poor man's just like a frog down a forty-foot well and no way to get out."

Scene Five

[*where a Humble Mountain Man speaks with the President-of-All-the-People*]

Dan Gibson is a man everyone around here looks up to, a kind of elder statesman of the people. White-haired, with the face of a college professor and two fingers missing from a mining accident, he is not about to take anything lying down.

"In 1960," he recalls, "the coal company was bulldozing on Frank Fugate's property, and ten of us went and put them out. They tried to come on these children's land and we were standing back of the fence. I had a shotgun and I told them bulldozer operators, 'You break that fence and you'll get what's in it.' We run them out, all right, and they got a warrant and arrested Frank Fugate. Then the company sued Frank in Circuit Court at Hindman and got a judgment for the company. Well you know, that always happens. But Frank took it to Federal Court, and he won. That's unusual. But the main thing is, they don't mess with Frank any more because he went to the clerk and got a copy of his deed, which says he deeded them mineral rights for deep mining only. The rest of our deeds is tampered with to suit the coal operators."

But if the Clear Creek landowners made sporadic attempts to stop the strippers, as a group they remained inchoate. Not until last April did they begin really to organize. They had gathered to draw up a "community action program," in the hope of obtaining a federal anti-poverty grant for recreation facilities, when it occurred to them: how can we sit here and talk about recreation when they are tearing up our land? Curious, but in an indirect way a federal program had given birth to the first serious movement to halt the strip mining on Clear Creek.

The mere fact of organization widens people's horizons. Matt Holiday even thought to call President Johnson: "Why can't I speak to the President? I help to pay his salary." State Representative Carl Perkins set it up for him and before he knew it, Holiday was on the line to LBJ.

"He said, 'This is the President, what can I do for you?' I told him how the strip mines were ruining our land. He said, 'I am with you, friend, but I am going to put you onto someone who can do you a lot more good than I can,' and the next thing I knew I was talking with Udall, the Secretary of the Interior. He said we may have to fight it all the way to the Supreme Court, but if the companies are destroying property then they'll have to pay for it."

The people here have little faith in courts which habitually decide in the company's favor, and few have the money to appeal. Nor are they impressed with schemes of compensation for damages. In the past, any compensation has been too little and too late to save the land and has provided no guarantees against future abuses. Recently a coal company was found guilty of polluting a stream and fined $800. The next day "that red, old, acid mine water" was pouring into the stream the same as ever. The mountain people will believe in Washington's good intentions the day the Federal Government says "no" to the pressure groups, the day Washington curbs the power of the coal companies, and their allies, to buy the legislatures, buy the courts, buy the freedom to do exactly as they please.

ACT TWO
STATE OF THE UNION

Scene One

[*where the Little People live on the Charity of the President-of-All-the-People*]

"Look at the muskrat," hooted the driver, peering from his coal truck at the man cleaning paper and debris from a creek bed.

The man straightened up and shook his fist. "I'd sooner be a musk-rat than a damn scab."

The "muskrat" was beautifying the countryside for $1.25 an hour under the federal-state "Jobless Fathers" program. He collects $175 a month and puts in 140 hours work for it. The "scab" was trucking coal from a nonunion mine for the same hourly wage. Both are noteworthy in that they have jobs at all in this area of southeastern Kentucky where the official unemployment figure is more than 10 per cent and unofficial estimates go as high as 50 per cent. Their shouting-match is sympto-matic of the diseases of their part of the country, and of the conflicts that divide the impoverished and enable a privileged few to prosper.

Estill Amburgey, 40, started work in the pits when he was 11. Today he supports his family of four on $60 worth of federal food stamps a month—one of nearly 2,000 families on the program in a county of 35,000 people. Occasionally he finds an odd job to perform with his truck. He could find work in one of a hundred small truck mines, which, because of their size, are not subject to the federal mine safety code. But he refuses on principle to work for a "scab" operator. And since low-paying, nonunion jobs are about the only ones available and recommended by the State Employment Service, his refusal to ac-cept them costs him unemployment compensation.

He lives in Perry County (Hazard), where only 15 per cent of persons over 25 have finished high school, and where the average adult has left school before the ninth grade. The median family income is $2,600; but if one excluded the incomes of coal operators, officials and businessmen, average family income would be closer to $1,600.

Amburgey belongs to the Appalachian Committee for Full Em-ployment, formed here in January, 1964, to represent the interests of the unemployed. Its members are ex-miners in an area where coal is the only industry and, for most of them, their sole source of income is either food stamps or a government check—retirement or disability, unem-ployment, "Aid to Families with Dependent Children" or "Jobless Fathers." A few have miners' pensions.

"The dole is a way of life around here," says Everette Tharp, secre-tary of the Committee. "The politicians put us on the dole to avoid interfering with the corporate monopolies that are responsible for the pitiful condition of our people."

Not all the needy benefit from the largesse of our government. Tharp charges that federal and state welfare programs are used polit-ically to reward "friends" of the coal companies and punish their enemies. "Workers in the scab mines have an easier time getting food stamps," he contends. "It's a kind of subsidy to keep them satisfied with low wages and no benefits. The Federal Government really thinks their money is helping the poor, the sick and disabled, and all the time their agents are denying these benefits to people in need. In any case the red tape is so thick many people give up."

Amburgey says they have threatened to cut off his food stamps if he fails to furnish proof of having applied for at least three (nonunion) jobs each week, "willingness to work" being one requirement for obtaining stamps in Kentucky. From the living room of their ramshackle house in the hollows near Kodak, his wife, Eunice, vows: "They can take our food stamps. They can take our furniture and all we have. We've still got our pride."

But this kind of defiance of the welfare bureaucracy is not usual. Thomas E. Gish, editor of the muckraking Mountain Eagle in nearby Whitesburg, says the typical welfare recipient here is "a political slave who knows his welfare payments can be withdrawn tomorrow if he steps out of line. This is the simple fact of life that has destroyed pride in the mountains, not because of welfare payments, but because of the price exacted to qualify for them—one's traditional independence and freedom."

Scene Two

[*where the Forces-of-Law-and-Order preserve the Values-of-Our-Civilization from the Forces-of-Anarchy*]

It was against this background of desperation that the Appalachian Committee was born, out of the remnants of the Roving Picket movement that ran its own stormy gamut in the last months of 1962. Berman Gibson, the Committee's founder and president, had emerged as leader of the Roving Pickets, a miners' group formed more or less spontaneously to protest low pay and dangerous working conditions in the nonunion mines.

Mine after mine had terminated contracts with the United Mine Workers of America (UMW) in preceding years, and many men had settled for less than union scale. Then, in September 1962, the union withdrew the miners' welfare cards entitling them to free medical care at miners' hospitals because coal operators were no longer contributing into the UMW welfare fund. It was the last straw.

Several thousand men converged on nonunion mining sites and coal tipples in seven counties. They picketed. They threatened. They threw rocks. The opposition—hirelings of the coal operators and "the law" itself—fought back. Beatings and shootings were attributed to both sides. A Hazard police lieutenant, Ira Kilburn, testified in court that the dynamiting of a rail tipple, blamed on the Roving Pickets, was in fact the work of other policemen in civilian clothes. Kilburn is no longer on the force.

The Roving Pickets, in the tradition of Kentucky mountaineers when their rights are threatened, were not exactly angels. But to them, it seemed the enemy had all the weapons, including the full force of the law. Gibson and seven other picket leaders were arrested in 1963 by FBI agents and state police and charged with conspiracy to blow up a rail bridge the previous year. Charges against Gibson were dismissed for lack of evidence. But four of his co-defendants were found guilty, on the basis of jailhouse confessions they later repudiated, and sentenced to six-year terms, pending appeal. Berman Gibson called it a frame-up.

On Election Day, 1963, Gibson was arrested again, along with six others, on a charge of assault with intent to kill. The arrests came as they were driving men to the polls to help reelect a circuit judge they considered fair. The judge lost, by 300 votes, to a man who has since handed down a nearly unbroken string of anti-labor decisions. The accused miners were later acquitted. Everette Tharp, a retired miner who once took a correspondence course in law and serves as the movement's intellectual and theorist, put it succinctly: "After the Election Day arrests, for a crime that allegedly took place over a year previous, we figured we were dead right: this was a political conspiracy to get rid of the movement."

Meanwhile, state mediation between the pickets and the Mine Operators' Association had resulted in an agreement to reestablish union pay and conditions in the mines, in return for a halt to picketing. Of the picket leaders, only Berman Gibson noticed there was no enforcement clause and refused to sign. The agreement has yet to be enforced. The UMW, which lost some 75 per cent of its members in the area since 1952 and all its members in Perry County, was weaker than ever, and the Roving Picket movement was dead. About half the pickets went back to the pits.

Suggestions for Further Reading

The standard works on white servants and laborers in the colonies are Abbot E. Smith, *Colonists in Bondage: White Servitude and Convict Labor in America, 1607–1776* (University of North Carolina Press, 1947), and Richard B. Morris, *Government and Labor in Early America* ° (Columbia University Press, 1946). Warren B. Smith examines the situation in a particular state in *White Servitude in Colonial South Carolina* (University of South Carolina Press, 1961). John Barth's novel *The Sot-Weed Factor* ° (Doubleday, 1960) gives a hilarious, bawdy, and authentic picture of life in colonial Maryland, in the process conveying a good deal of information about white servitude.

Post-Civil War attitudes and political activities of Southern whites are considered in Lawrence J. Friedman, *The White Savage: Racial Fantasies in the Postbellum South* ° (Prentice-Hall, 1970); A. D. Kirwan, *Revolt of the Rednecks: Mississippi Politics, 1876–1925* ° (University of Kentucky Press, 1951); and Paul Lewinson, *Race, Class and Party: A History of Negro Suffrage and White Politics in the South* ° (Oxford University Press, 1932). The plight of the American farmer is explored in Fred A. Shannon, *The Farmer's Last Frontier: Agriculture, 1860–1897* ° (Holt, Rinehart and Winston, 1945), and in Theodore Saloutos, *Farmer Movements in the South, 1865–1933* ° (University of California Press, 1960).

Moving descriptions of life in Appalachia are found in Harry W. Caudill, *Night Comes to the Cumberlands* ° (Little Press, 1963), and Jack E. Weller, *Yesterday's People: Life in Contemporary Appalachia* ° (University of Kentucky Press, 1965). Two basic studies of poverty and wealth in contemporary America are Michael Harrington, *The Other America: Poverty in the United States* ° (Macmillan, 1963), and John Kenneth Galbraith, *The Affluent Society* ° (Houghton-Mifflin, 1958). On the distribution of wealth in the United States, see Gabriel Kolko, *Wealth and Power in America: An Analysis of Social Class and Income Distribution* ° (Praeger, 1962). Dwight Macdonald helped bring the issue of poverty into the public eye with his article "Our Invisible Poor," *The New Yorker,* Vol. 38 (January 19, 1963), 82–132. In *Culture and Poverty* ° (University of Chicago Press, 1968), Charles Valentine challenges various common assumptions about the nature of poverty and its impact on culture.

° Available in paperback edition.

Labor

Industrial Workers
Struggle for Power

HERBERT G. GUTMAN

Too often the history of the workingman in the United States has been depicted as the slow, continual growth of the craft union and, until the Second World War, the spectacular failures of industrial unionism. This is only a partial view of the American worker, however, for at no time in the history of our country have a majority of the workers been enrolled in unions.

Labor organizations were not widespread before the end of the Civil War, and with the possible exception of the labor movement during the Jacksonian period, they rarely had either a consistent program or sufficient power to carry out any projects they began. Even the Jacksonian labor movement died in the Panic of 1837 and the ensuing waves of unemployment, which— along with an influx of poor white immigrants—placed power in the hands of the owners of industry. Craft workers, since they remained in relatively short supply, were able to sell their skills individually and had little to gain from collective bargaining. The unskilled and semiskilled workers of factories and mines, however, were put at a great disadvantage by increased competition for jobs, for their work required little training and they were easily replaceable. Ironically, it was the craft unions that attained the earliest successes, and the skilled workers were those protected by the first permanent national labor organization, the American Federation of Labor (the AFL), which was founded in 1881.

After the Civil War, industrial development in the United States took place at a rate perhaps unprecedented in the history of the world. The great wealth of natural resources, the abundant—indeed, superabundant—supply of labor, and fifty years of peace (the ten-week Spanish-American War of 1898 being only a minor diversion in American life) favored the United States in its competition with European industrial powers.

During this period of rapid industrial advance, each new wave of immigrants, chiefly from Eastern and Southern Europe, stiffened the competition for unskilled jobs. Profiting from the oversupply of labor, the owners of many industries drove wages down and thus increased profits at the expense of the workers. In the contest for jobs and profits, various groups of workers were often pitted against one another, thus increasing existing hostilities among different religious and ethnic groups. Anti-black sentiment, in particular, received an ominous boost as blacks were increasingly used to fill positions vacated by strikers. In fact, the use of black workers as strikebreakers and as a threat to would-be labor organizers continued in industrial work at least until the formation of the Congress of Industrial Organizations (the CIO) in 1936, and to this day it continues in the Southern textile industry, which is perhaps the most under-organized industry in America. Many blacks have sometimes found it impossible to get jobs except as a result of labor-management strife.

In the essay reprinted here, the author examines industrial workers' attempts to organize in the 1870's in the face of a growing alliance between industrial capitalists and state and national governments. In the process, he arrives at some surprising conclusions.

Although hardly any Negroes worked in coal mines before 1873, soon after the depression started mine operators in the Ohio Hocking Valley recruited hundreds from border and southern cities. Some had been sparingly employed in certain Indiana and Ohio mines, but attracted little attention. It was different in the Hocking Valley in 1874. A large number of white miners struck and showed an unusual degree of unanimity and staying power. The found support from members of the local middle class, and the operators, unable to wear down the strikers, brought in Negroes. Although the miners were defeated, the problems they raised for their employers indicated much the same so-

"The Workers' Search for Power" by Herbert G. Gutman from *The Gilded Age*, revised and enlarged edition, edited by H. Wayne Morgan (Syracuse, New York: Syracuse University Press, 1970), pp. 44 to 53, copyright 1963 and 1970 by Syracuse University Press. Reprinted by permission of the publisher.

cial environment as that in Braidwood and the Ohio Valley iron towns.

The railroad opened new markets for bituminous coal, and the years between 1869 and 1873 were a time of great prosperity. In 1870, 105,000 tons left the valley, and in 1873 just over 1,000,000 tons were shipped. Two years later, more than 20 percent of the coal mined in Ohio came from the Hocking Valley. Although entry costs were low, the ten largest firms in 1874 employed nearly two-thirds of the valley's miners.

The miners fell into two social groupings. Those born in and near the valley had spent most of their lives in the mines and often held local positions of public trust and esteem. A Cincinnati reporter found that miners held "a good position in society . . . as a class" and filled "a fair number of municipal, church, and school offices." These men had seen their status depersonalized as they quickly became part of a larger labor force, dependent on a distant and uncontrollable market. They unavailingly complained when operators brought in many more miners than needed for full-time work. A perceptive observer found that many of the older miners "have worked in these mines since they were boys and feel they have an actual property right to their places." Most of the new men who flocked to the valley after 1869 came from distant areas, and a good number were from England, Wales, and Ireland. The rapid growth of the industry made it difficult to support trade unions in the valley.

Economic crisis in 1873 suddenly punctured the region's prosperity. At best, miners found only part-time employment, and cash wages were less common than usual, for working miners were paid mostly in ninety-day notes and store credit. The operators complained that labor costs were too high and made the selling price of coal in a competitive but depressed market prohibitive. Talk of wage cuts, however, turned the miners toward trade unionism, and in December, 1873, they founded several branches of the newly established Miners' National Association. The operators in turn formed a region-wide trade association, and each of them posted a $5,000 bond as proof he would follow its directives. They also announced a sharp wage cut effective April 1, 1874, and entirely proscribed the new union.

Prominent union leaders lost their jobs. One operator closed his supply store "for repairs," and another locked his men in a room and insisted that they sign the new wage agreement. But the union thrived. Only nine "regular" miners favored the new contract, and no more than twenty-five or thirty regulars refused to join the union. The union men agreed to the lower wage but refused to abandon their organization. The operators remained adamant and insisted that the "progress or decay" of the region hinged on the destruction of the new union—"a hydra too dangerous to be warmed at our hearth." A strike over the right of labor organization started on April 1.

The strike brought trouble for the operators. Except for the *Logan Republican,* the weekly valley newspapers either supported the strikers or stood between them and the operators. No more than thirty regular miners accepted the new contract on April 1, and only seventy men entered the mines that day. Local public officials declined to do the bidding of prominent operators. The New Straitsville police deputized strikers, and after Governor William Allen sent the state inspector of mines to investigate reported miner violence, country and town officials assured him there was no trouble and a committee of merchants and "other property owners" visited Allen "to give him the facts."

New Straitsville town officials joined the miners to check the effort of operator W. B. McClung to bring in from Columbus "a posse" of nine special police armed with Colt revolvers and Spencer rifles. The miners felt it "unnecessary" for armed police to come to "their quiet town," and men, women, and children paraded the streets in protest. They made it uncomfortable for McClung's police, and he promised to close his mine and return the men to Columbus. But the mayor, on the complaint of a miner, issued a warrant for their arrest for entering the town armed, "disturbing the peace and quiet." Ordered to stand trial, the nine left town after McClung's superintendent posted their bond.

Except for the Nelsonville operators, other owners closed their mines on April 1 for two months and waited out the strikers. Toward the end of May, the operators divided among themselves. A few settled with strikers, but the largest rejected abritration and rebuked the union. Compromise was out of the question, insisted the more powerful operators, and they attacked the governor for not sending militia. The triumph of the union would soon lead to the "overthrow" of "our Government and bring upon us anarchy and bloodshed that would approach, if not equal, the Communism of Paris."

Unable to exert authority from within, the owners brought in between 400 and 500 Negroes in mid-June. Most came from Memphis, Louisville, and Richmond; few were experienced coal miners. They were offered high wages, told nothing of the dispute, and were generally misinformed about conditions. One employer admitted that "the motive for introducing the Negro was to break down the white miners' strike." Another boasted of his "great triumph over Trades-Unions" and called the use of Negroes "the greatest revolution ever attempted by operators to take over their own property." Gathered together in Columbus, the Negroes then were sped by rail to one of the mines, which was turned into a military camp. The county sheriff, twenty-five deputies, and the governor's private secretary were also there. Apparently with the approval of these officials, the operators armed the Negroes with "Government muskets," bayonets, and revolvers, and placed them on "military duty" around the property. No one could enter the area unless endorsed "by the operators or police." In the meantime, state militia were mobilized in nearby Athens, in Chillicothe, and in Cincinnati.

Anger swept the Hocking Valley when the strikers learned of this. The first day 1,000 miners and their families stood or paraded near the Negro encampment. No violence occurred, but the men called across picket lines of armed Negroes and urged them to desert the operators. The second day even more miners paraded near the encampment and urged the Negroes to leave. The miners succeeded in "raiding" the operators with an "artillery of words," and around 120 Negroes went back on the operators. Two of the defectors admitted they had been "led by misrepresentations to come North" and "wouldn't interfere with white folks' work." They defended unions as "a good thing" and advocated "plenty of good things" for everyone. The strikers housed the Negroes in union lodge rooms, and with the help of local citizens raised about five hundred dollars to help them return South. But this was only a small victory for the strikers. Enough Negroes remained to strengthen the hand of the operators and to demoralize the union men. Negroes went to other mines, even though strikers begged them not to work and "mothers held their children in their arms pointing out the negroes to them as those who came to rob them of their bread."

Outside the Hocking Valley, the press applauded the operators. The *Cleveland Leader* thought the strikers were "aliens"; the *Cincinnati Commercial* called them drunkards, thieves, and assassins. In the Hocking Valley, however, some residents complained of the "mercenary newspaper men and their hired pimps." The valley newspapers especially criticized the owners for using Negroes. Some merchants and other business folk also attacked the operators. Certain Nelsonville businessmen offered aid to the strikers and unsuccessfully pleaded with the operators to rehire all the miners. The police also were friendly, and the New Straitsville mayor prevented the sending of militia to his town.

Destruction of the union and the introduction of Negro workers did not bring industrial harmony. There were strikes over wage cuts in 1875 and 1877, and conflict between Negro and white miners. In 1875, when the men resisted a wage cut, the employers tacitly admitted that their power in the valley still was inadequate. Two of them, W. F. Brooks and T. Longstreth, visited Governor Allen and pleaded that he "restore order" in the valley towns. The governor was cautious, however, and sent no troops. But their pleas revealed the employers' anxieties and need for outside power.

Nothing better illustrated the differences between the small town and large city than attitudes toward public works for the unemployed. Urban newspapers frowned upon the idea, and relief and welfare agents often felt that the unemployed were "looking for a handout." The jobless, one official insisted, belonged to "the degraded class . . . who have the vague idea that 'the world owes them a living.' " Unemployed workers were lazy, many said, and trifling.

Native-born radicals and reformers, a few welfare officers, ambitious politicians, responsible theorists, socialists, and "relics" from the pre-Civil War era all agitated for public works during the great economic crisis of 1873–74. The earliest advocates urged construction of city streets, parks and playgrounds, rapid transit systems, and other projects to relieve unemployment. These schemes usually depended on borrowed money or fiat currency, or issuance of low-interest-rate bonds on both local and national levels. The government had aided wealthy classes in the past; it was time to "legislate for the good of all not the few." Street demonstrations and meetings by the unemployed occurred in November and December of 1873 in Boston, Cincinnati, Chicago, Detroit, Indianapolis, Louisville, Newark, New York, Paterson, Pittsburgh, and Philadelphia. The dominant theme at all these gatherings was the same: unemployment was widespread, countless persons were without means, charity and philanthropy were poor substitutes for work, and public aid and employment were necessary and just.

The reaction to the demand for public works contained elements of surprise, ridicule, contempt, and genuine fear. The Board of Aldermen refused to meet with committees of jobless Philadelphia workers. Irate Paterson taxpayers put an end to a limited program of street repairs the city government had started. Chicago public officials and charity leaders told the unemployed to join them "in God's work" and rescue "the poor and suffering" through philanthropy, not public employment.

The urban press rejected the plea for public works and responsibility for the unemployed. Men demanding such aid were "disgusting," "crazy," "loud-mouthed gasometers," "impudent vagabonds," and even "ineffable asses." They were ready "to chop off the heads of every man addicted to clean linen." They wanted to make "Government an institution to pillage the individual for the benefit of the mass." Hopefully, "yellow fever, cholera, or any other blessing" would sweep these persons from the earth. Depressions, after all, were normal and necessary adjustments, and workers should only "quietly bide their time till the natural laws of trade" brought renewed prosperity. Private charity and alms, as well as "free land," were adequate answers to unemployment. "The United States," said *The New York Times,* "is the only 'socialistic,' or more correctly 'agrarian,' government in the world in that it offers good land at nominal prices to every settler" and thereby takes "the sting from Communism." If the unemployed "prefer to cling to the great cities to oversupply labor," added the *Chicago Times,* "the fault is theirs."

None of the proposals of the jobless workers met with favor, but the demand by New York workers that personal wealth be limited to $100,000 was criticized most severely. To restrict the "ambition of building up colossal fortunes" meant an end to all "progress," wrote the *Chicago Times.* The *New York Tribune* insisted that any limitation on personal wealth was really an effort "to have employment without employers," and that was "almost as impossible . . . as to get into the world without ancestors."

Another argument against public responsibility for the unemployed identified this notion with immigrants, socialists, and "alien" doctrine. The agitation by the socialists compounded the anxieties of the more comfortable classes. Remembering that force had put down the Paris Communards, the *Chicago Times* asked: "Are we to be required to face a like alternative?" New York's police superintendent urged his men to spy on labor meetings and warned that German and French revolutionaries were "doing their utmost to inflame the workingman's mind." The *Chicago Tribune* menacingly concluded, "The coalition of foreign nationalities must be for a foreign, non-American object. The principles of these men are wild and subversive of society itself."

Hemmed in by such ideological blinders, devoted to "natural laws" of economics, and committed to a conspiracy theory of social change so often attributed only to the lower classes, the literate nonindustrial residents of large cities could not identify with the urban poor and the unemployed. Most well-to-do metropolian residents in 1873 and 1874 believed that whether men rose or fell depended on individual effort. They viewed the worker as little more than a factor of production. They were sufficiently alienated from the urban poor to join the *New York Graphic* in jubilantly celebrating a country in which republican equality, free public schools, and cheap western lands allowed "intelligent working people" to "have anything they all want."

The attitude displayed toward the unemployed reflected a broader and more encompassing view of labor. Unlike similar groups in small towns, the urban middle- and upper-income groups generally frowned upon labor disputes and automatically sided with employers. Contact between these persons and the worker was casual and indirect. Labor unions violated certain immutable "natural and moral laws" and deterred economic development and capital accumulation. The *Chicago Times* put it another way in its discussion of workers who challenged the status quo: "The man who lays up not for the morrow, perishes on the morrow. It is the inexorable law of God, which neither legislatures nor communistic blatherskites can repeal. The fittest alone survive, and those are the fittest, as the result always proves, who provide for their own survival."

Unions and all forms of labor protest, particularly strikes, were condemned. *The New York Times* described the strike as a "combination against long-established laws," especially "the law of supply and demand." The *New York Tribune* wrote of "the general viciousness of the trades-union system," and the *Cleveland Leader* called "the labor union kings . . . the most absolute tyrants of our day." Strikes, insisted the *Chicago Tribune,* "implant in many men habits of indolence that are fatal to their efficiency thereafter." Cleveland sailors who protested conditions on the Great Lakes ships were "a motley throng and a wicked one," and when Cuban cigar makers struck in New York, the *New York Herald* insisted that "madness rules the hour."

City officials joined in attacking and weakening trade unions. The mayor forbade the leader of striking Philadelphia weavers from speaking in the streets. New York police barred striking German cigar workers from gathering in front of a factory whose owners had discharged six trade unionists, including four women. Plain-clothes detectives trailed striking Brooklyn plasterers. When Peter Smith, a nonunion barrel maker, shot and wounded four union men—killing one of them —during a bitter lockout, a New York judge freed him on $1,000 bail supplied by his employers and said his employers did "perfectly right in giving Smith a revolver to defend himself from strikers."

Brief review of three important labor crises in Pittsburgh, Cleveland, and New York points out different aspects of the underlying attitude toward labor in the large cities. The owners of Pittsburgh's five daily newspapers cut printers' wages in November, 1873, and formed an association to break the printers' union. After the printers rejected the wage cut and agreed to strike if nonunion men were taken on, two newspapers fired the union printers. The others quit in protest. The *Pittsburgh Dispatch* said the strikers "owe no allegiance to society," and the other publishers condemned the union as an "unreasoning tyranny." Three publishers started a court suit against more than seventy union members charging them with "conspiracy." The printers were held on $700 bail, and the strike was lost. Pittsburgh was soon "swarming with 'rats' from all parts of the country," and the union went under. Though the cases were not pressed after the union collapsed, the indictments were not dropped. In 1876, the *Pittsburgh National Labor Tribune* charged, "All of these men are kept under bail *to this day* to intimidate them from forming a Union, or asking for just wages." A weekly organ of the anthracite miners' union attacked the indictment and complained that it reiterated "the prejudice against workingmen's unions that seems to exist universally among officeholders."

In May, 1874, Cleveland coal dealers cut the wages of their coal heavers more than 25 percent, and between four and five hundred men struck. Some new hands were hired. A foreman drew a pistol on the strikers and was beaten. He and several strikers were arrested, and the coal docks remained quiet as the strikers, who had started a union, paraded up and down and neither spoke nor gestured to the new men. Police guarded the area, and a light artillery battery of the Ohio National Guard was mobilized. Lumber heavers joined the striking workers, and the two groups paraded quietly on May 8. Although the strikers were orderly, the police jailed several leaders. The strikers did not resist and dispersed when so ordered by the law. In their complaint to the public, they captured the flavor of urban-industrial conflict:

> The whole thing is a calumny, based upon the assumption that if a man be poor he must necessarily be a blackguard. Honest poverty can have no merit here, as the rich, together with all their other monopolies, must also monopolize all the virtues. We say now . . . we entertain a much more devout respect and reverence for our public law than the men who are thus seeking to degrade it into a tool of grinding oppression. We ask from the generosity of our fellow citizens . . . to dispute [*sic*] a commission of honest men to

> come and examine our claims. . . . We feel confident they will be
> convinced that the authorities of Cleveland, its police force, and
> particularly the formidable artillery are all made partisans to a
> very dirty and mean transaction.

The impartial inquiry proved unnecessary; a few days later several firms rescinded the wage cut, and the strikers thanked these employers.

Italian laborers were used on a large scale in the New York building trades for the first time in the spring of 1874. They lived "piled together like sardines in a box" and worked mainly as ragpickers and street cleaners. They were men of "passionate dispositions" and, "as a rule, filthy beyond the power of one to imagine." Irish street laborers and unskilled workers were especially hard on Italians, and numerous scuffles between the two groups occurred in the spring of 1874. In spite of the revulsion toward the Italians as a people, the *New York Tribune* advised employers that their "mode of life" allowed them to work for low wages.

Two non-Italians, civil engineers and contractors, founded the New York Italian Labor Company in April, 1874. It claimed 2,700 members, and its superintendent, an Italian named Frederick Guscetti, announced: "As peaceable and industrious men, we claim the right to put such price upon our labor as may seem to us best." The firm held power of attorney over members, contracted particular jobs, provided transportation, supplied work gangs with "simple food," and retained a commission of a day's wages from each monthly paycheck. The company was started to protect the Italians from Irish "adversaries," and Guscetti said the men were willing to work "at panic prices." The non-Italian managers announced the men would work for 20 percent less in the building trades. Employers were urged to hire them "and do away with strikes."

Protected by the city police and encouraged by the most powerful newspapers, the New York Italian Labor Company first attracted attention when it broke a strike of union hod carriers. Irish workers hooted and stoned the Italians, but the police provided them with ample protection. The *Cooper's New Monthly* complained that "poor strangers, unacquainted with the laws and customs and language of the country," had been made "the dupes of unprincipled money sharks" and were being "used as tools to victimize and oppress other workingmen." This was just the start. The firm advertised its services in *Iron Age*. By the end of July, 1874, it had branched out with work gangs in New York, Massachusetts, and Pennsylvania.

There is much yet to learn about the attitude toward labor that existed in large cities, but over all opinion lay a popular belief that "laws" governed the economy and life itself. He who tampered with them through social experiments or reforms imperiled the whole structure. The *Chicago Times* was honest, if callous, in saying: "Whatever cheapens production, whatever will lessen the cost of growing wheat, digging gold, washing dishes, building steam engines, is of value.... The age is not one which enquires when looking at a piece of lace whether the woman who wove it is a saint or a courtesan." It came at last almost to a kind of inhumanity, as one manufacturer who used dogs and men in his operation discovered. The employer liked the dogs. "They never go on strike for higher wages, have no labor unions, never get intoxicated and disorderly, never absent themselves from work without good cause, obey orders without growling, and are very reliable."

The contrast between urban and rural views of labor and its fullest role in society and life is clear. In recent years, many have stressed "entrepreneurship" in nineteenth-century America without distinguishing between entrepreneurs in commerce and trade and those in industrial manufacturing. Reflecting the stresses and strains in the thought and social attitudes of a generation passing from the old pre-industrial way of life to the new industrial America, many men could justify the business ethic in its own sphere without sustaining it in operation in society at large or in human relationships. It was one thing to apply brute force in the marketplace, and quite another to talk blithely of "iron laws" when men's lives and well-being were at stake.

Not all men had such second thoughts about the social fabric which industrial capitalism was weaving, but in the older areas of the country the spirits of free enterprise and free action were neither dead nor mutually exclusive. Many labor elements kept their freedom of action and bargaining even during strikes. And the worker was shrewd in appealing to public opinion. There is a certain irony in realizing that small-town America, supposedly alien and antagonistic toward city ways, remained a stronghold of freedom for the worker seeking economic and social rights.

But perhaps this is not so strange after all, for pre-industrial America, whatever its narrowness and faults, had always preached personal freedom. The city, whose very impersonality would make it a kind of frontier of anonymity, often practiced personal restriction and the law of the economic and social jungle. As industrialism triumphed, the businessman's powers increased, yet he was often hindered—and always suspect—in vast areas of the nation which cheered his efforts toward wealth even while condemning his methods.

Facile generalizations are easy to make and not always sound, but surely the evidence warrants a new view of labor in the Gilded Age. The standard stereotypes and textbook clichés about its impotence and division before the iron hand of oppressive capitalism do not quite fit the facts. Its story is far different when surveyed in depth, carrying in it overtones of great complexity. And even in an age often marked by lust for power, men did not abandon old and honored concepts of human dignity and worth.

The IWW Fight
for Free Speech

MELVYN DUBOFSKY

For the most part, organized labor in America has been content to seek economic advantage for itself. On a few rare occasions, however, labor unions have participated in movements to restructure American society as a whole to bring about a more equal distribution of wealth and more humane conditions of life. The Knights of Labor, organized in 1869, was such an organization. A radical utopian union, it opened its membership to all workers, regardless of race, sex, age, nationality, or type of work. Its program included not only the typical labor demands, such as the eight-hour day and the abolition of child labor, but also demands for equal pay for both sexes, an income tax, and prohibition of the sale of alcoholic beverages. At the peak of its strength, the Knights had over 700,000 members. But a reputation for violence and radicalism caused it to decline rapidly after about 1885, and by the middle of the 1890's it had virtually disappeared.

The next significant radical labor organization was the Industrial Workers of the World (the IWW), better known as the Wobblies. The IWW was founded in 1905 as an outgrowth of the Western Federation of Miners. The purpose of the new organization, according to its chairman and guiding spirit, William D. ("Big Bill") Haywood, was to reorganize American government and economic life. The Wobblies advocated what has been called anarcho-syndicalism—that is, the organization of society into cooperative labor groups that would control the means of production, distribution, and exchange. In other words, they believed in socialism without the state. The IWW avoided political action, however, and concentrated on trying to organize the bottom strata of the American labor force, particularly the unskilled migrant workers of the Western mining, lumber, and agricultural industries. Like the Knights, the IWW was open to workers of all races, sexes, ages, nationalities, and types of work.

The Wobblies were perhaps the most colorful labor organization in American history, partly because of their leadership. One of the most renowned of the Wobbly leaders was Joe Hillstrom, also known as Joe Hill, who composed many of the marching songs used by future industrial workers in organization drives. Hill is perhaps best known for a statement he made just before his execution on a contrived murder charge in Utah: "Don't mourn for me. Organize." It was this spirit that captured the imagination of thousands of wandering workingmen in the West and that later spread to the East, where the IWW organized several successful strikes in northern mill cities.

Almost from the beginning of the IWW, the United States government as well as local governments and industries made every effort to destroy it. Although the Wobblies did not advocate violence, they stressed direct action in their organizing campaigns, and the violent reactions they sometimes evoked on the part of the authorities earned them the charge of inciting violence. In 1917, with the approval of President Wilson, the Justice Department attacked the IWW headquarters, confiscated all records, and arrested the leaders on charges of sedition, espionage, and interference with the war effort. Though the case against them was nonexistent, the Wobbly leaders were found guilty and imprisoned. The movement was thus effectively suppressed. Subsequently, many of the Wobbly leaders joined the Communist party to continue their work for social change.

This selection, dealing with the Wobblies' doctrine that the streets belong to the people and that all people have the right to free speech, gives an indication of the spirit that activated the movement as well as of the vicious response it drew from the dominant forces in American society.

"**Q**uit your job. Go to Missoula. Fight with the Lumber Jacks for Free Speech," the *Industrial Worker* encouraged its readers on September 30, 1909. "Are you game? Are you afraid? Do you love the police? Have you been robbed, skinned, grafted on? If so, then go to

"The IWW Fight for Free Speech" from *We Shall Be All: A History of the Industrial Workers of the World* by Melvyn Dubofsky, copyright © 1969 by Melvyn Dubofsky. Reprinted by permission of Quadrangle Books, Inc.

Missoula, and defy the police, the courts and the people who live off the wages of prostitution." Thus did the IWW proclaim the first of its many fights for free speech.

Many years after the IWW's free-speech fights had faded from public memory, Roger Baldwin, founding father of the American Civil Liberties Union, recalled that the Wobblies

> wrote a chapter in the history of American liberties like that of the struggle of the Quakers for freedom to meet and worship, of the militant suffragists to carry their propaganda to the seats of government, and of the Abolitionists to be heard. . . . The little minority of the working class represented in the I.W.W. blazed the trail in those ten years of fighting for free speech [1908–1918] which the entire American working class must in some fashion follow.

For Wobblies free-speech fights involved nothing so abstract as defending the Constitution, preserving the Bill of Rights, or protecting the civil liberties of American citizens. They were instigated primarily to overcome resistance to IWW organizing tactics and also to demonstrate that America's dispossessed could, through direct action, challenge established authority. To workers dubious about the results achieved by legal action and the reforms won through political action, the IWW taught the effectiveness of victories gained through a strategy of open, yet nonviolent confrontations with public officials. Roger Baldwin perceived as much when, writing long before the post-1954 civil rights movement had made the strategy of confrontation a commonplace of American protest movements, he commented about the IWW's approach: "Far more effective is this direct action of open conflict than all the legal maneuvers in the court to get rights that no government willingly grants. Power wins rights—the power of determination, backed by willingness to suffer jail or violence, to get them."

The IWW and its members did challenge the law and endure violence and imprisonment to win free speech—that is, the right for their soapboxers to stand on street corners, or in front of employment offices, and harangue working-class crowds about the iniquities of capitalism and the decay of American society. But behind the right to speak freely lay more important IWW goals. Many Wobblies considered street speaking the most effective means of carrying their gospel to Western workers. They had solid evidence for this belief. Experience had demonstrated that it was almost impossible for organizers to reach timber workers, construction hands, and harvesters out on the job where watchful employers harassed "labor agitators" and where workers were scattered over a vast geographical area. Only in the city did Western workers concentrate in sufficiently large numbers to be reached effectively by the handful of organizers proselytizing for the IWW, and only in the city did the "agitator" have a measure of freedom to recruit without interference by employers. Many an IWW recruit—among them, Richard Brazier, who later became a leader in the Northwest and also a member of the general executive board—testified to how urban soapboxers such as Joe Ettor aroused his initial interest in the IWW. The IWW and the Western workers also had a common enemy in the city: the employment agent or "shark." These "sharks," against whom the IWW directed most of its street-corner harangues, controlled employment in agriculture and lumber. With anti-union employers they maintained the heavy labor turnover among the unskilled workers—one on the way, one on the job, one leaving—that kept labor organization out of the fields and forests, wages low, and working conditions primitive. The heavy labor turnover guaranteed substantial commissions to the employment agencies that located jobs for the unemployed, as well as large payoffs to cooperating managers and foremen. If the IWW could break the links connecting the "shark," the employer, and the transient laborer, it could loosen the heavy chain of economic circumstances that kept the Western worker in semi-bondage.

Breaking the hold of the employment agencies on the job market would be the initial step in improving working conditions and raising wages, results which would themselves insure a sharp rise in IWW membership. With this in mind, IWW organizers, conceding that industrial conflict belonged in the *shop*, not on the street, stressed: ". . . To carry the war into the shop we must first get into the shop—in this case the camp. To control the source of supply in the industrial cities by forcing the employers to hire men through the I.W.W. is a great step in the direction of industrial control." Put differently, this meant that Western migratories had to be organized before going out on the job, which might last only a few days; and this, in turn, could be accomplished only by controlling the employment agencies, or abolishing them and replacing them with IWW hiring halls. Here is the primary reason the IWW demanded free speech in Spokane, Fresno, Missoula, Aberdeen, Minot, Kansas City, and scores of other Western cities where migratories laid over between jobs, or patronized employment agencies to find new jobs. Three of these many free-speech struggles reveal the pattern of IWW confrontations and their role in the history and development of the organization: Spokane, 1909–1910; Fresno, 1910–1911; and San Diego, 1912.

The first significant IWW struggle for free speech erupted in Spokane, Washington, the hub of the Inland Empire's agricultural, mining, and lumber industries and the central metropolis for all of western Washington, western Oregon, and northern Idaho. Here employers came to locate labor for the mines of the Coeur d'Alenes, the woods of the interior, and the farms of the Palouse and other inland valleys. Migratory workers came to rest up in Spokane during the winter after a long hard harvest summer or an equally arduous season of railroad construction work. In Spokane workers discovered cheap skid-row hotels and cheaper whisky and women to spend their skimpy savings on. When spring approached and savings dwindled, the migratories could turn to the "sharks," who for a price offered another season of employment out in the countryside or forest.

What the IWW accomplished in Spokane was in some respects truly remarkable. Recruiting largely among workers whose lives were often brutal and violent and who had a view of masculinity somewhat akin to the Latin idea of *machismo,* the IWW channeled working-class hostility toward employment agencies into constructive courses. Soapboxers warned angry workers that broken heads and shattered windows would not put the "sharks out of business." No! they thundered. "There is only one way you can get out of their hold. That is by joining the IWW and refusing to go to them for jobs."

The IWW's message was heard. Overalls Brigade "General" J. H. Walsh had come to Spokane after the 1908 convention, and within six months rejuvenated a previously moribund IWW local. The revitalized union leased expensive new headquarters which included a large library and reading room, ample office space, and an assembly hall seating several hundred. It held inside propaganda meetings four nights a week, operated its own cigar and newsstand, and even featured regular movies: from conventional one-reelers to illustrated rebel songs and dry economic lectures. When local authorities restricted street speaking, the Spokane local published its own newspaper, the *Industrial Worker,* which reached a wide local working-class audience. Walsh's local even retained a Spokane law firm on a yearly retainer, as well as maintaining a voluntary hospital plan for members. All this was supported from March to April 1909 by the dues of twelve hundred to fifteen hundred members in good standing and double that number on the local's books. For the first time, or so it now seemed, a labor organization had succeeded in reaching the Inland Empire's migratory workers.

IWW growth brought an immediate and inevitable reaction from Spokane's employers, "sharks," and officials. In March 1909 the city council, acting on complaints from the chamber of commerce, prohibited street-corner orations by closing Spokane's streets to Wobblies and all other "revolutionists." It did so partly because the soapboxers castigated organized religion and partly because IWW oratory had a greater effect than "respectable" citizens realized upon "the army of the unemployed and poorly paid workers." Spokane's city council's action was in accord with the observation made by a later federal investigator that the IWW's right to speak should be restricted when the organization denounced "everything we have been taught to respect from our earliest days . . . all kinds of religions and religious sects. . . ." Christianity and patriotism thus became the employment agents' first line of defense against the IWW onslaught. Thus, Spokane's initial street-speaking ordinance allowed religious groups, most notably the Salvation Army, the IWW's major competitor, the right to speak on the city's streets.

The IWW maintained that its organizers would continue speaking until the ordinance was repealed or made binding upon all organizations. On March 4 the city council placed religious groups under the ban, but the IWW remained unsatisfied. That very day J. H. Walsh himself mounted a soapbox and addressed his "fellow workers and friends," only to be hauled off to jail by local police. Later he was tried, convicted, and fined for violating the local street-speaking ordinance. For the next several days, as Walsh's legal appeals moved through the various courts, Wobblies spoke on Spokane's streets—and were promptly arrested and jailed. As the number of those arrested rose, so did the fines and the length of imprisonment. In March 1909 Spokane's jail filled with Wobblies, ten to twelve men crammed in cells built to accommodate only four. The free-speech prisoners, fed a diet of bread and water twice daily, could neither lie nor sit down. One Wobbly later recalled: "The misery in those cells was something never to be forgotten. . . ."

But the Wobblies refused to give up the struggle. Instead, they sang revolutionary songs, refused to work on the jail rock pile, held daily business meetings, made speeches, and preserved their militancy even within the prison walls. Those who passed by Spokane's jail during those March days must have thought it an odd prison, when they heard the words of the "Red Flag" or the "Marseillaise" filtering out from behind the bars.

As spring approached, the migratories began to leave Spokane for the countryside. Under these circumstances, city authorities released the imprisoned Wobblies, while state courts considered the constitutionality of Spokane's street-speaking ordinance. Spring and summer were not the time for the IWW to contend for free speech: it had to wait for its members to return for another winter in the city.

With the bulk of the migratories temporarily away, Spokane's officials acted to avert another winter of discontent and tumult. On August 10 the city council enacted a revised law that allowed religious groups to hold street meetings but required all other organizations to obtain permits before doing so. The *Industrial Worker* promptly warned the city fathers that the IWW would not ask permission to speak on streets its members had built. "The toad-eaters who make up the Spokane city council are afraid of the I.W.W.," a Wobbly rhetorician noted in an editorial. "Even the devil is not afraid of the Starvation Army." Thus a renewed clash between Wobblies and public authorities awaited summer's end.

Summer ended, the migratories returned to Spokane, and IWW soapboxers again took to the streets. The inevitable followed. On Monday, October 25, the police arrested Jim Thompson for street speaking without a permit. The IWW promptly demanded the inalienable right of free speech and also declared that it would send as many men to Spokane as were needed to win its struggle. Despite the IWW's threat and a legal ruling declaring the revised street-speaking ordinance discriminatory and unconstitutional, the battle continued to rage. On November 1, the day of the legal decision ruling the ban on speaking unconstitutional, the IWW initiated round-the-clock street meetings. Spokane's police promptly arrested each speaker who mounted a soapbox. Before long the city jail held every local IWW leader: Walter Nef, Jim Thompson, James Wilson, C. L. Filigno, and A. C. Cousins. Those not hauled off a soapbox were picked up in a police raid on IWW headquarters, which also netted three female sympathizers. The arrested Wobblies went to jail peaceably, for, as the *Industrial Worker* advised its readers, "it must be understood that any person, at any time, who would try to incite disorder or 'rioting' is an enemy of the IWW. Nothing of the kind will be tolerated at this time." Passive resistance and confrontation tactics as a form of direct action were being put to the test in Spokane.

The city fathers used every instrument of power they controlled to thwart the IWW. Before the battle ended almost four hundred Wobblies had been jailed. For a time, public officials reasoned that if they could incapacitate the IWW's leaders, the fight would dissipate. Such reasoning lay behind the city's decision to raid IWW headquarters on November 3, and to arrest local Wobblies on criminal conspiracy charges; it was also behind the move to arrest the editors of the *Industrial Worker*. None of this decisively stifled the Wobblies, however, for as one policeman remarked: "Hell! we got the leaders, but damned if it don't look like they are all leaders."

After their arrest Wobblies received a further taste of Spokane justice. When Frank Little appeared in court, the presiding magistrate asked him what he had been doing at the time of his arrest. "Reading the Declaration of Independence," Little answered. "Thirty days," said the magistrate. The prosecuting attorney demanded that the IWW "feel the mailed fist of the law," which for those leaders charged with criminal conspiracy meant four to six months in jail. For most Wobblies arrested for disorderly conduct the sentence was thirty days, then release, followed by further street speaking and another thirty-day sentence. This legal treatment, most Wobblies thought, justified their definition of government "as the slugging committee of the capitalist class."

In Spokane, indeed, slugging soon became more than merely rhetorical. Arresting police officers used their clubs liberally. Jail life proved even worse: twenty-eight to thirty Wobblies would be tossed into an eight-by-six-foot sweatbox, where they would steam for a full day while staring at bloodstained walls. After that they would be moved into an ice-cold cell without cots or blankets. Those who did not weaken from the heat of the first cell often collapsed from the chill of the second. Because Spokane's regular jails could not accommodate the hordes of IWW prisoners, the city converted an unheated, abandoned schoolhouse into a temporary prison. There in mid-winter jailers offered scantily clad prisoners two ounces of bread daily, soft pine for a pillow, and hardwood for a bed. Inside the schoolhouse guards woke the inmates at all hours of the night and then chased them from room to room. Under these conditions some Wobblies fell ill; others, no longer able to stand the strain, collapsed in the middle of the floor; still others maintained their spirits by walking around in a circle singing the "Red Flag." Once a week the school's jailers marched the prisoners out in order to have them bathe for allegedly sanitary reasons. Taken to the city jail, the Wobblies were stripped, thrust under an ice-cold shower, and then, frequently in frigid weather, marched back to their unheated prison.

The IWW estimated that, as a result of this treatment, 334 of the 400 men in prison for 110 days (from November through March) were treated in the emergency hospital a total of 1,600 times. Many left prison with permanent scars and missing teeth; the more fortunate walked away with weakened constitutions.

When police repression and prison brutality failed to weaken the Wobblies' resistance, the authorities resorted to different tactics. After raiding and closing IWW headquarters, they denied every hall in Spokane, except Turner Hall, to the Wobblies. Police seized copies of the *Industrial Worker* and arrested the men—even the boys—who peddled the paper. Unable to function in Spokane, the IWW moved its headquarters and all its defense activities to Coeur d'Alene City under the direction of Fred Heslewood, and published the *Industrial Worker* in Seattle. In the face of relentless repression, the IWW resisted.

The IWW ultimately triumphed because of the spirit and determination of its members. When IWW headquarters pleaded for volunteers to fight for free speech, scores of Wobblies descended upon Spokane. One Wobbly left Minneapolis on November 10, traveling across North Dakota and Montana atop a Pullman car despite sub-zero temperatures. Arriving in Spokane on November 21, somewhat chilled but ready to fight, he was arrested by police two days later. He was not alone: hundreds like him came to Spokane, and hundreds more were ready to come. All intended to make the free-speech fight an expensive and difficult proposition for Spokane's taxpayers. "Let them cry quits to their Mayor and police force if they do not relish it," threatened the Wobblies. "We can keep up the fight all winter."

No one better exemplified this IWW spirit than the "Rebel Girl," Elizabeth Gurley Flynn. Only nineteen years old and recently released from a Missoula jail (where another free-speech battle had ended), she was several months pregnant when she arrived in Spokane in November 1909. Local papers described her at that time as a "frail, slender girl, pretty and graceful, with a resonant voice and a fiery eloquence that attracted huge crowds." Another observer pictured her as a little woman, Irish all over, with "the Celt in her grey-blue eyes and almost black hair and in the way she clenches her small hands into fists when she's speaking." To Woodrow Wilson, she described herself in 1918 as

> an humble and obscure citizen who has struggled for democracy as her vision glimpsed it and who has suffered for espousing an unpopular and much misrepresented point of view. . . . For seven years I have supported my child, and helped to educate two sisters . . . and a brother. . . . This . . . has been a labor of love, but it is rather incompatible with the popular conception of a "labor agitator."

Elizabeth Gurley Flynn, however, was all agitator. Daughter of immigrant Irish parents, at fifteen or sixteen she made her first speech as a "materialistic socialist" before her father's radical club in Harlem; at seventeen she had been arrested for street speaking in New York; and at nineteen she was jailed, first in Missoula, then in Spokane. So adept an agitator was she that the Spokane authorities considered her the most dangerous and effective of Wobbly soapboxers. When a young attorney suggested to the city fathers that she not be tried along with the men on charges of criminal conspiracy, the local officials responded: "Hell, no! You just don't understand. She's the one we are after. She makes all the trouble. She puts fight into the men, gets them the publicity they enjoy. As it is, they're having the time of their lives."

Spokane brought Elizabeth Gurley Flynn to trial on charges of criminal conspiracy with a young Italian Wobbly named Charley Filigno. Not unexpectedly, the jury declared on February 24, 1910: "Filigno, guilty. Elizabeth Gurley Flynn, not guilty." An enraged prosecutor demanded of the jury foreman, "What in hell do you fellows mean by acquitting the most guilty, and convicting the man, far less guilty?" To which the foreman calmly replied: "She ain't a criminal, Fred, an' you know it! If you think this jury, or any jury, is goin' to send that pretty Irish girl to jail merely for bein' bighearted and idealistic, to mix with all those whores and crooks down at the pen, you've got another guess comin'."

But looks can be deceiving, and in Elizabeth Gurley Flynn's case they certainly were. After the fight in Spokane she proceeded to bigger and better battles. She was with the IWW at Lawrence, Paterson, and Everett. Still later, with Roger Baldwin, she helped found the American Civil Liberties Union, and fought to defend the rights of the poor and the exploited. Her vision of democracy as she glimpsed it took her from the Socialist party to the IWW to the ACLU and ultimately in the 1930's to the Communist party. During the forties and fifties she became American communism's leading female advocate as well as the only woman ever sentenced to a prison term under the Smith Act. While in Moscow attending a Soviet party congress in her capacity as chairman of the American Communist party, she died on September 5, 1964, at the age of seventy-four. From her first speech before the Harlem Socialist Club as a teen-ager to her last talk as a Communist, Elizabeth Gurley Flynn remained true to what she allegedly told theatrical producer David Belasco, upon turning down a part in a Broadway play: "I don't want to be an actress! I'm in the labor movement and I speak my own piece."

The piece she spoke in Spokane in the winter of 1909–1910 aided the IWW immeasurably. She won national attention and sympathy that no male agitator could. Her clash with local authorities, her arrest, and the despicable treatment she received in jail made nationwide headlines. She exemplified the IWW's determination to win free speech in Spokane. If repression could not break the spirit of a pregnant, slightly built, teenage girl, how could it crush the Wobblies' free-speech fighters flooding into Spokane in an unending stream?

Yet the Spokane struggle continued through the winter of 1910, as public officials resorted to further repressive measures. On February 22 Spokane officials crossed the state line into Idaho, raided IWW defense headquarters in Coeur d'Alene City, and arrested Fred Heslewood on a fugitive warrant. In response the IWW advised its members: "Let us go to Spokane, fill their jails and overthrow the whole tottering edifice of corruption misnamed the Spokane City Government." Five thousand volunteers were asked to demonstrate their contempt for the "slugging committee of the capitalist class."

Faced with this unrelenting nonviolent resistance, city officials finally weakened. From the IWW's point of view, Spokane's authorities chose a propitious moment for compromise, for by the end of February the Wobblies also were weakened in their resolve. St. John and other

IWW officials found it harder and harder to recruit volunteers for the Spokane fight. When spring came it would be even more difficult. Acting the part of realists, not visionary revolutionaries, a three-man IWW committee, including William Z. Foster, a new member, approached Spokane's mayor to discuss peace terms. The mayor at first proved unresponsive. He approved the IWW's defense of free speech, yet stressed that street speaking would not be tolerated when it interfered with the normal flow of traffic or the business of citizens—a decision that would be made by responsible public officials. The mayor further reminded the IWW committee that only the city council and the courts could determine the constitutionality of city restrictions on street speaking. Somewhat ominously, he warned that continued IWW free-speech activities would be more stringently repressed. The Wobblies, in turn, threatened that the "IWW is going to use the streets of Spokane or go down fighting." In truth, neither side had much stomach for continued warfare. For one thing, the city could not stand the expense of several hundred individual legal trials, including the ensuing appeals; for another, the IWW had exhausted campaigners and it lacked new recruits to take up the slack. Thus, on March 3, 1910, after a series of conferences between IWW representatives and various city officials, peace came to Spokane.

The IWW won its major demands. Indoor meeting places would no longer be denied to the organization, and it could also hold peaceful outdoor meetings without police interference. Spokane agreed to respect the IWW's right to publish the *Industrial Worker* and to sell it on the city's streets. Complicated terms were also devised to secure the release of those Wobblies still in prison. Significantly, the authorities assured the IWW that free speech would be allowed on city streets in the near future. Until that council enacted new speaking ordinances, it barred street corners to religious groups: the Salvation Army as well as the IWW would have to await the passage of a free-speech statute later that year.

Wobblies also won the secondary demands which had undergirded their fight for free speech. In the midst of the battle, Spokane officials had initiated reforms in the employment agency system, rescinding the licenses of the worst of the "sharks." After the battle, public officials throughout the Northwest attempted to regulate private employment agencies more closely.

As viewed by the Wobblies, the Spokane free-speech fight had been an impressive triumph for the twin principles of direct action and passive resistance. The discipline maintained by the free-speech fighters and the passivity with which they endured brutalities won the respect of many parties usually critical of or hostile to the IWW. During the struggle local socialists, Spokane's AFL members, and WFM miners in the Coeur d'Alenes, as well as "respectable" townspeople, contributed money, food, or just plain sympathy to the Wobbly cause. Passive resistance also showed what migratory workers who lacked the franchise might accomplish by more direct means. *Solidarity* grasped the lesson of Spokane when it observed: "By use of its weakest weapon —passive resistance—labor forced civic authorities to recognize a power equal to the state." If labor can gain so much through its crudest weapon, it asked, "what will the result be when an industrially organized working class stands forth prepared to seize, operate, and control the machinery of production and distribution?"

But free speech on the streets of Spokane did not guarantee successful labor organization among the workers of the fields, woods, and construction camps of the Inland Empire. In 1910 the IWW had only learned how to attract migratory workers during their winter layovers in town; it had not yet hit upon the secret of maintaining an everyday, effective labor organization out on the job among workers who moved freely. It had not yet discovered how to survive when employers set armed gunmen upon "labor agitators" and summarily discharged union members. Victory in Spokane did, however, inspire the soapboxers and organizer-agitators so prominent within the IWW to carry their campaigns for free speech to other Western cities where migratories gathered to rest or to seek employment.

California Growers Attack Migrant Labor Organizations

CAREY McWILLIAMS

Migrant farm workers have been and remain perhaps the most consistently depressed segment of the American labor force. Wandering from harvest to harvest, up and down both coasts, these low-paid agricultural laborers never have enough steady work to maintain even a passable standard of living. Their children rarely stay in one place long enough to have successful school experiences. Instead, they tend to pass the school years in the fields, while local truant officers look the other way. Because they have no home base, the migrant workers seldom have a chance to exercise their political rights. And because they are relatively few in number, they have little economic or social influence in the areas they frequent. Their labor serves primarily to put money in the pockets of those engaged in large-scale agriculture—the current "agribusiness."

An important factor in the success of large-scale agriculture in this country has been the cooperation of local, state, and national political and law-enforcement authorities with landowners. In industrial labor disputes, government forces have generally supported the factory owners and managers against the workers. They have demonstrated an even more negative attitude toward agricultural workers, as witnessed by the persistence of chattel slavery as a form of agricultural labor until the second half of the nineteenth century. In the South the emphasis was on making the labor force stay put, but in the West the important thing was to keep the labor force in motion—up through California, into Oregon and Washington, and back again, following the harvests of the fruits and vegetables for which the West Coast is famous.

Through the years, much of the migrant labor population in

California has been of non-European ancestry. Mexican-Americans, in particular, have often found that the only work available to them was at harvest time. Frequently, the structures of society have been marshaled against these minority populations in a manner suggestive of Jim Crow in the South. Segregated schools, segregated housing, and clearly discriminatory social and political practices have severely restricted their freedom of movement all along the West Coast. In addition, they have borne the brunt of vigilante justice and lynch law in the West—practices in which California has taken second place only to the South. Indeed, the lawlessness of the mining camps and of San Francisco's Barbary Coast in the nineteenth century is legendary. Currently, although large-scale agriculture has replaced mining as the state's leading industry, the patterns of coalition against minority workers' groups on the part of public officials, law-enforcement authorities, and leaders of business and industry remain much as they were in the nineteenth century.

Only in recent years has there been a successful drive to organize migrant farm workers into a viable economic force in California. Cesar Chavez and his Mexican-American grape-pickers have formed the United Farm Workers Organizing Committee (the UFWOC), which, after several years of striking against great odds, has been able to negotiate a contract with growers that promises to bring some improvement in the standard of living of both union members and other migrant agricultural laborers. The UFWOC is now turning its attention to crops other than grapes in an attempt to provide migrant workers with some measure of economic security throughout the year.

The following selection, first published in 1939, provides a vivid description of the difficulties faced by the migrant workers of the 1930's as they struggled for a better way of life.

Following the great wave of strikes which swept California in 1933, the farmers of the State began to form new organizations with which to combat the instinctive struggle of the State's 250,000 agricultural workers to achieve unionization. Farmers have never lacked organization in California; in fact, they have long set the pace for organizational activities among American farmers. They were pioneers in the field of co-operative marketing. Today every crop is organized

"California Growers Attack Migrant Labor Organizations" from *Factories in the Field: The Story of Migratory Farm Labor in California* by Carey McWilliams. Reprinted by permission of the author.

through a series of co-operative organizations, many of which are institutions of great power and wealth. For a great many years these organized farm groups have held the balance of political power in the State through their control of the State Senate. Holding a veto power on all State legislation, they have dictated to governors and defied the will of the people of the entire State. In addition to co-operative marketing organizations, the canning and packing houses have long been organized into powerful trade associations and, in 1926, the Western Growers Protective Association was formed, for the purpose of consolidating various smaller organizations of shippers and growers in the State. Shortly after the 1933 trouble, in February, 1934, American Institutions, Inc., was organized in California by Mr. Guernsey Frazer, a prominent American Legion official, for the purpose of selling the large shipper-growers a high-pressure pro-Fascism legislative program. This attempt to impose Fascism from the outside, so to speak, was not successful, but, by 1934, the large growers themselves recognized the necessity of organizing for the primary purpose of fighting labor organization. The organization which they effected, Associated Farmers of California, Inc., which today has membership in California of 40,000, has played an important role in the social history of the West. Inasmuch as it is the first organization of its type to appear in the United States, and as it has many points of similarity with organizations of a like character in Nazi Germany, it warrants careful scrutiny.

"FROM APATHY TO ACTION"

In 1933 the California Farm Bureau Federation and the State Chamber of Commerce appointed a joint committee to study farm-labor conditions in the State. At the conclusion of this survey the farmers of Imperial Valley—"the Cradle of Vigilantism"—formed a voluntary association known as Associated Farmers, "pledged to help one another in case of emergency. They agreed to co-operate to harvest crops in case of strikes and to offer these services to the local sheriff immediately as special deputies in the event of disorders arising out of picketing and sabotage." As soon as this group was organized, the State Farm Bureau and the State Chamber of Commerce each designated a representative to go from county to county "explaining the Associated Farmers idea to local Farm Bureaus, businessmen, and peace officers." Within one year, twenty-six counties had formed associated farmer groups, and, on May 7, 1934, a convention was held in Fresno for the purpose of creating a Statewide organization. I have a stenographic report of this organization meeting. It was presided over by S. Parker Frisselle [Mr. Frisselle was the first president and served for two years; his successor was Colonel Walter E. Garrison], who stated that the finances for the organization would unquestionably have to come from the banks and utility companies. The initial funds were, in fact, raised by Mr. Earl Fisher, of the Pacific Gas & Electric Company, and Mr. Leonard Wood, of the California Packing Company. At this meeting, it was decided that farmers should "front" the organization, although the utility companies and banks would exercise ultimate control.

Today the Associated Farmers have their headquarters in San Francisco and branch offices in practically every county of the State. Each farmer is supposed to pay one dollar a year, as membership dues, and an additional dollar for each thousand dollars a year spent in wages. In some counties, dues are levied on the basis of so many cents per ton of fruit and vegetables harvested. Every member pledges himself, "in case of trouble," to report at the local sheriff's office.

> Under agreement with the local sheriffs, no volunteer farmer will be asked to carry a gun or throw a gas bomb, even if he is deputized. He is armed with a pick handle about twenty inches long. A good many of the Associated Farmers would prefer fire-arms. But they had been overruled by cooler heads who say that in the heat of defending their homes by invading strike pickets, the embittered farmers might use their guns too effectively and turn public opinion against the organization.

The "idea" back of these mobilizations, according to Mr. Taylor, "is to muster a show of force when required." How effectively some of the mobilizations have been organized may be indicated by the fact that in the Salinas strike, 1,500 men were mobilized for deputy duty in less than a day; in the Stockton strike, 2,200 deputies were mobilized in a few hours and in Imperial Valley 1,200 deputies were recently mobilized on a few minutes' notice. When one realizes that in 1933 a large percentage of the farm lands in Central and Northern California were controlled by one institution—the Bank of America—the irony of these "embittered" farmers defending their "homes" against strikers becomes apparent.

An efficient espionage system is maintained by the Associated Farmers. In 1935, I inspected the "confidential" files of the organization in San Francisco. At that time, they had a card-index file on "dangerous radicals" containing approximately one thousand names, alphabetically arranged, with front- and side-view photographs of each individual, including notations of arrests, strike activities, affiliations, and so forth. Each reference contained a number which referred to a corresponding identification record in the archives of the State Bureau of Criminal Identification. Sets of this file have been distributed to over a hundred peace officers in the State and lists have been sent to members of the association. Local offices or branches of the Associated Farmers maintain elaborate records of a similar nature, including a "check-up" system whereby workers with a reputation for independence may be readily identified and rousted out of the locality. The State Bureau of Criminal Identification, the State Highway Patrol, and local law-enforcement agencies work in the closest co-operation with agents of the association; in a sense, the association may be said to direct the activities of these public agencies. The State Bureau of Criminal Identification had its private investigators sleuthing for the Tagus Ranch in the San Joaquin Valley and it employed, at one time or another, the various stool pigeons upon whose testimony the Sacramento criminal-syndicalism prosecution was based.

In addition to its espionage activities, the Associated Farmers maintain a carefully organized propaganda department. Regular bulletins, heavily larded with "anti-Communist" information, are sent to the members; special articles are reprinted and distributed throughout the State; and a steady flow of statements and releases are supplied to the press. In recent years, the association has begun to dabble in a more ambitious type of propaganda. One of its spokesmen, Mr. John Phillips, a State Senator, recently visited Europe. Upon his return, Mr. Phillips published a series of articles in the *California Cultivator* (February 1 and 15, 1936), on his travels. One article was devoted to Mr. Phillips' impressions of the Nazis (he was in Nuremberg when the party was in session). Mr. Phillips particularly noticed the new type of German citizenship—the *Reichsburger*—under which "you simply say that anybody who agrees with you is a citizen of the first class, and anybody who does not agree with you is a non-voting citizen." His admiration for Hitler is boundless: "I would like to tell you how the personality of Hitler impressed me and how I feel that he has a greater personal appeal, a greater personal influence on his people than many of the nations realize." "Hitler," he said in a speech on January 18, 1938, "has done more for democracy than any man before him." Some years ago, Frances Perkins, Secretary of Labor, issued a statement repudiating a circular which the Associated Farmers had distributed in which they had attempted to make out, by reference to a faked marriage license, that she was a Jewess. Throughout California in 1936 and 1937, the Associated Farmers sponsored and organized meetings for the Reverend Martin Luther Thomas, of Los Angeles, who heads a "Christian American Crusade," and who is a notorious anti-Semite and Red-baiter. As a result of Mr. Thomas' harangues, the authorities in Riverside County employed a special detective, at a salary of $1,800 a year, to spy on the "subversive activities" of school children in the Riverside public schools. Mr. Phillips, who is frequently teamed with the Rev. Mr. Thomas at anti-Communist meetings sponsored by the Associated Farmers, was, for a time, holding a county office in Riverside County, designated as "labor co-ordinator." More recently the Associated Farmers have sponsored Samuel J. Hume, of the California Crusaders, who has spoken throughout the State inveighing against labor organization.

Shortly after its formation, the Associated Farmers launched a campaign, in the rural counties, for the enactment of the anti-picketing and so-called "emergency-disaster" ordinances. Anti-picketing ordinances have, as a consequence, been enacted in practically every rural county. The alleged justification for the "emergency-disaster" ordinances, which provide for a mobilization of all the forces of the community in case of a "major disaster," was the earthquake which occurred in Southern California in March, 1933. Today practically every county in the State, and most of the cities and towns, have such ordinances in effect. There is nothing in the wording of most of these ordinances to prevent their use in case of a "strike," which, in the eyes of the farmers during harvest, is certainly a "major disaster." The ordinances provide, in elaborate detail, for the formation of a kind of "crisis," or extra-legal governmental machinery, which is to come into existence, with broad powers, upon the declaration by the appropriate executive officer in the community that a state of emergency exists. The purpose back of the campaign for the enactment of these ordinances has been clearly indicated. For example, on December 18, 1936, the county counsel in Los Angeles was instructed to draft legislation which "would permit counties to spend funds for erecting concentration camps for use during major disasters." Thus the governmental apparatus for a kind of constitutional Fascism actually exists in California today.

It would be suggested, of course, that I am exaggerating the importance of these ordinances and misstating the purpose for which they were enacted. But other evidence exists which points to the real intention back of these measures. Concentration camps are to be found in California today. I described, in some detail, such a camp in an article which appeared in *The Nation* (July 24, 1935). It is located a few miles outside of Salinas, California. Here a stockade has been constructed which is admittedly intended for use as a concentration camp. When local workers inquired of the shipper-growers why such a curious construction had been established, they were told that it was built "to hold strikers, but of course we won't put white men in it, just Filipinos." A similar stockade at one time existed at the farm factory of the Balfour-Guthrie Company (a large British-owned concern) at Brentwood, California. During a strike at this farm in 1935, "a substantial fence surmounted by plenty of barbed wire" was built about the workers' camp, with "the entrance guarded night and day." When questioned about this camp, the growers protested that "agitators continually refer to it as a stockade, a cattle corral, or a prison, and its inhabitants as slaves or prisoners." Mr. P. S. Bancroft, President of the Contra Costa unit of the Associated Farmers, in defending the camp, said that "obviously the fence and guard were there to keep the lawless element out, not to keep the contented workmen in." When the striking workers in the Imperial Valley set up a camp and strike headquarters in 1934, however, the camp was raided by local police, because, to quote from the *Shipper-Grower Magazine* (March, 1934), "it was a concentration camp in which the workers were being kept against their wishes." The burning question, therefore, would seem to be: When is a concentration camp not a concentration camp? At the Tagus Ranch, in 1934, a huge moat was constructed around an orchard in order "to protect the properties," with armed guards stationed at the entrance and with a machine gun mounted on a truck. "All roads leading to the ranch with the exception of the main entrance, where guards are stationed, are blocked by barbed wire and flooded with water by dikes. Fifty old employees report nightly to the ranch manager regarding the conduct of employees under suspicion." There is much similar evidence, all tending to show that the great farm factories of California take on the appearance of fortified camps under military surveillance whenever a strike is threatened.

Throughout the year 1934 the Associated Farmers stimulated many "trial mobilizations." On July 23, 1934, Sheriff O. W. Toland at Gridley announced that a "trial mobilization" of American Legion men and special deputies had come off perfectly: "All Legionnaires were at the hall in ten minutes and in forty-five minutes the entire assembly was present." Many Legion Posts throughout the State practiced similar mobilizations which were timed to coincide with organizational activity among agricultural workers. From Merced, on July 14, 1934, came word that the California Lands, Inc. (Bank of America), and the California Packing Company had demanded forty extra deputy sheriffs, "equipped sufficiently to cope with violence." From Hanford, July 16, 1934, came the report that county officials had organized an Anti-Communist League "to co-operate with county officers in case of emergencies." Most of this viligante recruiting has been done by elected officials, sheriffs, and district attorneys, and peace officers. For example, in 1934 Sheriff Howard Durley, according to the *Fillmore Herald*, "prepared to organize a county-wide vigilante group for the purpose of handling emergencies. Approximately 200 special deputies were sworn in, chosen from prepared lists, and these will be organized into smaller units of ten men each in all sections of the county." I could quote an abundance of similar evidence.

In the following year, 1935, the strategy was carried a point further, when the growers began to order "preventive" arrests. On December 30, 1935, the Sheriff of Imperial Valley (where 4,000 gun permits had been issued in the summer), at the opening of the winter harvest season, "launched a valley-wide roundup of professional agitators, Communists and suspects *to avert a possible strike* among lettuce workers." Commenting upon this move, the *Los Angeles Times* stated editorially: "Professional agitators who are busily engaged in fomenting new labor trouble in the Imperial Valley winter lettuce [harvest] will find the authorities ready for them. Sheriff Ware and his deputies have *the jump on them this time*," i.e., arrests were made before a strike could be called and in advance of the season.

Needless to say, the Associated Farmers have a powerful legislative lobby in Sacramento and an elaborate legislative program. In general, they have sponsored the enactment of laws restricting labor's right to organize on the avowed theory that such legislation "would help cut down the cost of labor"; the incorporation of all labor unions; laws prohibiting sympathetic strikes; measures designed to prevent the unionization of governmental and utility-company employees;

provisions limiting the right of strikers to relief; and a number of other measures, such as laws making it illegal to interfere with the delivery of food or medical supplies, outlawing the Communist Party, and prohibiting all picketing. At present, the farm groups are fighting strenuously against a proposal for a unicameral legislative body in California, for, under the present system, they actually hold a legislative veto through their control of the State Senate. Until this hold is broken, democratic processes cannot function.

SANTA ROSA

Encouraged by their success in 1934 in crushing unionization activities among agricultural workers, the Associated Farmers determined in 1935 to stamp out the last vestiges of revolt and to prevent an organizational campaign from getting under way. As part of this strategy, they organized a systematic terrorization of workers in the rural areas on the eve, so to speak, of the various crop harvests. Without waiting for organizational activity to start, and in advance of the season, fiery crosses burned on the hilltops and wholesale arrests were made, usually accompanied by an elaborate Red-baiting campaign in the local press to build up the idea, in the mind of the community, that grave danger threatened. In February, 1935, the leaders of the Associated Farmers sponsored the formation in Sacramento of the California Cavaliers, a semi-military organization, which announced that its purpose was to "stamp out all un-American activity among farm labor." Mr. Herman Cottrell, an official of the Associated Farmers and an organizer of the California Cavaliers, publicly stated: "We aren't going to stand for any more of these organizers from now on; anyone who peeps about higher wages will wish he hadn't." As the harvest season approached, statements such as the foregoing were accompanied by overt acts of terrorization. At San Jose, on June 10, 1935, on the eve of the apricot-crop harvest, three fiery crosses blazed on the hills near a workers' camp where, two years previously, a mob of vigilantes had raided the camp, kidnaped a score of "radical" leaders, held them for two hours, beaten them, and then driven them across the county line. Confident that they had the situation well in hand, the Associated Farmers, in a radio broadcast on June 14, 1935, told their members "to go ahead and don't worry about agitators this season."

In general this confidence was justified, for 1935 was marked by only one major "incident," that of Santa Rosa. In August, the workers, assembled in the Santa Rosa and Sebastopol sections for the apple harvest, voted to strike. As the season was somewhat delayed, the growers ignored the strike vote until some two hundred packing-house employees decided to join the pickers in a general walkout. On August 1, 1935, two Communist Party officials were speaking at a mass meeting of pickers and packing-house workers in Santa Rosa, when the hall was raided by a group of 250 vigilantes, who jerked the speakers from the platform, broke up the meeting, and engaged in a general free-for-all fight with the workers. As the crop matured and workers were not immediately forthcoming in the superabundance demanded by the growers, a delegation of orchard owners went to the relief agencies and demanded that a large number of relief clients be dropped from the rolls and ordered into the orchards. A few days later, on August fifth, a committee of six men, "saying they represented 300 vigilantes," called on the local WPA administrator and demanded that "all Communists, Reds, and radicals" be dropped from the payroll of the WPA, stating that if this ultimatum were not complied with in forty-eight hours, they would take matters into their own hands. The WPA administrator stalled for time, and the committee reluctantly agreed to extend the deadline.

On August 23, 1935, "with sunset this evening set as the new deadline," a mob of vigilantes seized Solomon Nitzburg and Jack Green, together with three other men, dragged them through the streets of Santa Rosa, and after the three men had kissed the American flag on the courthouse steps and promised to leave the community, released them. Nitzburg and Green, refusing to comply with the demand, were kicked, beaten, tarred and feathered, and paraded around the courthouse in Santa Rosa, and driven out of the county. In seizing Nitzburg, the mob fired volley after volley of rifle fire through his home, and followed up this attack with the use of tear-gas bombs. The entire evening of August twenty-third was a Saturnalia of rioting, intimidation, and violence, described as "the wildest scene in the history of Sonoma County." The whole affair was carried out brazenly, with no attempt at concealment, and the *San Francisco Examiner,* which played up the incident as provocatively as possible, openly stated that "the tar and feather party was hailed in Sonoma County as a direct American answer to the red strike fomentors." The leaders of the mob consisted of the following men: a local banker, the Mayor, the head of the local Federal Re-employment Bureau, several motor cops, a member of the State Legislature, numerous American Legionnaires, and the President of the local Chamber of Commerce. Later twenty-three business and professional men in the community were indicted in connection with the riot, but were quickly acquitted; and, later, when Nitzburg and Green sued for damages, the court found in favor of the defendants.

Santa Rosa, the first major "incident" after the Cannery and Agricultural Workers Industrial Union had been smashed in 1934, was significant of the rising tide of potential Fascism in California. The division of social forces was clear-cut. On the one hand were the migratory workers in the field and the packing-house employees who were, for the most part, local residents, together with a few miscellaneous local sympathizers. Arrayed against this group were a few large growers and the packing-house companies utilizing the local towns-people as a vigilante mob to crush a pending strike. The form of constitutional government was swiftly brushed aside and mob rule openly sanctioned. This exhibition of Fascist insurrection not only went unpunished, but received open public support throughout the State and the tacit approval of State officials. The strike, of course, was crushed. In fact, the strike was crushed so thoroughly that it backfired on the growers. "The mob action," according to the United Press, "of the vigilantes has frightened away from the county so many workers that the county is 20 per cent under the number of pickers needed. Pay was increased one-fourth cent a pound, with payment of transportation, to induce pickers to come here, but the increase has had little effect in this regard." Soon the local growers were wailing about a "labor shortage" and announcing that four thousand pickers were needed immediately "to save the crop." This demonstration of the shortsightedness of employer violence, however, made no impression upon the Associated Farmers, who continued to use the Santa Rosa technique throughout 1935, 1936, and 1937.

Suggestions for Further Reading

The standard history of the American workingman is John R. Commons et al., *History of Labour in the United States* (4 vols.; Macmillan, 1918–35). A specialized survey of labor during the Gilded Age is Norman J. Ware, *The Labor Movement in the United States, 1860–1895* ° (Appleton-Century-Crofts, 1929). For the philosophy behind the labor movement, see Gerald N. Grob, *Workers and Utopia: A Study of Ideological Conflict in the American Labor Movement, 1865–1900* ° (Northwestern University Press, 1961), and Herbert G. Gutman, "Protestantism and the American Labor Movement: The Christian Spirit in the Gilded Age," *American Historical Review,* Vol. 62 (October, 1966), 74–101.

Important labor conflicts are treated in Leon Wolff, *Lockout: The Story of the Homestead Strike of 1892* ° (Harper and Row, 1965); Almont Lindsey, *The Pullman Strike: The Story of a Unique Experiment and of a Great Labor Upheaval* ° (University of Chicago Press, 1942); D. L. McMurray, *Coxey's Army: A Study of the Industrial Army Movement of 1894* ° (Little, Brown, 1929); and R. V. Bruce, *1877: Year of Violence* ° (Bobbs-Merrill, 1959).

Patrick Renshaw has written a short history of the IWW entitled *The Wobblies* ° (Doubleday, 1967). Apart from Melvyn Dubofsky's work, *We Shall Be All: A History of the Industrial Workers of the World* (Quadrangle, 1969), the best available source of information on the Wobblies is the collection of documents from the movement edited by Joyce L. Kornbluh, *Rebel Voices: An I.W.W. Anthology* ° (University of Michigan Press, 1964).

On the history of labor in the early twentieth century, see John Laslett, *Labor and the Left: A Study of Socialist and Radical Influences in the American Labor Movement, 1881–1924* (Basic Books, 1970); Irving Bernstein, *The Lean Years: A History of the American Worker, 1920–1933* ° (Houghton-Mifflin, 1960); and David Brody, *Labor in Crisis: The Steel Strike of 1919* ° (Lippincott, 1965).

For the history of the labor movement during the Depression, see Irving Bernstein, *Turbulent Years: A History of the American Worker, 1933–1941* (Houghton-Mifflin, 1970). An important labor dispute of the period is described in Sidney Fine, *Sit-Down: The General Motors Strike of 1936–1937* (University of Michigan Press, 1969).

Carey McWilliams treats the problems of migrant labor in *Ill Fares the Land: Migrants and Migratory Labor in the United States* (Little, Brown, 1942). A powerful fictional treatment of attempts to organize farm workers in California is John Steinbeck's *In Dubious Battle* ° (Viking, 1938). The classic statement on the westward movement of poor migrants is John Steinbeck's monumental *Grapes of Wrath* ° (Vi-

° Available in paperback edition.

king, 1939). For a general study of the homeless wanderers who proliferated during the Depression, see Henry Hill Collins, *America's Own Refugees: Our 4,000,000 Homeless Migrants* (Princeton University Press, 1941). The continuing problems of migrant workers are considered in Dale Wright, *They Harvest Despair: The Migrant Farm Worker* (Beacon, 1965), and in T. E. Moore, *The Slaves We Rent* (Random House, 1965).

Chinese-, Japanese-, and Spanish-Americans

Anti-Chinese Sentiment
in California

ELMER C. SANDMEYER

Too often the study of immigration in American history deals only with the Atlantic migration, overlooking the fact that there were several waves of immigration from East Asia. The first major wave of Pacific migration was a large-scale movement of Chinese into California and the West during the gold rush, beginning in 1848. The second was an influx of Japanese settlers on the West Coast around the turn of the twentieth century.

Toward the middle of the nineteenth century, political unrest in China displaced many peasants and urban poor. Many of the latter migrated to Latin America and the American tropics under a system of contract labor that was much like indentured servitude. There they sometimes replaced African slaves, whose numbers were dwindling because of the abolition or suppression of the Atlantic slave trade. These Oriental laborers were called "coolies," which in China meant merely unskilled laborers but which in the Western Hemisphere soon acquired the meaning of bound, or involuntary, laborers. Actually, most of the Chinese immigrants to the United States had belonged to the free peasantry in China and thus had roots in the same class that produced the Irish and German immigrants of the period.

If it was difficult for white European immigrants to find a place in the relatively stable Eastern society at mid-century, it was even more difficult for East Asians to move into the highly fluid, rapidly changing, energetic society of California. Next to the blacks, the Chinese were the immigrant group most different from the dominant whites. Their physical appearance was distinctive, and they tended to preserve their own language, religion, customs, and culture. Over half of these immigrants were married men who had left their families in China and who found it necessary to work hard and to live extremely frugally in order to send money home, to visit their families in China, or to return to China permanently. All these factors tended to set the Chinese apart from white America, though by 1852 the Chinese in California alone numbered 25,000 and made up 10 percent of the state's total population.

Although the Chinese were at first fairly well received because of a desperate shortage of unskilled labor in California, they found themselves less and less welcome as more white laborers became available. They soon came to dominate both the restaurant and the laundry businesses in San Francisco and in the northern part of the state. Furthermore, they demonstrated an ability to take over apparently worthless mining claims and make them pay by working harder and longer than the white miners. This phenomenon produced so much hostility in the mining camps that the Chinese were frequently barred from owning or working claims. The willingness of the East Asian immigrants to work long hours at low pay, which had originally worked in their favor, came to be seen by white migrants from the East and the South as unfair competition.

As early as 1852 attempts were made to bar the Chinese from admission to the West Coast. Anti-Chinese sentiment culminated in the passage of the Chinese Exclusion Act in 1882. Although this law was intended to halt immigration for only a ten-year period, it virtually put a stop to Chinese migration to the United States. Ironically, it had the effect of opening the West Coast to Japanese immigration, which was stimulated by the need to fill various jobs in the expanding economy that would earlier have been filled by the Chinese.

The selection reprinted here discusses the development of antagonism toward the Chinese among white Californians and the discriminatory behavior suffered by Chinese immigrants to America during the years of the gold rush.

No single cause furnished the motivation of the anti-Chinese movement in California. It was only through the combination of a variety of motives, appealing to diversified groups, together with an auspicious political situation, that the movement for the exclusion of the Chinese was able to succeed.

The range of the motives which served as the bases of the anti-

"Anti-Chinese Sentiment in California" from *The Anti-Chinese Movement in California* by Elmer C. Sandmeyer. Reprinted by permission of University of Illinois Press.

Chinese sentiment in California may be seen in two statements made in 1876. According to the first of these, Californians were convinced,

> That he is a slave, reduced to the lowest terms of beggarly economy, and is no fit competitor for an American freeman.
>
> That he herds in scores, in small dens, where a white man and wife could hardly breathe, and has none of the wants of a civilized white man.
>
> That he has neither wife nor child, nor expects to have any.
>
> That his sister is a prostitute from instinct, religion, education, and interest, and degrading to all around her.
>
> That American men, women and children cannot be what free people should be, and compete with such degraded creatures in the labor market.
>
> That wherever they are numerous, as in San Francisco, by a secret machinery of their own, they defy the law, keep up the manners and customs of China, and utterly disregard all the laws of health, decency and morality.
>
> That they are driving the white population from the state, reducing laboring men to despair, laboring women to prostitution, and boys and girls to hoodlums and convicts.
>
> That the health, wealth, prosperity and happiness of our State demand their expulsion from our shores.

The official spokesman of San Francisco before the Joint Special Committee of Congress expressed a similar view:

> The burden of our accusation against them is that they come in conflict with our labor interests; that they can never assimilate with us; that they are a perpetual, unchanging, and unchangeable alien element that can never become homogeneous; that their civilization is demoralizing and degrading to our people; that they degrade and dishonor labor; that they can never become citizens, and that an alien, degraded labor class, without desire of citizenship, without education, and without interest in the country it inhabits is an element both demoralizing and dangerous to the community within which it exists.

These charges were repeated in so many speeches, editorials, and other forms of expression that one can hardly escape the conviction that they represented widely prevalent belief.

The contents of these charges may be considered under three heads: the economic, the moral and religious, and the social and political. Of the charges which may be designated as economic none was more frequently nor more persistently used than that of coolieism.

While the evidence thus far presented indicates that the motivating influences of Chinese immigration were essentially like those operating among Europeans, Californians were convinced that Chinese laborers came to this country under servile or "coolie" contracts. Senator Sargent had the support of widespread public opinion when he insisted that, in spite of laws forbidding the importation of coolies, the Chinese coming to California were not free, but were bound to service for a term of years, the faithful performance of their contracts being secured by their families at home, and that while these contracts were void under our laws, they were made effective by the superstitions of the coolies.

These charges were not new to Californians. The attempt to pass the Tingley Bill in 1852 for the enforcement of contracts made in China had been defeated only after bitter debate. The following year members of the Chinese Companies admitted that they had imported men under contract but, finding it unprofitable, had discontinued the practice. Californians were inclined to accept this evidence, and the statements of Frederick F. Low to the effect that Chinese laborers were too poor to finance their passage and of Thomas H. King that practically all Chinese men came under contract for a definite period of years, rather than the report of a special committee of the legislature in 1862 or the later statement of the attorney of the Six Companies denying the existence of coolie contracts among the Chinese in California. Public opinion, as represented in the press, tended to identify Chinese labor with Negro slavery in the south, a slavery not of law, but of condition and custom.

> Coolies are such pauper Chinese as are hired in bulk and by contract at Chinese ports, to be hired out by the contracting party in this or any other foreign country to which by the terms of the contract they are to be shipped. The contracting parties for California are the Six Companies, and they have imported more than nine-tenths of all the Chinese who have come to this state. . . . When the coolie arrives here he is as rigidly under the control of the contractor who brought him as ever an African slave was under his master in South Carolina or Louisiana. There is no escape from the contractor or the contract.

This conviction of Californians was buttressed by the knowledge that traffic in Chinese "coolie" or contract labor was being carried on to the West Indies and South America. The term "coolie" had been applied to the Chinese by foreigners, and in the sense in which it generally was used it meant simply common laborers, with no implication whatever of involuntary servitude. But the term came to be applied to the system of transporting contract laborers to the mines and plantations of the Spanish and British, and was soon current in connection with the Chinese in California. The "coolie traffic" to the West Indies and South America had begun before the middle of the century, and by 1871 more than one hundred thousand had been sent to Cuba alone.

Most of this traffic centered at Macao, Amoy, and Hong Kong. The recruiting, which was handled either by "coolie brokers" on a commission basis or by merchants as a speculative proposition, was permeated with fraud and graft, kidnapping, and inveigling into gambling debts. The Chinese spoke of the traffic as "the buying and selling of pigs." Conditions in transit can be compared only with the horrors of the "middle passage" of the African slave trade. Little provision was made for the comfort of the coolies, and instances were not infrequent of revolts among them, resulting often in death and destruction. The risks involved in the traffic made it difficult to procure ships.

The reprehensible methods of many of those engaged in the traffic furnished many perplexing problems for the consuls in China. The Chinese government was opposed to the traffic, but did little about it, largely because of the lack of consuls in foreign countries. In 1862 Americans were prohibited from participating in it. Within the British Empire the government had exercised a certain amount of supervision over the trade from the beginning, and by 1874 had assumed full control so far as its own subjects and territories were concerned. The worst elements came to center at Macao, and the supervision of the Portuguese government was very lax. Finally, through the efforts of the British and Chinese governments and by action of Portugal, the Macao traffic was terminated, leaving only Hong Kong and the treaty ports. The Chinese government, however, barred the traffic from the treaty ports after the report of an investigating committee sent to Cuba in 1876. There is evidence, however, that the trade continued illegally for some years longer.

What connection, if any, existed between this traffic and the immigration of Chinese to California? As we have seen, American ships had been rather extensively engaged in the traffic. Reports of consular officials, admissions by members of the Chinese Companies, and the attempt to pass the Tingley "Coolie Bill" are evidence that in the early years Chinese came to California under such contracts. Californians were convinced that the traffic was being continued long after it had been prohibited. As proof they pointed to the apparent control exercised by the Chinese Six Companies over the immigrants, to the fact that Chinese laborers were brought into the country in large numbers for the railroads and other corporations, and to the plausible statements of men who were presumed to know the facts. On the other hand, the Chinese Six Companies earnestly denied that they controlled these laborers, and the men who knew them best insisted that they were not imported under the notorious coolie system. The difference, however, seems to have been chiefly one of degree rather than of kind. The evidence is conclusive that by far the majority of the Chinese who came to California had their transportation provided by others and bound themselves to make repayment. In the words of one of the most thorough students of this problem,

> There is no doubt that the greater part of the Chinese emigration to California was financed and controlled by merchant brokers, acting either independently or through Trading Guilds. . . . Under the credit-ticket system Chinese brokers paid the expenses of the coolie emigration. Until the debt so incurred by the coolie was paid off the broker had a lien on his services—a lien that might or might not be sold to a bona fide employer of labor. . . . By the credit-ticket system . . . was made possible the large emigration of Southern Chinese to [the] U.S.A., Canada and Australia which commenced during the fifties of [the] last century and continued until it was gradually restricted or prohibited by the legislatures of these English-speaking states.

Foreigners in China differed in their statements regarding this traffic. Peter Parker, S. Wells Williams, and Sir Arthur Edward Kennedy, colonial governor at Hong Kong, declared that the shipments to California were not of the notorious contract coolie order, and that they were so recognized by the Chinese. United States Consuls Denny and Bailey, however, insisted that there was no difference between those going to California and those bound for Cuba and other places in the West Indies and South America. The most evident difference was that, while the contracts of the "coolie traffic" were sold and the coolie had nothing to say as to whom he should serve, the broker retained the "credit ticket" of the California immigrant. In other words, the laborer's obligation was direct to the broker, and while the latter exercised a close supervision over him, the laborer was free to choose his employer so long as he made his monthly payments.

Californians, in constantly increasing numbers, either doubted that this difference existed or discounted its significance, holding that the living and working conditions of the Chinese were those of slavery, even if legal evidence were lacking. The absence of tangible evidence was accounted for on the ground that the agreements were never brought into American courts but were enforced by Chinese methods. Substantial proof of this was found in the control exercised by the Companies through an agreement with the shipping concerns, that no ticket should be sold to a Chinese unless he presented a certificate from his Company to the effect that all of his obligations had been met. When notice was posted that the legislature had prohibited this practice the Six Companies posted a counterblast: "If anyone does not pay what has been expended, the companies will get out a warrant and arrest him and deliver him over to the American courts, and then if the Chinaman loses his baggage and passage ticket it will not be any concern of the companies." Whatever the actual conditions may have been, appearances convinced the average Californian that in the Chinese laborer he was meeting competition that had many of the earmarks of slavery. And the Civil War was altogether too recent to make those earmarks attractive.

No charge against the Chinese was made more frequently nor with more sympathetic hearing than that relating to their low standard of living. Practically all of the Chinese laborers in California were single men and lived in very restricted quarters. In most cases they came, not to settle permanently, but to accumulate an amount sufficient to enable them to return to China and live in comparative comfort. Accustomed to living on a few cents a day, with the higher wage scale in California the laborer hoped to be able to attain his goal in a relatively short time, even with the increased cost of supplies. Hence, ". . . they work on patiently for years, saving every cent, living cheaply and working cheaply."

Those who opposed Chinese cheap labor urged that the American laborer, with his ideal of a home and family, could not compete with the Chinese because he could not live on the Chinese level of wages. Hence, American immigrants, so greatly desired in California, would not come, or if they came, would not stay. Comparisons were made with Gresham's Law of money, and with conditions in the south, where free labor was unable and unwilling to compete with slave labor. As a sample of outside opinion concerning California labor conditions the *Denver News* was quoted, "Give California a wide berth, for the laborer is not worthy of his hire in that state, even when there is work for him to do." The presence of Chinese laborers was held responsible for an increasing number of "hoodlums" among the young men of California, because the Chinese preempted the opportunities for finding work, and their wage scale degraded labor to a level so low that white boys would not engage in it. At the same time commodity prices to the consumer were not lowered.

Many employers welcomed the Chinese laborer because his low wage scale enabled them to inaugurate undertakings which otherwise might not have been able to compete with the older establishments in the East. Others claimed that white labor was not available, while some insisted that the Chinese created additional labor for the whites, of a higher grade than that done by the Chinese. This was one phase of the question on which California disagreed with the East. Postmaster General Key, after a visit to California, spoke very highly of Chinese laborers. "It is wonderful to see how little a Chinaman can live on." What was, perhaps, a common view in the East was:

> If the people of California were capable of viewing their own interest without passion or prejudice, they would perceive they have a great advantage over the rest of the country in the cheapness of Chinese labor. It favors a rapid development of the resources of that wonderful state. It enables them to undersell in all markets every exportable article which their soil, climate and mineral wealth enable them to produce.

Especially irritating to opponents of the Chinese were the statements of Easterners, on the basis of very meager information, belittling the problem of Chinese labor. When President Anderson of Chicago University and Henry Ward Beecher, after short visits to California, gave lectures and interviews deriding the opposition to the Chinese and accusing Californians of gross exaggeration regarding the danger from Chinese immigration, the press answered with bitter denunciation. The *Post*, which was probably the most radical anti-Chinese newspaper in the state, said,

It is difficult to preserve good temper in the face of such balder-dash from such a source. This sensational word-monger [Beecher] taunts us with the theory of evolution, and twittingly declares that if least fitted to survive, then we should go to the wall. . . . But only let the general government release our people from federal obligations, and with our own state laws and local enactments we will free ourselves from the leprous evil, or, failing in that, with the same right arms that founded this western empire, will prove to the world that the imperial Saxon race, though but a million strong, can maintain its claim even against four hundred million serfs to possess and forever hold untrammeled the fair continent of America. . . . The silence of the grave would be all that would tell of the Chinaman's existence here.

Many Californians opposed Chinese labor because it represented a standard upon which no European could live. As one writer insisted, the Chinese were denounced, not because they sold their labor cheaply, but because their civilization was such that they *could* sell cheaply. In other words, Californians objected to the Chinese because they were willing to be the mudsills of society. And it was considered a turn in the tide when an Eastern writer pointed out that the reason why the white laborers could not compete with the Chinese was that the standard of living of the whites made larger and more diverse require-ments than the narrow range of wants of the Chinese, and that "the survival of the fittest" was not a valid argument; one might just as well argue the superiority of the Canadian thistle because it over-comes useful grasses.

This phase of the working of a low standard of living was not ap-preciated by all Californians. Some of those who favored their em-ployment claimed that Chinese cheap labor had an effect very much like that of machinery, apparently depriving men of work but actually providing more jobs. This argument was opposed by Henry George. He insisted that "the essential thing about Chinese laborers is that they are cheap laborers." While the principal effect of labor-saving ma-chinery is on production, increasing and cheapening it, the effect of cheap labor is chiefly on distribution. With cheap labor production remains practically the same, but the laborer has less purchasing power. Actually, the higher labor is, the more efficient it is likely to be. Thus cheap labor may even raise the cost of production, since there may be less units produced, due both to the lower efficiency and to the lower purchasing power of cheap labor. George's argument was too involved to become a popular one, but even the ordinary citizen could see the force of his statement that the cheap laborer compels other laborers to work cheaply.

This cheap labor made an insidious appeal to Californians because it offered comforts at small cost and relief from the unusually high prices of white labor. Many even of those opposed to the Chinese patronized them. William Wellock, one of Denis Kearney's lieutenants, charged that the product of the more than ten thousand Chinese cigar-makers in San Francisco was being consumed, not by Stanford, Crocker, Flood and other wealthy men, but by the workingmen. Asserting that the Chinese came and remained because Californians were profiting by their presence, editors complained:

> The Chinaman is here because his presence pays, and he will re-main and continue to increase so long as there is money in him. When the time comes that he is no longer profitable *that* genera-tion will take care of him and will send him back. We will not do it so long as the pockets into which the profit of his labor flows continue to be those appertaining to our pantaloons.
>
> They do not go because the people of California, while pro-testing against their presence, continue to utilize their labor in a hundred ways. In this matter private interest dominates public in-terest.

The decades of most intensive anti-Chinese agitation were bur-dened with problems of railroad, land, and other monopolies, and anything smacking of monopoly was certain to arouse instant antago-nism. Californians saw in the Chinese a developing monopoly of sinister mien. As they entered one field of activity after another it was claimed that they not only drove out American laborers but also tended to monopolize the industry. This was charged particularly in regard to cigar and shoe making and certain types of garment manufacture. They were credited with great imitative skill, and it was claimed that the only industry into which the Chinese had gone without monopo-lizing it was that of woolen manufacture, and that this was due to the large amount of capital required. "Where little capital is required, there the Mongol is sure to triumph."

When Eastern interests objected to the anti-Chinese agitation on the ground that it would injure our trade opportunities in China, Californians replied that this trade was very one-sided. Figures were quoted showing that our exports to China in 1878 totaled more than

$23,000,000 and our imports over $18,000,000, but that some $16,-000,000 of our exports were in gold and silver bullion, very largely remittances by Chinese in California, covering not only about five million in savings, but also purchases of Chinese goods. It was charged that the Chinese purchased most of their food and clothing in China, and that factories for the duplication of American goods were being set up in China.

> We may sell them samples of goods, but in a short period they will make goods as good as the sample. . . . It is not at all improbable that within twenty years we shall find the East demanding protection from Chinese cheap labor in China as loudly as California now demands protection from the same kind of labor within her own limits. The fundamental fact of this question is that at home or abroad the Chinese can produce cheaper than any other people in existence.

The Chinese were charged with contributing to monopoly in connection with the great landholders and the railroads. The latter had received large grants from the government, while the former had acquired the Spanish and Mexican holdings, and were included in the general anti-monopoly agitation. Since these landed interests were among the most ardent advocates of continued Chinese immigration the charge was frequently voiced that California was in danger of having a "caste system of lords and serfs" foisted upon it, the great holders of land and the railroads being represented as "Chinese emigration bureaus" and the largest "Chinese employment offices" on the coast. The anti-Chinese element in California looked upon these "monopolists" as among the chief mainstays of the Chinese. The claim of Eastern newspapers that the "better class" of Californians favored the Chinese was answered with, "Nobody is in favor of anything of the kind but the cormorants, desert-grabbers and other Judas Iscariots of their race, who would sell the whole land—people, liberties, institutions and all—for their own private aggrandizement. . . ." These great landowners were regarded as worse than the plantation owners of slave days. The only way to solve the situation was to break up the large holdings into small farms. "The Mongolian will be ground out with the growth of genuine American circumstances." When J. C. G. Kennedy appeared in Washington on behalf of the Chinese Six Companies and of the "agricultural interests" of California, it was alleged that he had been connected with the slave interest before the Civil

War and that President Lincoln had removed him from office because of his activities in this cause. His actions were denounced. "It is the nearest to an open declaration upon the part of the Mexican grant-holders of California of a deliberate purpose to make a struggle for 'Chinese cheap labor' that has yet come to our notice. The great land-owners are evidently on the warpath."

From an economic viewpoint employers and those seeking employment differed widely concerning the effect of the Chinese in the state. With few exceptions employers considered them beneficial as a flexible supply of labor, cheap, submissive, and efficient; but those whose only capital was their ability to work were almost unanimous in the opinion that the Chinese were highly detrimental to the best interests of the state. Each group saw the problem through the spectacles of its own economic interests.

Anti-Japanese Sentiment
after Pearl Harbor

JACOBUS tenBROEK, EDWARD N. BARNHART,
and FLOYD W. MATSON

In 1882, when Congress passed the Chinese Exclusion Act which virtually ended Chinese immigration to the United States, there were fewer than two hundred Japanese in this country. The exclusion of the Chinese, however, produced a drastic shortage of labor on the West Coast, thus stimulating immigration from Japan. Although the rulers of Japan had long been opposed to emigration (in fact, prior to 1854 it was a crime punishable by death), in the late nineteenth century they were persuaded to change their policy, and there was a large movement of Japanese citizens into the Western Hemisphere. In the first ten years of the twentieth century, over ninety thousand Japanese entered the United States.

The immigrants were at first welcomed because they filled necessary slots in the expanding economy, but antagonisms quickly began to mount. Since the turn of the century, Japan had been rising to prominence as a world power, and many Californians saw the influx of Japanese laborers as a prelude to invasion by the Japanese state. Workingmen's groups, fearing competition from foreign labor, worked with an inflammatory press and opportunistic politicians to have the Japanese excluded from the United States along with the Chinese under the act of 1882. In 1900, the Japanese government consented to curb the emigration of labor to the United States by denying passports to would-be emigrants. Then, in 1907, when the Japanese government protested the increasing racial discrimination faced by the Japanese in California, President Theodore Roosevelt arrived at what was called the "Gentlemen's Agreement" with the rulers of Japan, under which both the United States and Japan were to take measures to stop immigration between the two countries. Finally, virtually all immigration from East Asia was permanently halted by the Immigration Act of 1924.

Because the Naturalization Act of 1790 had limited the privilege of naturalization to "free white persons," East Asian migrants to this country legally remained "aliens." This condition was used against them when California passed the Alien Land Act of 1913 barring "aliens ineligible for citizenship" from owning land in the state. Meanwhile, other discriminatory practices were spreading in the West. Many of the stereotypes that white Americans had developed with regard to the Chinese were transferred to the Japanese. They were accused of being devious, unreliable, and dishonest. They were seen as a threat to Christian civilization, to the democratic way of life, to the virtue of white women. Because of the fear of "moral contamination," the San Francisco School Board barred Japanese children from public schools in 1906. The racism inherent in the attitudes of the dominant whites of the West was demonstrated in increased agitation against the "yellow peril."

In the 1930's, Japanese incursions into China built up increasing hostility toward the Japanese-Americans living on the West Coast. Then, on December 7, 1941, when the Japanese bombed Pearl Harbor, shock and outrage swept over the American people—much of which was to be vented on the West Coast Japanese. On the eve of the war, there were 126,947 persons of Japanese ancestry living in the United States, 112,935 of whom were concentrated in the states of California, Oregon, Washington, and Arizona. Of the latter group, 41,089 were foreign born, or Issei; the remainder were Nisei, citizens of the United States who were born in this country to foreign-born parents.

In the early months of 1942, the war went well for the Japanese army and navy in the Pacific but badly for the Japanese residents of the United States. Racist feelings were intensified by wild rumors of sabotage and espionage, and a variety of groups demanded the expulsion of Japanese-Americans from the West Coast. Then, under the direction of the United States Army and the War Relocation Authority set up by President Franklin Roosevelt, the Japanese living along the coast were urged to move from their homes to "resettlement centers" in the nation's interior. When voluntary relocation failed, the army forcibly moved over one hundred thousand persons to the centers and held them there under armed guard. Gradually, the "security" of the camps relaxed, and many of the prisoners—none of whom had been proven guilty of disloyalty —were allowed to work and to move around outside the so-called critical areas. In 1944, some Japanese-Americans were allowed to return to the coast; and in 1946, the last of the shameful internment camps was closed.

The following selection describes the process by which existing hostilities toward the Japanese were activated by the attack on Pearl Harbor. It was the anti-Japanese hysteria generated in the early months of the war that led ultimately to the unconstitutional imprisonment of tens of thousands of Americans.

Half a century of agitation and antipathy directed against Japanese Americans, following almost fifty years of anti-Chinese and antiforeign activity, had by 1941 diffused among the West Coast population a rigidly stereotyped set of attitudes toward Orientals which centered on suspicion and distrust. This hostility reached maturity in the early twenties with the passage of the Alien Land Law and the Oriental Exclusion Act, and although thereafter it became relatively inactive it was kept alive during the thirties by the stimuli of Japanese aggression and economic depression. In the weeks and months following the attack upon Pearl Harbor the traditional charges were widely revived and the stereotype recalled in detail; public attitudes toward the Japanese minority soon crystallized around the well-worn themes of treachery and disloyalty, and expressions of opinion came more and more to be characterized by suspicion, fear, and anger.

The Japanese stereotype was not created at Pearl Harbor; the basic ingredients had been mixed years before. But the enemy bombs of December 7 exploded the mixture on a vaster scale and with more far-reaching consequences than ever in the past. The rumors that emerged from Pearl Harbor gave new sustenance to racist belief in the yellow peril, to romantic movie-fed ideas of the treacherous and inscrutable Asiatic, to undefined feelings of hostility and distrust compounded of the xenophobia of superpatriots and the rationalizations of competitors. Once revitalized by enemy bombs, however, the Japanese stereotype had no need to depend upon the myth of sabotage at Pearl Harbor. Long after the rumors had been disproved, by repeated ref-

From *Prejudice, War and the Constitution: Causes and Consequences of the Evacuation of the Japanese Americans in World War II*, pp. 68–72 and 91–96 by Jacobus tenBroek, Edward N. Barnhart, and Floyd W. Matson, published by the University of California Press, 1954. Reprinted by permission of The Regents of the University of California.

utations from the highest authorities, the stereotype remained and Americans along the Western slope and far inland were more suspicious, fearful, and angry than ever before. The very absence of anything resembling subversive activity by resident Japanese was seized upon as "disturbing and confirming" evidence that an "invisible deadline" of disaster was approaching. As weeks passed, the superstructure of rationalizations and defenses built upon this foundation grew more insensibly elaborate.   ‣

DECEMBER: WAR

The Japanese attack on Pearl Harbor came as a profound shock, if not a complete surprise, to residents of the Pacific Coast states. Although for many years most citizens had been aware that war was a possibility, many refused to believe the first reports from Honolulu and were convinced only by repeated broadcasts and ubiquitous black headlines. But the full import of the news soon became apparent as all service personnel was ordered to report to stations, as jeeps and convoys in war regalia appeared on the streets, and military aircraft began to roar overhead. By midafternoon of December 7, 1941, thousands of citizens were rushing to recruiting stations to enlist or offering their services in any capacity.

Before they could recover from the initial shock, West Coast residents were confronted with more bad news. Coincident with the Pearl Harbor attack enemy forces had struck with disastrous effect at Hong Kong, Manila, Thailand, Singapore, Midway, Wake, and Guam. Japanese bombers had at a single blow destroyed the air defenses of Hong Kong, and within a few days occupied Kowloon peninsula and placed the British crown colony in jeopardy. On December 10 the "impregnable" British warships *Repulse* and *Prince of Wales* were sunk by Japanese planes, thus upsetting the balance of naval power in the far Pacific. The little kingdom of Thailand had surrendered on December 8, and the enemy began a swift southward movement through the British Malay states toward Singapore. Other Japanese troops landed in the Philippines on December 10 and were converging on Manila. Guam was captured on December 11, the fate of Wake Island appeared sealed (it fell on December 23), and Midway was imperiled by an enemy task force. Meanwhile, dispatches which had filtered through censorship suggested that American losses at Pearl Harbor were far worse than at first indicated. It was freely predicted that Alaska and the Pacific Coast itself were next in line for Japanese attack and even attempted invasion.

People everywhere were frightened, and their fear was heightened by a feeling of helplessness. The threat of bombings and invasion, plus the absence of precise information as to events in Hawaii, quickly bred rumors of total disaster. It was whispered that the entire Pacific fleet had been destroyed; that every reinforcing ship sent out from the mainland had been sunk off the coast by Japanese submarines.

Almost at once rumors about the resident Japanese began. Japanese gardeners were said to be equipped with short-wave transmitters hidden in garden hose; Japanese servants and laborers who failed to appear for work on December 7 (a Sunday) were accused of prior knowledge of the Hawaii attack. Japanese farmers were charged with smuggling poison into vegetables bound for market, and cans of seafood imported from Japan were said to contain particles of ground glass. Signaling devices similar to those reported found in Hawaii were alleged to have been set up in coastal areas. A number of anxious Californians, according to one report, went so far as to plow up "a beautiful field of flowers on the property of a Japanese farmer," because "it seems the Jap was a fifth columnist and had grown his flowers in a way that when viewed from a plane formed an arrow pointing the direction to the airport."

These rumors and accusations arose largely as a result of the stories of fifth-column activity at Pearl Harbor which were rapidly accumulating in the press. After an inspection of the Pacific base, Secretary of the Navy Knox was quoted as saying that sabotage at Pearl Harbor constituted "the most effective fifth-column work that's come out of this war, except in Norway." Newspaper headlines on the Knox report generally stressed this aspect: "Secretary of Navy Blames Fifth Columnists for the Raid," "Fifth Column Prepared Attack," "Fifth Column Treachery Told." Other stories told of secret signalling and faked air-raid alerts by Hawaiian Japanese at the time of the attack, of arrows cut in the cane fields to aid enemy pilots, and roadblocks improvised to tie up military traffic.

In opposition to the rumors and scare stories was a succession of official assurances that all dangerous enemy aliens had been apprehended, that necessary precautions had already been taken, and that Japanese Americans as a whole were loyal to the United States. This viewpoint was, moreover, echoed in the editorials of most California newspapers during the first days of war. Despite these assurances, however, Americans became increasingly restive as the prospect of Japanese attack or invasion grew more plausible. For half a century they had heard of the treachery and deceitfulness of resident Japanese —of how the "Japs" were concentrated in strategic areas of the state; of how by "peaceful invasion" they hoped to take over first California and ultimately the nation; of how they formed a network of spies and soldiers in disguise, patiently awaiting the Imperial signal to rise against the white man.

The news from the battle-fronts, recording new Allied losses almost daily, made the most alarmist forebodings seem realistic. Charges of fifth-column plots multiplied rapidly and broadened in scope, soon including the mainland as well as Hawaii, and possible future actions as well as past events. It was reported, for example, that a Los Angeles naval sentry had seen signal lights in a Japanese waterfront colony; that the suicide of a Japanese doctor had uncovered a spy ring in the same area; that members of the notorious Black Dragon Society had been planted in cities and fishing communities; that the fifth-column character of Japanese schools in America had been exposed. The halls of Congress echoed with such exposures; Senator Guy Gillette of Iowa warned that "Japanese groups in this country planned sabotage and subversive moves," and Congressman Martin Dies of Texas announced the discovery of a book revealing Japanese plans to attack the United States.

Meanwhile the war was being brought steadily closer to home. On December 20 it was announced that Japanese submarines were attacking West Coast shipping; and on the same day two tankers were reportedly torpedoed off California. Two days later newspapers told of the shelling of a freighter by an enemy sub near Santa Barbara; the next day two more tankers were said to have been attacked off the California coast. Residents of the coastal states began to feel that their shores were under virtual blockade by enemy submarines.

The refugees from Hawaii, arriving in late December, brought new rumors of sabotage by island Japanese on December 7. It was said that Japanese had placed obstructions on the road to Pearl Harbor to keep reinforcements from getting through; that they had sabotaged the planes on the landing fields; that one group had entered Hickam Field in a milk truck, let down the sides, and turned machine guns on American pilots as they ran to their planes.

Impressive "confirmation" of these rumors was contained in a sensational dispatch by a United Press correspondent, Wallace Carroll, who visited Honolulu shortly after the attack. Repeating with an air of authority most of the charges made by Honolulu refugees, the report declared that numbers of Hawaii Japanese had had advance knowledge of the bombing, and that Japanese produce merchants delivering to warships had been able to report on United States fleet movements. Carroll speculated that newspaper advertisements placed by Japanese firms may have been coded messages, and asserted that the enemy raiders had been aided by improvised roadblocks and arrows cut in the cane fields. The hands of Japanese pilots shot down during the assault were, he said, adorned with the rings of Honolulu High School and of Oregon State University. The dispatch continued:

> Japanese of American nationality infiltrated into the Police Departments and obtained jobs as road supervisors, sanitary inspectors or minor government officials. Many went to work in the postoffice and telephone service, ideal posts for spies. . . .
> An American resident, who had studied Japanese methods in Manchuria and North China, told me that the Japanese fifth column and espionage organizations in the islands were similar to those which had been used to undermine the Chinese.

Accounts such as this, together with reports of new Allied reverses and tales of atrocities in the Philippines, goaded some Filipino Americans into direct retaliation against their Japanese neighbors. On December 23 a Japanese American, honorably discharged from the United States Army, was found stabbed to death on a Los Angeles sidewalk; his assailants were reported to be Filipinos. On Christmas Day in Stockton, windows of numerous Japanese business houses were smashed, assertedly by gangs of Filipinos. The next day in the same city an alien Japanese garage attendant was shot to death by a Filipino; newspapers prominently featured the incident, under such headlines as "Jap, Filipino District Under Guard; 1 Slain," "Stockton Jap Killed by Filipino; Riots Feared; Area Under Guard." By the end of December similar incidents were publicized almost daily. On December 29, a Japanese waiter was shot to death by a Filipino in Chicago. On December 30 an alien Japanese was shot and wounded in Sacramento; on New Year's Day a Japanese and his wife were murdered in the Imperial Valley. Other cases were reported from Gilroy and Livermore, and even from Utah.

Thus, within the first three weeks of war, the familiar Japanese stereotype was again visible on the Pacific Coast, and aroused individuals and groups were militantly reacting to it. The surprise attack of December 7, occurring in the midst of peace negotiations, seemed a definite confirmation of the old remembered tales of Japanese deceitfulness. Although for a time many citizens were reluctant to blame resident Japanese for the actions of Japan, and newspaper comment frequently was on the side of tolerance, the accumulating "evidence" of sabotage and espionage gradually put an end to toleration. Popular anger and apprehension rose in proportion to the continuing successes of the enemy, and by the end of 1941 suspicion and animosity were the most frequently expressed attitudes toward the Japanese Americans.

❖   ❖   ❖

THE STEREOTYPE

The Japanese stereotype, as reconstructed in the early months of war, was a composite image reflecting a diversity of hates and fears on the part of the West Coast population. Frequently inconsistent and even mutually exclusive, the public expressions of these underlying attitudes were alike in their hostility and in the suspicion they revealed concerning the loyalty of resident Japanese. As rumor and opinion, they circulated through public resolutions and private declarations, while coastal residents in the weeks of crisis cast about for arguments to embody their growing anger and frustration. The arguments they found were with few exceptions neither logical nor original, but represented the tarnished banners of long-past campaigns—the yellow-peril charges of the unionists and politicians, the economic rationalizations of the farm groups, the racist outbursts of the patriots—the alarms and excursions of fifty years of agitation which had merged and recombined to form the popular stereotype of the Japanese character.

Sabotage. Foremost among the traditional beliefs to be revived in the public mind was the myth of the yellow-peril invasion, the identification of America's Japanese as actual or potential spies and saboteurs. Emerging as an explanation of the shocking and calamitous events of December 7, the Pearl Harbor legend described such purported actions as the destruction of airplanes on the ground, the cutting of arrows in cane fields, and the deliberate obstruction of traffic into military installations. The truth of these accounts, which circulated widely with the arrival of refugees from Hawaii, was seldom doubted.

The widespread belief in the actuality of sabotage in Hawaii provided the basis for virtually all organized agitation to oust the West Coast Japanese; it stimulated the circulation of anonymous chain letters throughout California in January and February, and was shown regularly in letters to newspapers, to the United States Attorney General, and to congressmen.

The immediate significance of the Pearl Harbor legend to Pacific Coast residents was, of course, its portent of disaster for themselves. The Sacramento *Bee* voiced a common concern in pointing out that "the experience with the fifth column in Hawaii is overwhelming evidence that... the authorities must take no chances with possible Jap or Axis sympathizers," and many Californians shared the opinion of their attorney general that "we are just being lulled into a false sense of security.... Our day of reckoning is bound to come ... we are approaching an invisible deadline." This anticipation of disaster was heard with increasing frequency during February and March, as popular fears mounted despite the refusal of Japanese Americans to demonstrate their "disloyalty" through subversive acts. Local, state, and national officials voiced the conviction that the absence of sabotage in the present made it all the more certain in the future, and the same viewpoint was expressed by private spokesmen and popular commentators. It was eventually incorporated into the final report of General DeWitt as a primary factor justifying evacuation: the absence of sabotage was, according to the general, "a disturbing and confirming indication that such action would be taken."

Most of those who expressed fear over the threat of sabotage argued that American citizens of Japanese ancestry were as much suspect as aliens. This racist belief, summarized in the phrase "Once a Jap always a Jap," was publicized by congressmen such as Rankin and Stewart and appears to have made its way into the official reasoning of General DeWitt. Various officials of the three Pacific Coast states conceded that some Japanese Americans might be loyal to the United States but deemed it impossible, because of racial factors, to distinguish between the loyal and disloyal. The governor and attorney general of California and the mayors of Los Angeles, Seattle, and Portland, among others, adopted this viewpoint; minor law-enforcement officers in California endorsed an equivalent line of reasoning in pleas for evacuation. The theory was greatly advanced by the accumulating stories of fifth-column plots on the mainland, and further encouraged by dramatic press descriptions of spot raids by the FBI.

There is no need to recapitulate here the official denials and refutations which established conclusively that there had been no sabotage or other fifth-column activity at Pearl Harbor, either during or after the Japanese attack. On the other hand, it is impossible to disprove objectively the thesis of "latent sabotage," the argument that West Coast Japanese were awaiting an Imperial signal to rise in concerted fifth-column action. The "facts" on which this thesis was based were soon shown to be mythical; the various rumors of poisoned vegetables, undercover signal devices, messages and arrows in the fields, and so on were one by one proved false. Moreover, the total inability of the FBI to uncover saboteurs among the Japanese population was frankly admitted by Attorney General Biddle in a memorandum to President Roosevelt in May, 1942.

Geographical concentration. Despite their shadowy character and the frequency of denials, both the Pearl Harbor rumors and the accounts of plans for sabotage remained in wide circulation among the West Coast population throughout the war. The general credence given these beliefs provided support for other traditional apprehensions regarding the Japanese Americans, one of the most persistent of which concerned their alleged "concentration" in strategic military and industrial areas. Numerous persons complained in letters to the Attorney General of the presence of Japanese near "Oil Fields, Tank Farms, Air Ports, and other vital defense industries"; "our coast line"; "the foot of our mountains and the entrances to our canyons, which lead to the dams and water reservoirs"; "vantage places in harbor fisheries ... strange isolated promontories of our unguarded coastline, and ... our aircraft plants." An extensive statement charging the Japanese with deliberate settlement in strategic areas was presented before the Tolan Committee by Attorney General Warren of California—a statement with which many California newspapers seemed to agree.

Disloyalty. Increasingly, under the stress of war, old and half-forgotten suspicions against the Japanese were dusted off and reintroduced as "evidence" of their disloyalty. Once again it was widely proclaimed that they were racially unassimilable. It was charged that their language schools were instruments of Imperial propaganda; that Nisei children educated in Japan had returned as spies or at least as indoctrinated Japanese fanatics; that the dual citizenship of the second generation was a mask for allegiance to the homeland; that community clubs and associations were manipulated from Tokyo; that Buddhism and Shintoism were agencies of Emperor worship; and that the occupation of farmlands by Japanese was a peaceful invasion which would end in domination of the American mainland.

This mélange of legends, distortions, and half-truths subsequently played a prominent role in the official arguments advanced in defense of mass removal of the Japanese—arguments by which both evacuation and detention were initially justified by the military and ultimately confirmed by the courts. One of the most prevalent of the hostile beliefs took its departure from the apparent approval of Japan's victories in China by some resident Japanese before the outbreak of war with the United States. From this the suspicion grew that many had possessed prior knowledge of the December 7 attack, and that plans for future sabotage operations by individual members were foreknown in the Japanese community. Mayor Bowron of Los Angeles, for example, asserted that many resident Japanese "knew what was coming" and "overplayed their hand" in the year before the war by an excessive pretense of loyalty to America.

Cultural lag. The retention of old-world culture by Japanese Americans was frequently invoked as proof of their disloyalty. In language, education, religion, and family patterns, they were suspected of willfully avoiding Western ways and favoring alien customs. Letter writers declared that "any Japanese child that attends a Japanese school will . . . be . . . a potential enemy," and that "all of them have been back to Japan for certain educational periods." Attorney General Warren sweepingly condemned as anti-American the language schools, religious organizations, and vernacular press of the resident Japanese, and considered the Japanese tongue itself a suspicious bond with the old country. Attendance at a language school, membership in an organization, or even passive acceptance of old-world customs was held to be sufficient cause for barring Japanese Americans from state employment. In a formal notice of discharge sent to all persons of Japanese ancestry employed by the state, the California State Personnel Board declared that "the defendant does read and write the Japanese language, and . . . subscribed to a Japanese newspaper . . . the defendant did attend a Japanese school . . . the defendant is a member and officer of certain Japanese organizations."

Coolie labor. The familiar accusations of cheap labor and unfair competition, which had long underlain the agitation of farm and labor groups, were once again heard as agriculturists and other interested groups joined the clamor against the Japanese. Despite their declarations that Japanese monopolized farmlands and vegetable production, the farmers saw no inconsistency in also maintaining that their removal would not hamper production. Officials of the California Farm Bureau, the Western Growers Protective Association, and the Grower-Shipper Vegetable Association wrote letters demonstrating that mass evacuation of the Japanese would not affect the food supply. California's Governor Culbert L. Olson conceded that some loss of "squat labor" might follow evacuation but did not consider it serious; Attorney General Warren declared that estimates of the importance of Japanese farm labor were based on "fantastic figures."

Less often heard, but still in evidence, was the old yellow-peril warning against the alleged high birth rate of the Japanese. As always, the Native Sons were especially vociferous on this point, declaring that war might have been avoided had Japan been "denied the privilege of using California as a breeding ground for dual citizens." The Joint Immigration Committee likewise declared that the Japanese were "hardy of stock, militant opponents of race suicide, able to labor and thrive under living conditions impossible to an American."

Race hatred. The threat of riots and acts of violence against the Japanese, assertedly arising from "race hatred," constituted a potent argument for mass evacuation. The traditional Japanese stereotype included a belief in the existence of mutual hostility between the "white" and "yellow" races which it was thought must inevitably culminate in rioting and vigilantism—unless one or the other group should withdraw. This thesis, of course, was not without historical basis. California, and to a lesser extent Washington and Oregon, had a long history of vigilante activity, especially against the dark-skinned and Oriental minorities. Added to this tradition, in the months after Pearl Harbor, were the frustrating reports of Japanese victories and the accompanying tales of atrocities which were sufficient in themselves to stimulate public anger and the desire for revenge.

From the evidence that has accumulated it is possible to make an approximate appraisal of the extent of violence and vigilantism in the three coastal states during the months before evacuation. At least seven murders of Japanese Americans are known to have occurred, including among the victims a Los Angeles veteran of World War I and a middle-aged couple of Brawley, California. The number of physical assaults was substantially larger. Six Filipinos attacked a Japanese in Seattle; another Filipino shot and wounded a Japanese in Sacramento. Gunfire from moving automobiles wounded several persons (including a ten-year-old boy) in Gilroy. Similar events occurred at Costa Mesa, at Mount Eden, and at various points in Alameda County. Stockton Filipinos reportedly attacked Japanese with knives on three occasions. Robbery and assault were combined at least twice, in Seattle and in Rio Vista, California. Rape or attempted rape was recorded twice (in one case by men posing as FBI agents who were later identified as state prison guards). In Seattle, a Negro truck driver shot a Nisei drugstore owner because he "wanted to get a Jap," and at Kingsburg, California, a Chinese American shot a Japanese American and then committed suicide in his jail cell.

Pacific Coast newspapers generally gave much more prominence to these incidents than was customary in ordinary crime coverage. There can be little doubt that the appearance of vigilantism in the press was more substantial than the reality; but there is no less doubt that the lurid news reports both confirmed and influenced public attitudes toward the Japanese minority. Many citizens felt strongly enough to demand that the government sweep away constitutional restraints in acting against the Japanese; to the extremists there seemed no contradiction between combating fascism abroad and embracing its methods at home. The crowning irony of their demand was that it was expressed almost invariably in terms of solicitude for the welfare of the Japanese who were to be its victims.

The vast assortment of rumors and suspicions, epithets, and accusations, directed at Japanese Americans in the first month of war was almost totally fictitious in content and wholly tragic in effect. Its historical importance, however, lies less in the degree of truth or falsity of specific charges than in its revelation of the prevailing state of mind among the population of the Pacific Coast; a deeply rooted and broadly diffused attitude of suspicion and distrust toward all persons of Japanese descent, which demonstrated scant regard for distinctions of birth or citizenship, for "minute constitutional rights," for the record of political loyalty or the facts of social assimilation. The wave of anti-Japanese sentiment which was set in motion by the attack on Pearl Harbor, and subsequently given more impetus by an unbroken series of war disasters, swept all opposition before it and carried in its wake numbers of responsible public officials and organized private groups. By mid-February the tide of hostility reached its crest, and soon thereafter it broke over the heads of the Japanese Americans— engulfing more than 100,000 persons, citizens and aliens alike, in a vortex of popular anger and official acquiescence.

The Alianza Movement of New Mexico

FRANCES L. SWADESH

In 1848, when the Treaty of Guadalupe Hidalgo was signed ending the Mexican War, about half the territory of Mexico was incorporated into the United States. With the land came its inhabitants, of whom many were Mexican citizens of Spanish or Spanish-Indian descent but the majority were Indians. Under the terms of the treaty, former Mexican citizens were granted American citizenship. But the Indians were treated in the traditional American fashion, and the subsequent history of the Mexican-American has been one of dispossession and discrimination.

In the 1960's, however, a widespread revolt began among the Spanish-speaking citizens of the United States. This segment of the American population is divided into three major groups: the **chicanos**, or Mexican-Americans; the **latinos**, immigrants from other Latin American countries; and Puerto Ricans. In the past there has been little cooperation among these various groups, who have different historical and cultural backgrounds and are concentrated in different areas of the country. Under chicano leadership, however, a movement to unify the Spanish-speaking people of the country is now taking place, and a Denver-based organization known as the "Crusade for Justice" has held several national meetings for the express purpose of binding together the various elements of **La Raza** (the race), a term used in reference to all Spanish-speaking Americans.

Among the issues that concern the leaders of La Raza are the use of Spanish as the primary language of instruction in schools in Spanish-speaking communities; land reform, including the restoration to chicanos of land taken from them after the Mexican War; economic protection for migrant farm workers, many of whom are chicano, latino, or Puerto Rican; and the development of cooperative economic institutions that will allow the communities themselves to benefit from their labor.

One of the most dramatic episodes in the growing chicano revolt has been the successful organization, led by Cesar Chavez and the United Farm Workers Organizing Committee, of the migrant workers in California. This campaign has been conducted largely in the Spanish language, and its rallying cries of **huelga** (strike) and **la causa** (the cause) have echoed through the vineyards of California, doing much to unify members of La Raza. Fittingly, the union's symbol is the Mexican eagle, and organizers have made frequent use of appeals to the Mexican heritage and religious tradition.

On the local level, one of the most effective attempts at chicano organization took place in Crystal City, Texas—the "Spinach Capital of the World." Here, 85 percent of the population is chicano, but only 5 percent of the farms are chicano-owned. For decades, the town has been run by the Anglos, largely for their own benefit. But recently, as a result of political organization, the chicanos were able to take over the town government, an event that promises in the future to focus attention on the needs of the majority of the town's inhabitants.

The most startling program of land reform to emerge from the revolt of the 1960's is that proposed by Reies Lopez Tijerina in New Mexico. His movement, known as the **Alianza,** is attempting to make the United States government honor the terms of the Treaty of Guadalupe Hidalgo and restore to the chicanos of the state the land guaranteed to them in perpetuity by the treaty. The story of the background of Tijerina's claims is told in the following selection.

The most controversial of all the organizations representing Spanish-speaking people in the United States is the "Alianza" (Alliance of Free City-States) with headquarters in Albuquerque, New Mexico. The Alianza has been variously described as a nativistic cult movement, a criminal conspiracy, and a movement for social and political change whose leader, Reies Lopez Tijerina, is its major catalytic agent.

"The Alianza Movement of New Mexico," by Frances L. Swadesh from *Minorities and Politics*, edited by H. J. Tobias and C. E. Woodhouse, copyright 1969, The University of New Mexico Press. Reprinted by permission of The University of New Mexico Press.

"Whatever happens in the courts to Reies Tijerina, 41, leader of thousands of poverty-worn Spanish-Americans in northern New Mexico, he may have been the instrument of social and political change in the state and he himself may become a legendary figure" (*Los Angeles Times,* 2/5/1968).

The Alianza made front-page headlines in newspapers around the world on June 5, 1967, when about twenty of its members raided the Rio Arriba County Courthouse at Tierra Amarilla in northern New Mexico. They supposedly had intended to make a "citizen's arrest" of the district attorney, Alfonso Sanchez, on the grounds that he had illegally arrested some of their fellow Alianza members and had forcibly prevented the holding of a public meeting on land-grant demands.

BACKGROUND OF THE LAND-GRANT CONTROVERSY

Alianza members are descendants of grantees of lands in New Mexico, Colorado, Arizona, Texas, Utah and California, donated in the seventeenth and eighteenth centuries by the kings of Spain and, from 1822 to 1846, by the Mexican government.

These lands were granted under Castilian laws, exported and adapted to the settlement policies of the New World. In the vast arid lands of what is now the Southwestern United States, volunteer settlers were moved onto lands not occupied by the sparse indigenous population, to live as independent yeomen growing irrigated crops and raising livestock, chiefly sheep.

Under the body of law defining Spanish and Mexican land grants, donations of land could be made to individuals but were more characteristically made to towns or to groups of families desiring to found new communities. Part of each grant was composed of house lots and irrigable lands specifically assigned to individual families. These could be sold by the recipient family or its heirs after the conditions of settlement had been met: building a house, clearing a field, digging an irrigation ditch, growing crops and defending the area from the attacks of nomadic Indians for a period of several years.

By far the largest portion of most grants, however, was the "ejido" (common holding) of the community, which was inalienable and not subject to individual appropriations. Within this category were included irrigated town pastures, usually enclosed, plus the surrounding, unenclosed range and forest lands which, in New Mexico and some other areas, were mountainous and not suitable for agriculture.

Ejido lands throughout Hispanic America have been lost, especially as a market economy began to break down the economic self-sufficiency of subsistence-oriented, traditional, rural communities. The older system of bartering persisted in some underpopulated areas, including northern New Mexico. With the entry of cash transactions, some people inevitably became indebted to others and were forced to pay their debts with their land.

In the United States, however, the loss of the ejido lands on grants was primarily owing to the failure of United States authorities to recognize the ejido principle of land ownership, even though the 1848 Treaty of Guadalupe Hidalgo guaranteed protection of the personal, cultural and property rights of those Mexican citizens who remained north of the newly extended United States border. As a result of this lack of recognition, the grant heirs lost their subsistence base as well as access to such vital resources as timber for fuel and construction and the mineral wealth beneath their former ejido lands. These losses account partially for the fact that more than one-third of all Spanish-speaking families in the Southwest—41% in New Mexico and over 50% in Texas—have incomes below $3,000 per year, a figure which falls well within the designated poverty levels.

The central programmatic demand of the Alianza is for a thorough investigation of wholesale violations of the guarantees of the Treaty of Guadalupe Hidalgo. The Alianza claims that these violations have denied personal and cultural rights as well as property rights. This demand has been interpreted in some quarters as a "con game" designed to enrich Reies Tijerina and his associates. In other quarters the Alianza is seen as a standing threat to law and order; and only some observers see the Alianza demands as reasonable premises for negotiations patterned on the Indian claims cases.

Such contradictory interpretations have affected public opinion on the purposes and leadership of the Alianza. This instability of opinion, in turn, has affected the very pattern of development of the Alianza.

VIEW FROM THE SOUTH

The views expressed in the press of Mexico, which have potential influence upon future developments, are well exemplified by a series of six articles, published in November, 1967, by Manuel Mejida, a reporter for the Mexico City daily, *Excelsior*. Mejida had toured the Hispano villages of New Mexico and had interviewed many villagers, seeking to enlighten his Mexico City readers on the precipitating causes of the Tierra Amarilla raid.

As a Mexican citizen, Mejida evaluated the land problems of New Mexico from the standpoint of the ejido lands in Mexico. These lands, in substantial areas, had been monopolized by "latifundistas" (plantation owners) who reduced the small farmers to peonage. In the 1930's, a sweeping movement of agrarian reform restored and developed the ejidos in the hands of the communities to which they originally belonged.

Mejida, on the precedent of Mexican experience, considered the grievances of the New Mexicans to be justified. He was impressed by the fact that the land-grant heirs, young and old alike, could state with fair precision the boundaries of their original grants and the acreage which had been appropriated for the public domain, to become, eventually, part of National Forest or state lands, or else to be sold to wealthy Anglo ranchers. Each villager knew the details of who, when, for what purpose and with which consequences areas of their lands had been lost, and each felt the community's loss as a "wound to his own self-esteem."

Mejida found virtual idolatry among the poverty-stricken villagers for Reies Tijerina, whom they saw as the "incarnation of the justice denied them for one hundred years." Although well-to-do Hispanos tended to see Tijerina and his followers as a "bunch of agitators and bandits," the poor were touchingly confident that, through the Alianza, they could recover their lost subsistence base in the forest and range of their ancestral grants. Some who had been forced to leave the home village to seek livelihood elsewhere expressed hope that their situation was "temporary" and that soon they could return to their traditional life as small independent agriculturalists and stockmen.

In view of the violent events of the Tierra Amarilla raid, Mejida found the villagers surprisingly mild-mannered and free of hatred. Many expressed reluctance to take a stand against their own government for, as Mejida had to remind his Mexico City readers, these were people who valued their United States citizenship, had paid taxes, and served in the armed forces without complaint. But they were determined: "We are waiting for the hour of justice . . . never mind how many years our battle for justice takes, we shall win."

Women as well as men had devoted vast amounts of time and effort, as well as what little money they had, to the Alianza's cause and they were prepared for more sacrifices in the future. Conversing as individuals or groups, the villagers displayed optimism and determination.

Mejida felt, nonetheless, that he was witnessing "the twilight of Hispanoamerican life in New Mexico." The villages had become so severely depopulated that the Hispano population of New Mexico, long the majority, had sunk below thirty percent in the 1960's. Forced by lack of training (in fields other than farming and livestock) into the ranks of migrant farm labor, many Hispanos had experienced the disruption of community and family life in the process of moving from one state to another in search of jobs. Despite their stubborn loyalty to kin- and community-based values of Hispanic rural culture, the culture was in the grip of disintegrating forces.

Mejida doubted that this poverty-stricken minority group, contemptuously accorded the treatment of a "Beggar's Army," could prevail against the forces of Anglo-dominated wealth and vested interest in confronting their federal government.

Interviewing Governor David Cargo of New Mexico, Mejida found him cautious about gambling his political future on sustained support of the land issues whose validity he acknowledged. Reluctantly, Mejida came to the conclusion that the realities and expediencies of contemporary life in the United States dictate the final extinction of the Hispano way of life in New Mexico.

DOMINANCE AND THE ETHNOCENTRIC VIEW

Manuel Mejida's melancholy prediction has been voiced for years by people who eagerly anticipate the extinction of the Hispano way of life in New Mexico. Crudely stated, their widespread belief is that the Hispanic culture of the Southwest is incurably inferior to the dominant Anglo culture; its language is a broken patois which must be rapidly forgotten in favor of English; besides, they maintain, the normal fate of all ethnic minority groups in the United States is to plunge headfirst into the Melting Pot and come out "Real Americans"—even if you wouldn't want your daughter to marry one.

This belief, often operating at deeply unconscious levels of otherwise informed minds, has tragically affected dominant-group views of the problems of three groups—the Negro, Indian and Spanish-speaking people of the United States.

Negroes, in the overwhelming majority, did not voluntarily come to the United States seeking a better life, but were brought in chains and subjected to centuries of enslavement followed by social discrimination and exclusion from the economic opportunities others enjoyed. Indians and Hispanos lived in territories which were seized by the United States, since which time they have lived as second-class citizens. Puerto Ricans too became United States citizens by force of arms. The ideology of the Melting Pot, therefore, has no basis in reality for these groups.

Dominant-group ethnocentrism has profoundly affected the political functioning of the above three groups. In the case of the New Mexicans, this ideology provided the rationale for keeping New Mexico in the status of a territory long after statehood should have been granted, with the result that certain semi-colonial characteristics were strengthened and perpetuated to the disadvantage of the Hispano and Indian populations.

Here is how the editor of the *Harper's Weekly* reacted in 1876 to Senate passage of a statehood bill for New Mexico:

> Of the present population, which is variously estimated, and at the last census was 111,000, nine-tenths are Mexicans, Indians, "greasers," and other non-English-speaking people. About one-tenth or one-eleventh part of the population speak the English language, the nine-tenths are under the strictest Roman Catholic supervision. ... The proposition of the admission of New Mexico as a State is, that such a population, in such a condition of civilization, of industries, and intelligence, and with such forbidding prospects of speedy improvement or increase—a community almost without the characteristic and indispensable qualities of an American State— shall have a representation in the national Senate as large as New York, and in the House shall be equal to Delaware. It is virtually an ignorant foreign community under the influence of the Roman Church, and neither for the advantage of the Union nor for its own benefit can such an addition to the family of American States be urged. There are objections to a Territorial government, but in this case the Territorial supervision supplies encouragement to the spirit of intelligent progress by making the national authority finally supreme.

When this diatribe was published, Colorado had already been granted statehood, although its population in 1870 only totaled 39,864 and its mining camps were hardly known for the refinement of their "civilization." By 1910, New Mexico's population had more than tripled, but statehood was delayed another two years. In the interim, the ruling circles of the Anglo minority had formed a partnership with a selected few of the Hispano majority, who were rewarded with material benefits and positions of nominal leadership in exchange for keeping their people under control.

The heritage of this partnership was the characteristic political patronage system of New Mexico, which is often represented as a traditional Hispanic form. In fact, this system overthrew the established democratic forms of Hispanic municipal government, in which the principle of seniority was dominant within a framework of full manhood suffrage, and replaced it with the "paid election," reinforced by threats and promises. By the time New Mexico achieved statehood, the Hispano majority was reduced in ratio and in its capacity to function in its own interest. It had been effectively saddled with a "leadership" that owed its first loyalty to the dominant clique of Anglos.

The Hispano majority managed to impose its will on occasion, for instance, by including in the New Mexico State Constitution a pledge to abide by the terms of the Treaty of Guadalupe Hidalgo. This pledge, however, has been so little honored that it is now widely believed by Anglos that the Treaty and its terms are irrelevant to discussions of the current status of Hispanos.

The descendants of the Spanish-speaking people who became United States citizens under the Treaty, however, believe that its terms are the "supreme law of the land," taking precedence over other laws. They consider the Treaty permanently binding upon *both* signatories. For this reason, the Alianza has, from the beginning, sought to win the active support of the Mexican government to its demand for an investigation into the charges of Treaty violations. The Mexican government, thus far, has avoided taking a position on the matter; on the other hand, the issues involved have stirred widespread popular sympathy when discussed in such press reports as the Mejida series. In Mexico, the New Mexican Hispanos are seen as "the brothers outside."

Such public support might persuade the Mexican government or another government with representation in the United Nations to instruct its delegates to lodge an official request for investigation of possible violation of the Universal Declaration of Human Rights, as the Alianza has been requesting for several years. What is most surprising, in fact, is that New Mexicans have not previously sought a remedy through international channels. Previous failure to utilize means that are nominally available is the result of the lack of political experience and of a genuine political leadership among the Hispanos. Functioning within the existing political structure of New Mexico, Hispanos can only perpetuate their own subordination.

RELATIVE DEPRIVATION AND THE TACTICS OF DESPAIR

A common line of questioning the intentions and methods of the Alianza begins with the query: Why does the Alianza focus its efforts so sharply on the land question? When it is pointed out that traditional Hispano family and community life depend on a land base, the further questions are raised: Why did the Hispanos wait so long to protest the loss of their lands, and why don't they now seek a remedy through the courts instead of resorting to violence?

Such questions can only be answered by examining the direction of Hispano changes over periods of time, with particular attention to those periods when rapid changes entailing social dislocations have forced groups of Hispanos to action.

The following paragraphs draw upon the author's previous researches, amplified by a series of scholarly articles published in *El Dia*, a Mexico City daily newspaper, by Agustin Cue Canovas and entitled "The Forgotten People."

The Canovas articles reviewed the provisions of the Treaty of Guadalupe Hidalgo from the standpoint of maneuvers by the Mexican leadership to protect the rights of its former citizens now incorporated in the United States. Articles 8, 9 and 10 of the Treaty specified the civil and property rights of the transferred citizens, and were ratified by the Mexican government. Article 9 was modified by the United States Senate, but the United States envoys who negotiated the final draft signed a protocol saying that the new wording had the same protective coverage as the earlier draft. Article 10 made provision that all land grants in the territories in question would be "respected as valid and of the stated extension," and that grants whose confirmation had not been completed prior to the United States invasion would be completed or forfeited within a period of two years. The Senate suppressed Article 10 and Canovas surmised that failure to provide for the speedy and automatic confirmation of all valid land grants, as previously pledged, was a prelude to the wholesale and violent expropriations which followed. By failing to specify a procedure and a time period for the confirmation of the grants, Congress set the stage for interminable delays in processing claims, while the Colonial and Mexican Archives were seized and systematically pillaged by the enemies of the grantees.

The grantees were forced to hire lawyers at their own expense and produce what title papers they could; to go through a lengthy and complex procedure before the Land Commissioner, District Court and Supreme Court; and then seek confirmation by the Surveyor General and, once again, in the Supreme Court. In California, the influx of gold prospectors in 1849 brought about immediate and wholesale violations of the terms of the Treaty; in Texas the picture was even worse.

Mexican authorities protested illegal expropriations, evictions and assassinations, continuing to do so along the Texas border until well into this century, but to no avail. Ironically, President Manuel Peña y Peña, the Mexican president who signed the Treaty of Guadalupe Hidalgo, would have been willing to make even greater territorial concessions to the United States in order to secure the rights of his former fellow-citizens, but he was assured that their freedom was guaranteed and their rights and interests would be protected.

Contrary to the rapid and violent expropriation of grant lands in California and Texas, the same process was more delayed and more veiled in New Mexico. From the time of the arrival of the first New Mexico Surveyor General in 1854 until well after the Civil War, the land-grant heirs presented their claims with little apparent evidence that they would fail to be confirmed. The fact that the overwhelming majority of the population continued to be Hispano masked their growing loss of property and civil rights, for the ejido lands which the Surveyor General immediately began to assign to the public domain continued to be unfenced and available for grazing, and the Anglo population was nowhere large enough to present a real threat.

By 1888, however, Antonio Joseph protested to the House of Representatives the situation provoked by denial of statehood to New Mexico. He pointed out that of more than one thousand land-grant claims submitted only 71 had so far been confirmed. Land-grant heirs, despite the Treaty promise to protect them from depredations by nomadic Indian tribesmen, had suffered more than five million dollars' worth of uncompensated damages in the hostilities between the United States and the Navahos and Apaches. Joseph made pointed reference to the distinguished Civil War service rendered by the new citizens from New Mexico.

The protests of Antonio Joseph had little effect. A Court of Private Land Claims was established in 1891 to expedite matters and, when it closed its deliberations in 1904, less than two million acres of land out of thirty-five million acres claimed by the heirs had been confirmed. Of this acreage, a large portion had remained in the hands of lawyers representing the heirs; for instance, one half the acreage of the Cañon de San Diego Grant.

Even so, until grazing lands were fenced off, and the heirs were reduced to their limited agricultural lands, the Hispanos never seem to have recognized the existence of a policy designed systematically to deprive them of their property rights. Each local group, as access was lost, reacted sharply, often with violence, to what they considered an outrage. Starting in the 1880's and continuing to the present, these local groups resorted to vigilante action—cutting fences, burning barns and haystacks and slashing livestock. This was the beginning of the tactics of despair.

During a brief period of years, the ever-deepening impoverishment of the New Mexican Hispano population was relieved by federal and state programs to restore their economy and meet their educational needs. In the 1930's, community studies conducted under the Soil Conservation Service of the U.S. Department of Agriculture focused on the relationship between loss of the subsistence base, land, and social dislocation. In a few communities, direct measures were taken to restore some of the lost ejido lands to the community. The development of a few stockmen's cooperatives promised to modernize grazing practices for general community benefit. The Taylor Grazing Act of the 1930's was intended to increase the grazing lands available to the poverty-stricken communities of northern New Mexico, but its actual long-term effect has been to strengthen the domination of corporate livestock interests.

After this brief respite, the condition of the Hispano villages took a rapid plunge into deeper impoverishment, as a result of the wholesale loss of most of their young men to military service in World War II. When the local population temporarily could not maintain the livestock industry to the required levels of meat production for the armed forces, a sharp increase in leasing of the National Forest range by corporate out-of-state interests took place, and the villagers have never recovered access to substantial segments of their traditional range.

Forced emigration from the villages in search of wage work, which for many years had been a seasonal or temporary means of meeting subsistence needs for the younger men, now took entire families away and increased the number of ghost towns in New Mexico. Between

1950 and 1960, the percentage of New Mexico Hispanos living in rural communities dropped from nearly 60% to less than 43%.

While urbanization is a worldwide trend, the cultural shock for people of a traditional culture, as that involved in such a forced movement, brings social disaster in its wake. The majority of former villagers who are now obliged to live in the slums of New Mexico's towns and cities constantly express the desire to return to the country, even if they could not hope for better than a marginal subsistence. In large measure, even this thin hope is barred by existing welfare regulations, which deny aid to families owning even the tiniest plot of land which might produce a supplement to their benefits. People forced to go on the welfare rolls, therefore, can only do so after they have sold their land and spent the proceeds.

Comparing life as it is today with what it used to be, forcibly urbanized Hispanos express a keen sense of loss. It is this sense of relative deprivation which is the main motivating force of the Alianza. Even those who have managed to make a livelihood in the city feel that only as small village landholders can they maintain the core values of their culture: the cooperative unity of the enlarged kin group, the firm rules of "respect and honor" handed down from one generation to the next and the proud sense of their hereditary status, bestowed on them by Philip II, of "hijosdalgo de solar conocido"—landed gentlemen.

Suggestions for Further Reading

The Chinese immigration to the West Coast of the United States has received very little attention from historians. Virtually the only works on the subject are Mary Coolidge, *Chinese Immigration* (Henry Holt, 1909), which was written with the hope of reopening immigration after it was brought to a halt by the Chinese Exclusion Act of 1882, and Gunther Barth, *Bitter Strength: A History of the Chinese in the United States, 1850–1870* (Harvard University Press, 1964). A recent study of the reception met by Chinese immigrants in America is Stuart C. Miller, *The Unwelcome Immigrant: The American Image of the Chinese, 1785–1882* (University of California Press, 1969). For an account of some of the problems that the Chinese faced in the United States, see Herbert Ashbury, *The Barbary Coast: An Informal History of the San Francisco Underworld* ° (Knopf, 1933).

For the background to anti-Japanese sentiment at the outbreak of the Second World War, see Roger Daniels, *The Politics of Prejudice: The Anti-Japanese Movement in California and the Struggle for Japanese Exclusion* ° (University of California Press, 1962), and Carey McWilliams, *Prejudice: Japanese Americans, Symbol of Racial Intolerance* (Little, Brown, 1944). Two pertinent works published under the auspices of the University of California Education and Resettlement Study are Dorothy Swaine Thomas and Richard Nishimoto, *The Spoilage: Japanese American Evacuation and Resettlement* ° (University of California Press, 1946), and Dorothy Swaine Thomas, Charles Kikuchi, and James Sakoda, *The Salvage* (University of California Press, 1952). Eugene V. Rostow published two articles that were harshly critical of the Japanese-American evacuation: "The Japanese-American Cases—A Disaster," *Yale Law Journal,* Vol. 54 (June, 1945), 489–533, and "Our Worst Wartime Mistake," *Harper's,* Vol. 191 (September, 1945), 193–201. The political aspects of the Japanese-American internment are analyzed by Morton Grodzins in *Americans Betrayed: Politics and the Japanese Evacuation* (University of Chicago Press, 1949). Recent studies of the events surrounding the evacuation include Bill Hosokawa, *Nisei: The Quiet Americans* (Morrow, 1969), and Andrie Girdner and Anne Loftis, *The Great Betrayal* (Macmillan, 1969).

The history of the Mexican-American is told in Carey McWilliams, *North from Mexico* ° (Lippincott, 1949), and in Manuel P. Servín (ed.), *The Mexican-Americans: An Awakening Minority* ° (Glencoe, 1970). The contemporary situation of America's chicanos is explored in Julian Samora (ed.), *La Raza: Forgotten Americans* ° (University of Notre Dame Press, 1966), and in Stan Steiner, *La Raza: The Mexican Americans* ° (Harper and Row, 1970). Peter Nabokov tells the story

° Available in paperback edition.

of the Alianza in *Tijerina and the Courthouse Raid* ° (University of New Mexico Press, 1969). The California grape-pickers' strike led by Cesar Chavez is described in John Gregory Dunne, *Delano* ° (Farrar, Straus and Giroux, 1967), and in Peter Matthiessen, *Sal Si Puedes: Cesar Chavez and the New American Revolution* ° (Random House, 1969).

On the Puerto Ricans in the United States, see Oscar Handlin, *The Newcomers: Negroes and Puerto Ricans in a Changing Metropolis* ° (Harvard University Press, 1959); Clarence Senior, *The Puerto Ricans: Strangers—Then Neighbors* ° (Quadrangle, 1961); and Patricia Cayo Sexton, *Spanish Harlem* ° (Harper and Row, 1965). A more personal view of Puerto Rican life in this country is presented in Piri Thomas' autobiographical *Down These Mean Streets* ° (Knopf, 1967) and in Oscar Lewis' *La Vida: A Puerto Rican Family in the Culture of Poverty —San Juan and New York* ° (Random House, 1967).

Women

The Cult
of True Womanhood:
1820–1860

BARBARA WELTER

The decades before the Civil War resounded with the cry of reform. Hardly an institution in American life escaped the scrutiny of some group determined to change it. There were campaigns for the abolition of slavery, for penal reform, for better care of the insane, for temperance, for communal living, for industrial socialism, and for many other schemes to improve the status quo. Not the least of these was a campaign for women's rights led by such impressive figures as Elizabeth Cady Stanton, Frances Wright, and the Grimké sisters.

Women had always been a valuable commodity in colonial America. In seventeenth-century Virginia, wives were actually sold by the Virginia Company, which transported young women from England and exchanged them for one hundred and fifty pounds of good tobacco. The rigors of frontier life and the dangers of continuous child-bearing without proper hygienic or medical care made the female mortality rate—along with that of infants—extremely high. Indeed, it was not unusual for a hardy male settler to go through three or four wives in his lifetime.

As long as American society was primarily agricultural, there was a fairly clear-cut distinction between the functions of men and women. Most of the woman's time was taken up with housework and child-rearing. When she had time, she joined the men in the fields, where there was always plenty of work for both sexes.

With urban society, however, came challenges to the traditional division of labor between the sexes. As industrialization proceeded and the income of factory workers dropped, it became necessary for some women to leave the home to take factory jobs alongside their husbands. Thus, instead of finding themselves with more free time as a result of increasing mechanization, they found themselves working at two full-time jobs—as factory operative and housewife. "Woman's work" of caring for the home had by this time acquired a taboo for most men, and a double standard of behavior that bore no relation to the actual circumstances of society or the differences between the sexes was fast taking root.

For the growing ranks of middle-class women, however, the Industrial Revolution brought an increase in leisure time. These women did not have to work outside the home, and the multiplication of labor-saving household devices, coupled with the availability of household servants as a result of recent immigration, freed them considerably for new interests and activities. It was this newly leisured class of women that produced most of the members of the ante-bellum women's rights movement. In fact, many of the leaders of this campaign were women who had become interested in the anti-slavery movement but found themselves excluded from active participation in it merely on the basis of their sex.

The following study describes the ideal of "True Womanhood" that was exalted in the popular literature of the day— partly as a reaction against the rising ambitions of many middle-class women. This literature, which stressed the desirability of such "feminine" traits as submissiveness and domesticity, ran decidedly counter to the movement for women's rights. Apparently, the literature enjoyed a wider and more influential audience than did the feminists.

The attributes of True Womanhood, by which a woman judged herself and was judged by her husband, her neighbors and society, could be divided into four cardinal virtues—piety, purity, submissiveness and domesticity. Put them all together and they spelled mother, daughter, sister, wife—woman. Without them, no matter whether there was fame, achievement or wealth, all was ashes. With them she was promised happiness and power.

Religion or piety was the core of woman's virtue, the source of her strength. Young men looking for a mate were cautioned to search first for piety, for if that were there, all else would follow. Religion belonged to woman by divine right, a gift of God and nature. This "peculiar susceptibility" to religion was given her for a reason: "the vestal flame of piety, lighted up by Heaven in the breast of woman" would throw its beams into the naughty world of men. So far would its candle power reach that the "Universe might be Enlightened, Improved, and Harmonized by WOMAN!!" She would be another, better Eve, working in cooperation with the Redeemer, bringing the world back "from its revolt and sin." The world would be reclaimed for God through her suffering, for "God increased the cares and sorrows of woman, that she might be sooner constrained to accept the terms of salvation." A popular poem by Mrs. Frances Osgood, "The Triumph of the Spiritual over the Sensual," expressed just this sentiment, woman's purifying passionless love bringing an erring man back to Christ.

Dr. Charles Meigs, explaining to a graduating class of medical students why women were naturally religious, said that "hers is a pious mind. Her confiding nature leads her more readily than men to accept the proffered grace of the Gospel." Caleb Atwater, Esq., writing in *The Ladies' Repository,* saw the hand of the Lord in female piety: "Religion is exactly what a woman needs, for it gives her that dignity that best suits her dependence." And Mrs. John Sandford, who had no very high opinion of her sex, agreed thoroughly: "Religion is just what woman needs. Without it she is ever restless or unhappy. . . ." Mrs. Sandford and the others did not speak only of that restlessness of the human heart, which St. Augustine notes, that can only find its peace in God. They spoke rather of religion as a kind of tranquilizer for the many undefined longings which swept even the most pious young girl, and about which it was better to pray than to think.

One reason religion was valued was that it did not take a woman away from her "proper sphere," her home. Unlike participation in other societies or movements, church work would not make her less domestic or submissive, less a True Woman. In religious vineyards, said the *Young Ladies' Literary and Missionary Report,* "you may labor without the apprehension of detracting from the charms of feminine delicacy." Mrs. S. L. Dagg, writing from her chapter of the Society of Tuscaloosa, Alabama, was equally reassuring: "As no sensible woman will suffer her intellectual pursuits to clash with her domestic duties" she should concentrate on religious work "which promotes these very duties."

The women's seminaries aimed at aiding women to be religious, as well as accomplished. Mt. Holyoke's catalogue promised to make female education "a handmaid to the Gospel and an efficient auxiliary in the great task of renovating the world." The Young Ladies' Seminary at Bordentown, New Jersey, declared its most important function to be "the forming of a sound and virtuous character." In Keene, New Hampshire, the Seminary tried to instill a "consistent and useful character" in its students, to enable them in this life to be "a good friend, wife and mother," but more important, to qualify them for "the enjoyment of Celestial Happiness in the life to come." And Joseph M'D. Mathews, Principal of Oakland Female Seminary in Hillsborough, Ohio, believed that "female education should be preeminently religious."

If religion was so vital to a woman, irreligion was almost too awful to contemplate. Women were warned not to let their literary or intellectual pursuits take them away from God. Sarah Josepha Hale spoke darkly of those who, like Margaret Fuller, threw away the "One True Book" for others, open to error. Mrs. Hale used the unfortunate Miss Fuller as fateful proof that "the greater the intellectual force, the greater and more fatal the errors into which women fall who wander from the Rock of Salvation, Christ the Saviour. . . ."

One gentlemen, writing on "Female Irreligion," reminded his readers that "man may make himself a brute, and does so very often, but can woman brutify herself to his level—the lowest level of human nature—without exerting special wonder?" Fanny Wright, because she was godless, "was no woman, mother though she be." A few years ago, he recalls, such women would have been whipped. In any case, "woman never looks lovelier than in her reverence for religion" and conversely, "female irreligion is the most revolting feature in human character."

Purity was as essential as piety to a young woman, its absence as unnatural and unfeminine. Without it she was, in fact, no woman at all, but a member of some lower order. A "fallen woman" was a "fallen angel," unworthy of the celestial company of her sex. To contemplate the loss of purity brought tears; to be guilty of such a crime, in the women's magazines at least, brought madness or death. Even the language of the flowers had bitter words for it: a dried white rose symbolized "Death Preferable to Loss of Innocence." The marriage night was the single great event of a woman's life, when she bestowed her greatest treasure upon her husband, and from that time on was completely dependent upon him, an empty vessel, without legal or emotional existence of her own.

Therefore all True Women were urged, in the strongest possible terms, to maintain their virtue, although men, being by nature more sensual than they, would try to assault it. Thomas Branagan admitted in *The Excellency of the Female Character Vindicated* that his sex would sin and sin again, they could not help it, but woman, stronger and purer, must not give in and let man "take liberties incompatible with her delicacy." "If you do," Branagan addressed his gentle reader, "you will be left in silent sadness to bewail your credulity, imbecility, duplicity, and premature prostitution."

Mrs. Eliza Farrar, in *The Young Lady's Friend,* gave practical logistics to avoid trouble: "Sit not with another in a place that is too narrow; read not out of the same book; let not your eagerness to see anything induce you to place your head close to another person's."

If such good advice was ignored the consequences were terrible and inexorable. In *Girlhood and Womanhood: or, Sketches of My Schoolmates,* by Mrs. A. J. Graves (a kind of mid-nineteenth-century *The Group*), the bad ends of a boarding school class of girls are scrupulously recorded. The worst end of all is reserved for "Amelia Dorrington: The Lost One." Amelia died in the almshouse "the wretched victim of depravity and intemperance" and all because her mother had let her be "high-spirited not prudent." These girlish high spirits had been misinterpreted by a young man, with disastrous results. Amelia's "thoughtless levity" was "followed by a total loss of virtuous principle" and Mrs. Graves editorializes that "the coldest reserve is more admirable in a woman a man wishes to make his wife, than the least approach to undue familiarity."

✿   ✿   ✿

Purity, considered as a moral imperative, set up a dilemma which was hard to resolve. Woman must preserve her virtue until marriage and marriage was necessary for her happiness. Yet marriage was, literally, an end to innocence. She was told not to question this dilemma, but simply to accept it.

Submission was perhaps the most feminine virtue expected of women. Men were supposed to be religious, although they rarely had time for it, and supposed to be pure, although it came awfully hard to them, but men were the movers, the doers, the actors. Women were the passive, submissive responders. The order of dialogue was, of course, fixed in Heaven. Man was "woman's superior by God's appointment, if not in intellectual dowry, at least by official decree." Therefore, as Charles Elliott argued in *The Ladies' Repository,* she should submit to him "for the sake of good order at least." In *The Ladies' Companion* a young wife was quoted approvingly as saying that she did not think woman should "feel and act for herself" because "when, next to God, her husband is not the tribunal to which her heart and intellect appeals —the golden bowl of affection is broken." Women were warned that if they tampered with this quality they tampered with the order of the Universe.

The Young Lady's Book summarized the necessity of the passive virtues in its readers' lives: "It is, however, certain, that in whatever situation of life a woman is placed from her cradle to her grave, a spirit of obedience and submission, pliability of temper, and humility of mind, are required from her."

Woman understood her position if she was the right kind of woman, a true woman. "She feels herself weak and timid. She needs a protector," declared George Burnap, in his lectures on *The Sphere and Duties of Woman.* "She is a measure dependent. She asks for wisdom, constancy, firmness, perseverance, and she is willing to repay it all by the surrender of the full treasure of her affections. Woman despises in man every thing like herself except a tender heart. It is enough that she is effeminate and weak; she does not want another like herself." Or put even more strongly by Mrs. Sandford: "A really sensible woman feels her dependence. She does what she can, but she is conscious of inferiority, and therefore grateful for support."

Mrs. Sigourney, however, assured young ladies that although they were separate, they were equal. This difference of the sexes did not imply inferiority, for it was part of that same order of Nature established by Him "who bids the oak brave the fury of the tempest, and the alpine flower lean its cheek on the bosom of eternal snows." Dr. Meigs had a different analogy to make the same point, contrasting the anatomy of the Apollo of the Belvedere (illustrating the male principle) with the Venus de Medici (illustrating the female principle). "Woman," said the physician, with a kind of clinical gallantry, "has a head almost too small for intellect but just big enough for love."

This love itself was to be passive and responsive. "Love, in the heart of a woman," wrote Mrs. Farrar, "should partake largely of the nature of gratitude. She should love, because she is already loved by one deserving her regard."

Woman was to work in silence, unseen, like Wordsworth's Lucy. Yet, "working like nature, in secret" her love goes forth to the world "to regulate its pulsation, and send forth from its heart, in pure and temperate flow, the life-giving current." She was to work only for pure affection, without thought of money or ambition. A poem, "Woman and Fame," by Felicia Hemans, widely quoted in many of the gift books, concludes with a spirited renunciation of the gift of fame:

> Away! to me, a woman, bring
> Sweet flowers from affection's spring.

"True feminine genius," said Grace Greenwood (Sara Jane Clarke), "is ever timid, doubtful, and clingingly dependent; a perpetual childhood." And she advised literary ladies in an essay on "The Intellectual Woman"—"Don't trample on the flowers while longing for the stars." A wife who submerged her own talents to work for her husband was extolled as an example of a true woman. In *Women of Worth: A Book for Girls*, Mrs. Ann Flaxman, an artist of promise herself, was praised because she "devoted herself to sustain her husband's genius and aid him in his arduous career."

Caroline Gilman's advice to the bride aimed at establishing this proper order from the beginning of a marriage: "Oh, young and lovely bride, watch well the first moments when your will conflicts with his to whom God and society have given the control. Reverence his *wishes* even when you do not his *opinions*."

Mrs. Gilman's perfect wife in *Recollections of a Southern Matron* realizes that "the three golden threads with which domestic happiness is woven" are "to repress a harsh answer, to confess a fault, and to stop (right or wrong) in the midst of self-defense, in gentle submission." Woman could do this, hard though it was, because in her heart she knew she was right and so could afford to be forgiving, even a trifle condescending. "Men are not unreasonable," averred Mrs. Gilman. "Their difficulties lie in not understanding the moral and physical nature of our sex. They often wound through ignorance, and are surprised at having offended." Wives were advised to do their best to reform men, but if they couldn't, to give up gracefully. "If any habit of his annoyed me, I spoke of it once or twice, calmly, then bore it quietly."

A wife should occupy herself "only with domestic affairs—wait till your husband confides to you those of a high importance—and do not give your advice until he asks for it," advised *The Lady's Token*. At all times she should behave in a manner becoming a woman, who had "no arms other than gentleness." Thus "if he is abusive, never retort." *A Young Lady's Guide to the Harmonious Development of a Christian Character* suggested that females should "become as little children" and "avoid a controversial spirit." *The Mother's Assistant and Young Lady's Friend* listed "Always Conciliate" as its first commandment in "Rules for Conjugal and Domestic Happiness." Small wonder that these same rules ended with the succinct maxim: "Do not expect too much."

As mother, as well as wife, woman was required to submit to fortune. In *Letters to Mothers* Mrs. Sigourney sighed: "To bear the evils and sorrows which may be appointed us, with a patient mind, should be the continual effort of our sex. . . . It seems, indeed, to be expected of us; since the passive and enduring virtues are more immediately within our province." Of these trials "the hardest was to bear the loss of children with submission" but the indomitable Mrs. Sigourney found strength to murmur to the bereaved mother: "The Lord loveth a cheerful giver." *The Ladies' Parlor Companion* agreed thoroughly in "A Submissive Mother," in which a mother who had already buried two children and was nursing a dying baby saw her sole remaining child "probably scalded to death. Handing over the infant to die in the arms of a friend, she bowed in sweet submission to the double stroke." But the child "through the goodness of God survived, and the mother learned to say 'Thy will be done.' "

Woman then, in all her roles, accepted submission as her lot. It was a lot she had not chosen or deserved. As *Godey's* said, "The lesson of submission is forced upon woman." Without comment or criticism the writer affirms that "to suffer and to be silent under suffering seems the great command she has to obey." George Burnap referred to a woman's life as "a series of suppressed emotions." She was, as Emerson said, "more vulnerable, more infirm, more mortal than man." The death of a beautiful woman, cherished in fiction, represented woman as the innocent victim, suffering without sin, too pure and good for this world but too weak and passive to resist its evil forces. The best refuge for such a delicate creature was the warmth and safety of her home.

The true woman's place was unquestionably by her own fireside— as daughter, sister, but most of all as wife and mother. Therefore domesticity was among the virtues most prized by the women's magazines. "As society is constituted," wrote Mrs. S. E. Farley, in the "Domestic and Social Claims on Woman," "the true dignity and beauty of the female character seem to consist in a right understanding and faithful and cheerful performance of social and family duties." Sacred

Scripture reenforced social pressure: "St. Paul knew what was best for women when he advised them to be domestic," said Mrs. Sandford. "There is composure at home; there is something sedative in the duties which home involves. It affords security not only from the world, but from delusions and errors of every kind."

✿   ✿   ✿

The American woman had her choice—she could define her rights in the way of the women's magazines and insure them by the practice of the requisite virtues, or she could go outside the home, seeking other rewards than love. It was a decision on which, she was told, everything in her world depended. "Yours it is to determine," the Rev. Mr. Stearns solemnly warned from the pulpit, "whether the beautiful order of society . . . shall continue as it has been" or whether "society shall break up and become a chaos of disjointed and unsightly elements." If she chose to listen to other voices than those of her proper mentors, sought other rooms than those of her home, she lost both her happiness and her power—"that almost magic power, which, in her proper sphere, she now wields over the destinies of the world."

But even while the women's magazines and related literature encouraged this ideal of the perfect woman, forces were at work in the nineteenth century which impelled woman herself to change, to play a more creative role in society. The movements for social reform, westward migration, missionary activity, utopian communities, industrialism, the Civil War—all called forth responses from woman which differed from those she was trained to believe were hers by nature and divine decree. The very perfection of True Womanhood, moreover, carried within itself the seeds of its own destruction. For if woman was so very little less than the angels, she should surely take a more active part in running the world, especially since men were making such a hash of things.

Real women often felt they did not live up to the ideal of True Womanhood: some of them blamed themselves, some challenged the standard, some tried to keep the virtues and enlarge the scope of womanhood. Somehow through this mixture of challenge and acceptance, of change and continuity, the True Woman evolved into the New Woman—a transformation as startling in its way as the abolition of slavery or the coming of the machine age. And yet the stereotype, the "mystique" if you will, of what woman was and ought to be persisted, bringing guilt and confusion in the midst of opportunity.

The women's magazines and related literature had feared this very dislocation of values and blurring of roles. By careful manipulation and interpretation they sought to convince woman that she had the best of both worlds—power and virtue—and that a stable order of society depended upon her maintaining her traditional place in it. To that end she was identified with everything that was beautiful and holy.

"Who Can Find a Valiant Woman?" was asked frequently from the pulpit and the editorial pages. There was only one place to look for her —at home. Clearly and confidently these authorities proclaimed the True Woman of the nineteenth century to be the Valiant Woman of the Bible, in whom the heart of her husband rejoiced and whose price was above rubies.

The Woman Movement

WILLIAM L. O'NEILL

Some standard narrative histories of America give the impression that the only issues capable of stirring women to organize politically were prohibition and women's suffrage. This is certainly not the case, although it is true that over-concentration on these issues and the heavy publicity that centered around them tended to divert attention from other aspects of feminism that may have been of more profound importance both for the women of America and for society at large.

At the time of the 1848 convention on women's rights in Seneca Falls, New York—the event from which the women's rights movement usually dates itself—feminists saw disfranchisement as only one of a whole array of serious legal and social disabilities faced by women. Women were not allowed to own property—in most cases, not even the clothes they wore. A working wife was not allowed to keep her wages but was required to turn them over to her husband. In the case of separation or divorce, a woman had no legal claims on her husband and was not allowed to keep the children. She had no legal status, which meant that she was not permitted to bring suit or to give testimony in the courts. Often, she was not permitted to inherit property or to make a will. She was barred from public office and excluded from public life generally. For the most part, women lacked opportunities for education, vocational training, and professional employment. The national consensus was that women belonged in the home, and determined efforts were made to see that they stayed there.

In the beginning, there was a good deal of confusion and

disagreement among the feminists as to the best method of improving their situation. Some women instituted petition campaigns and direct lobbying in their states. Others sought the help of friendly legislators, hoping to bring informal influence to bear. Eventually, most of the efforts of the women's movement were focused on securing the right to vote, for it seemed that only the use of the franchise could generate the pressure necessary to eliminate legal discrimination against women.

Today it may be difficult to understand why the idea of female suffrage was so furiously opposed by the American public, both male and female, in the closing years of the nineteenth century. The opponents of female suffrage often used the argument that women were too frail, too pure, too noble, to participate in the political arena. Indeed, the Gilded Age was one of the most corrupt periods in American political life, and men may actually have seen the extension of the franchise as a step toward the corruption of a new segment of society. Or, believing their own rhetoric, they may have feared that women voters would force overly rigorous reforms on the existing political and social structures. In the South, the vote of black women was viewed as an even more unthinkable threat to the status quo than the vote of white women. Any explanation that could be given here would be simplistic. But, generally, the opposition to the women's movement can be understood as part of a wide-ranging defensive reaction against the breakdown of the traditional family system that was proceeding, hand in hand with urbanization, in the entire Western world.

When women's suffrage was finally achieved in 1920, after over half a century of struggle, the women's movement was too divided within itself to mobilize the new vote for any better purpose than prohibition. Because class interests tended to take precedence over sex interests, women voters failed to function as a political interest group. On the contrary, they tended to join the men in conventional party politics and hence had virtually no effect on national policy. Having won a major victory, many of the feminist leaders retired from the public eye, and the agitation for women's rights largely died out, to be revived only in the 1960's.

The following article points out some of the conflicts and difficulties of the women's rights movement before 1920.

The phrase most commonly used by women in the nineteenth and early twentieth centuries to describe their expanding activities was "the woman movement." This movement included not only those things pertaining to women's rights but almost any act or event that enlarged woman's sphere, increased her opportunities, or broadened her outlook. It covered everything from woman suffrage and social reform down to the individual accomplishments of gifted, ambitious women. "Feminism," a more limited word, related specifically to the advancement of women's legal and political rights. The feminist movement, in turn, was broadly divided into two wings, but, because feminists themselves did not recognize this until the very end of the period, i.e., in the 1920's, I have coined the phrases "social feminism" to describe that part of the movement that put social reform ahead of women's rights and "hard-core" or "extreme feminists" to describe those who put women's rights before all else. A "suffragist" was simply one who worked for equal suffrage, irrespective of her views on other questions.

❋   ❋   ❋

In the 1830's women were stirred by the currents of reform that were sweeping the country, and those who were moved to action discovered that their status as women told against their ambitions as abolitionists, temperance workers, or whatever. Sarah M. Grimké was inspired to write the first American feminist tract of consequence because some clergymen objected to her anti-slavery work. Elizabeth Cady Stanton was started on her career as a women's rights leader after she was denied a seat, by reason of her sex, at a World Anti-Slavery Convention in London. Susan B. Anthony became a feminist after she was discriminated against by her male colleagues in the temperance movement.

In 1848 these separate streams of dissent came together at the first Women's Rights Convention in Seneca Falls, New York. The "Declaration of Sentiments" that was adopted by the meeting indicated another element that infused the early feminist movement: the libertarianism of the age of reform. Modeled in part on the Declaration of Independence, this manifesto declared that "the history of mankind is a history of repeated injuries and usurpations on the part of man toward woman, having in direct object the establishment of an absolute

Abridged from "Feminism as a Radical Ideology" originally published in *Dissent: Explorations in the History of American Radicalism,* edited by Alfred F. Young, © 1968 by Northern Illinois University Press, DeKalb. Reprinted by permission of the publisher.

tyranny over her." It was, in fact, a decidedly radical document—not that it called for an end to private property, or anticipated a good society along socialist lines, but in storming against every iniquity from votelessness to the double standard of morals it made demands that could not be satisfied without profound changes in the social order. The most sophisticated feminists appreciated, in some measure at least, that they were not merely asking for their rights as citizens, that what they wanted called for new institutions as well as new ways of thinking. They seem to have been feeling their way toward a new domestic order. Mrs. Stanton, who denounced marriage as "opposed to all God's laws," wanted to begin its reformation by liberalizing divorce. The magazine she and Susan B. Anthony ran after the Civil War, *Revolution*, was full of references to the "marriage question" at a time when no orthodox person was willing to admit that there was a marriage question.

Logic alone had forced extreme feminists to sail these dangerous waters because even then it was clear that if women were fully emancipated by law, their domestic obligations would nevertheless prevent them from competing with men on an equal basis. There were only two (by no means mutually exclusive) ways of dealing with this problem: either women must be supported by the kind of welfare measures (guaranteed maternity leaves with pay, family allowances, and the like) that the advanced social democracies have devised, or marriage and the family must be more flexibly defined.

Because the first alternative did not exist in the mid-nineteenth century, far-sighted women had to consider how the essential domestic institutions could be revised to free women from the tyranny of home and family; they had some precedents to guide them. For their own reasons the Mormons practiced polygamy, while the Shaker communities went to the opposite extreme by abolishing not only marriage but sexual relations as well. A number of perfectionist groups explored the varieties of free love, such as John Humphrey Noyes, who (at Oneida, New York) combined the equality of the sexes, perfectionism, socialism, and "complex marriage" (the sharing of spouses) in a bizarre but strikingly successful way. In such an atmosphere it was natural for the boldest feminists to flirt with radical approaches to the domestic problem. It is impossible to tell where these speculations would have led Mrs. Stanton and her followers, but the Victoria Woodhull affair suggests a likely possibility.

Victoria Woodhull and her equally vivid sister, Tennessee Celeste

Claflin, burst upon the New York scene in 1868. Although nominally lady stockbrokers, they were agitators and evangelists by persuasion, and enthusiasts for everything radical, or just plain wild—socialism, spiritualism, or women's rights. Their magazine, *Woodhull and Claflin's Weekly*, promoted such causes, as well as the peculiar interests of their mentor, Stephen Pearl Andrews, a self-proclaimed universal philosopher and linguist. The surprising thing about the raffish sisters is that they rapidly became celebrated champions of the cause of women, admired by such shrewd and experienced figures as Elizabeth Cady Stanton and Susan B. Anthony. In 1871, for example, Victoria Woodhull persuaded a congressional subcommittee to hold hearings on woman suffrage, and she testified before it with great effect.

Their *Weekly* was interested in marriage from the beginning. Stephen Pearl Andrews believed in free love in the usual Victorian sense (that is, in extramarital sexual relationships contracted as a matter of principle), and the Claflin sisters had practiced free love long before they understood its theoretical possibilities. Having thrown out a good many hints, Mrs. Woodhull finally called a mass meeting and on the stage of Steinway Hall declared herself a free lover. She seems to have been genuinely astonished at the ferocious reaction to this public confession; newspapers hounded her, cautious feminists snubbed her, and the sisters fell on hard times, financially and emotionally. Victoria struck back by disclosing that Henry Ward Beecher, the most famous preacher of the day and a good friend of woman suffrage, had been having an affair with the wife of Theodore Tilton, Mrs. Woodhull's friend, her biographer, and perhaps her lover. The ensuing scandal destroyed the Claflins and the Tiltons; but Beecher survived it, thanks to his great reputation, considerable courage, and influential friends.

The effect of this debacle on the suffrage movement's fortunes is hard to determine because the cause was already in bad shape when the Claflins took it in hand. Suffragists had been disappointed at the end of the Civil War when they were asked to sacrifice votes for women to secure votes for Negro men. Some of them refused to admit that the freedman's need was greater than theirs and, because of this and other frictions, the suffrage movement had divided into two organizations: the staid, Boston-based American Woman's Suffrage Association and the more aggressive National Woman's Suffrage Association, led by Miss Anthony and Mrs. Stanton. Both groups were tarnished by the Beecher-Tilton affair, but the AWSA suffered less because it had always been anti-Claflin. The NWSA came in for a larger measure of abuse because of its closer association with the sisters, but the unquestionable virtue and integrity of its leaders saved it from total eclipse. It used to be thought that the affair had set back equal suffrage for decades; today, however, the movement's temporary decline seems to have been only one feature of the conservative backlash of the Gilded Age. Suffragists had expected too big a reward for their services during the Civil War as nurses, propagandists, and sanitary commission volunteers. The country was grateful to them, but not all that grateful —as the defeat of woman suffrage in the hotly contested Kansas referendum of 1866 demonstrated. In freeing and enfranchising the Negro, America, it seemed, had exhausted its supply of liberalism.

The Woodhull affair had one lasting effect, however: it reaffirmed the general conviction that suffrage politics and radical speculations, particularly those affecting marriage and the family, did not mix. In consequence the movement, although it never disowned the social goals that women's votes were presumably to implement, emphasized the most conservative aspects of the suffrage question. The vote was shown to be compatible with the existing domestic economy, and—at best—with those reforms that would elevate and refine domesticity to the level of perfection for which society yearned. Suffragists thereafter, vigorously resisting the temptation to think seriously about the domestic institutions that ruled their lives, made sexual orthodoxy their ruling principle.

In the long run these shocks had two important consequences: feminism rapidly became more conservative and more altruistic. Its conservatism—not the doing of Victoria Woodhull—stemmed from the tightening up of morals and manners that occurred in the high Victorian era. Bills like the Comstock Act (1873) made it impossible for John Humphrey Noyes and other sexual radicals to use the mails, choking off the lively debate that had flourished earlier. The porous or open quality that had characterized American life in the age of reform gave way to the censorious prudery we associate with Victorianism. It is very likely that the extreme feminists would have had to abandon their tentative explorations, if only because of social purity. Earlier there had been sporadic attempts by organized women to eliminate the double standard of morals by holding men to a higher level of conduct. The radical feminists who toyed with free love approached the same goal from an opposite direction, by proposing a sort of convergence in which men and women would occupy a middle ground between the old extremes of absolute license and complete chastity. After the war, however, all doubts as to which line feminists would follow were relieved by the social purity movement, which enlisted the energies of public-spirited women all over the country in a crusade to abolish prostitution and infidelity. Mrs. Stanton continued to advocate free divorce, to the great embarrassment of her younger followers, but she was very much the exception.

At the same time that feminists abandoned their more advanced positions they took on a great range of activities that often had little to do with women's rights. Extreme feminists, for example, displayed a keen sense of self-interest in the struggle over Negro suffrage after the Civil War. The Stantonites as a rule were more radical and more sensitive to the needs of others than the Boston faction, but when they were forced to choose between the Negroes' interests and their own they unflinchingly went down the line for feminist objectives.

The feminism of later years, however, was much more generous and diffuse. A hardy band of suffragists fought the good fight for the vote while most feminists devoted themselves to charities, philanthropies, and reforms. As social workers, settlement house residents, members of women's clubs, advocates of the reform of child labor and women's working conditions, of municipal government, public health, education, and housing, and as temperance workers and conservationists they submerged their interests as women in a sea of worthy enterprises. These social justice activities became the principal justification for feminism and are what historians most admire about the movement, but feminists paid a high price for their good deeds in two important ways. First, these activities drained off personnel from the women's rights movement and protracted the suffrage struggle. Second, they led to ideological confusions that played a large role in the collapse of feminism once the vote was won.

Social feminism also perpetuated the confusion between class and sex, that false sense of solidarity that characterized the entire woman movement. In a way this was natural, because all women suffered from disabilities that were imposed upon men only discriminatingly. It was not possible to have a "man movement" because most men enjoyed all the rights and opportunities that God and nature presumably intended them to have. Equal rights for women, however, did not mean the same thing to a factory girl that it meant to a college graduate, and feminists invariably refused to admit that differences in station among women were of any importance. In the beginning this hardly mattered, because the early feminists were mainly bourgeois intellectuals who were struggling to improve their own immediate circumstances. As the woman movement matured, however, its sociological evasions and self-deceptions attained critical proportions.

This analytic failure, which was characteristic of a movement that (with the notable exceptions of Elizabeth Cady Stanton and Charlotte Perkins Gilman) produced few intellects of the first rank, was compounded by an insistence that women were united in a selfless sisterhood by their maternal capacities, real or potential. "Women," it was declared over and over again, "stand relatively for the same thing everywhere and their first care is naturally and inevitably for the child." Maternity was not only a unifying force but the enabling principle that made the entrance of women into public life imperative. As another suffragist put it in 1878, "the new truth, electrifying, glorifying American womanhood today, is the discovery that the State is but the larger family, the nation the old homestead, and that in this national home there is a room and a corner and a duty for mother." Not only was the nation a larger home in need of mothering, but, by impinging upon the domestic circle, it made motherhood a public role.

As Jane Addams saw it, "many women today are failing properly to discharge their duties to their own families and household simply because they fail to see that as society grows more complicated it is necessary that woman shall extend her sense of responsibility to many things outside of her own home, if only in order to preserve the home in entirety." Thus the effort to escape domesticity was accompanied by an invocation of the domestic ideal: women's freedom road led in a circle, back to the home from which feminism was supposed to liberate them. Feminism was made respectable by accommodating it to the Victorian ethos that had forced it into being.

Given the plausibility and flexibility of this contention, women were (perhaps inevitably) lured into using it to secure their immediate aims; but in retrospect it does not seem to have been an unqualifiedly successful ploy. The Women's Christian Temperance Union is a case in point. Although one historian recently hailed Frances Willard's "supreme cleverness" in using "this conservative organization to advocate woman suffrage and child labor laws and other progressive legislation always in the name of purity and the home," the history of the WCTU illustrates the weakness of an argument that begins by accepting the opposition's premise. In conceding that better homes were of equal importance to feminists and anti-feminists alike, these women reduced their case from one of principle to a mere quarrel over tactics. All the opposition had to do to redeem itself was prove that its tactics were superior. This apparently is what happened to the WCTU after the death of Frances Willard (which coincided with a significant change in its social composition), when new leaders came to believe that temperance was more crucial to the home than suffrage, child welfare, and other progressive causes. Perhaps this new orientation would have come about in any event, but surely such WCTU suffragists as Frances Willard made it much easier by their willingness to utilize the cult of domesticity in pursuit of quite separate and distinctively feminist objectives.

The truth was that while these feminists resented the demands made upon them in their roles as wives and mothers, they were insufficiently alert to the danger presented by even a partial accommodation to the maternal mystique. Gravely underestimating the tremendous force generated by the sentimental veneration of motherhood, they assumed they could manipulate the emotions responsible for the condition of women without challenging the principles on which these feelings rested. Moreover, while denying that under the present circumstances mothers could be held accountable for the failings of their children, they implied that, once emancipated, women could legitimately be indicted for their progenies' shortcomings. In 1901 Susan B. Anthony declared that "before mothers can rightfully be held responsible for the vices and crimes, for the general demoralization of society, they must possess all possible rights and powers to control the conditions and circumstances of their own and their children's lives." Her remark would seem to mean that, once granted political equality, mothers would have to answer for all the ills of society. This was a great weight to lay on female posterity, and such statements contributed to the unhealthy and unrealizable expectations that feminism encouraged.

A further hazard of the feminist emphasis on motherhood was the support it lent the notion that women were not only different from men, but superior to men. Julia Ward Howe, a moderate and greatly admired feminist, persistently implied that emancipation was intended to make women better mothers as well as freer persons.

> Woman is the mother of the race, the guardian of its helpless infancy, its earliest teacher, its most zealous champion. Woman is also

the home-maker, upon her devolve the details which bless and beautify family life. In all true civilization she wins man out of his natural savagery to share with her the love of offspring, the enjoyment of true and loyal companionship.

Definitions like this left men with few virtues anyone was bound to admire, and inspired women to think of themselves as a kind of super-race that had been condemned by historical accident and otiose convention to serve its natural inferiors.

Such indeed was the case with women who, encouraged by the new social sciences (especially anthropology, which demonstrated that matriarchies had existed and may once have been common, if not universal), took themselves with a new seriousness that few men could share. Elizabeth Cady Stanton argued that prehistoric women had been superior to men, or at least equal to them, but that Christianity, and especially Protestantism, had driven the feminine element out of religion and had subordinated women to the rule of men. Society thereby had lost the beneficent moral and conservative forces of the female intellect and the mother instinct.

With this line of argument, Walter Rauschenbush, no enemy of women's rights, was compelled to take issue. Alarmed by what he regarded as the feminists' moral pretensions, he wrote: "Many men feel that women are morally better than men. Perhaps it is right that men should instinctively feel so. But it is a different matter when women think so too. They are not better. They are only good in different ways than men." Rauschenbush believed in the emancipation of women, but he reminded his readers that the feminine virtues could easily be exaggerated, and that in recent times both Christian Science and theosophy had demonstrated a particular appeal to women even though both stressed authority and unexamined belief.

As Rauschenbush's observation suggests, the attempt to demonstrate women's superior nature led nowhere. In essence it was just one more variation of the Victorian mystique, another way of exploiting the belief that woman's unique power was rooted in the mystery of her life-giving capacities. Taken one way, it led back to a preoccupation with motherhood. Read differently, it supported so complete a rejection of men that women could retain their integrity and spirituality only in spinsterhood. Or—by subscribing to the principles of Ellen Key, who elevated motherhood even above marriage and made the right to have illegitimate children the central aspect of feminism—women could have their cake and eat it too. They could realize their generative and instinctual potential without an unseemly dependence on the contaminating male. Deliberately having an illegitimate child necessitated an act of masculine cooperation, and in a delicious reversal of ancient custom man became an instrument of woman's purpose and his ungoverned passion the means to her full emancipation. This was radicalism with a vengeance, but a radicalism that had curiously little to do with the normal objects of revolutionary ardor.

Most organized women, however, were neither radical nor especially feministic. The woman movement as a whole, and most social feminists in particular, were satisfied with the comparatively modest programs of the WCTU and the General Federation of Women's Clubs. These programs, despite the fears of conservatives, were no threat to what Mrs. Gilman scornfully called the domestic mythology; in fact, they rested largely on the domestic and maternal mystique that was characteristic of the Victorian era. Not only did organized women continuously invoke "home and mother," for the most part their serious enterprises dealt with such related social matters as pure foods and drugs, child welfare, and working mothers. Whenever suffragists were able to tie in the ballot with a specific problem of special interest to women, they gained adherents. Through most of the nineteenth century suffragists maintained that women were entitled to vote as a matter of right and that they needed the vote to protect themselves and to advance the causes that were important to them. Neither argument was very persuasive in the age of Victoria, and always the suffragists' greatest obstacle was the indifference of their own sex.

As late as 1908 Theodore Roosevelt could comfortably, and quite rightly, say that "when women as a whole take any special interest in the matter they will have suffrage if they desire it." But only a few years later the picture had changed entirely. In 1914 the General Federation of Women's Clubs endorsed women suffrage in the name of its two million members; in 1917 membership of the NWSA soared to something like two million; and in that same year 500,000 women in New York City alone put their signatures to a suffrage petition. By 1917 it was obvious that women wanted the vote, and by 1920 they had it.

Few feminists seemed to realize that although winning the vote had been a feminist victory, it had not been won for feminist reasons. Suffragists had merely persuaded the organized middle-class women, who had become a potent force for reform in the Progressive era, that they needed the vote in order to secure the healthier and broader domestic life that was their main objective; feminists had not, however, convinced bourgeois women that they were greatly deprived and oppressed and that they had vast unrealized capabilities. From a strictly feminist point of view, the vote had been wrongly obtained. It neither reflected nor inspired a new vision of themselves on the part of most American women. Moreover, the suffrage could not but demoralize feminists who had worked so hard for so long, only to find that success had little effect upon the feminine condition.

The immediate consequence of feminine emancipation, then, was the fading away of the woman movement as it became apparent that the great organizations had less in common than they supposed. Moreover, the organizations themselves were changing in character. The WCTU was obsessed with prohibition (although it did not entirely lose interest in other social problems during the 1920's). The NWSA was transformed into the League of Women Voters; and although the league struggled valiantly to advance the old causes beloved of women reformers, it lacked the drive, funds, and numerical membership of its predecessor. The General Federation suffered least, because it had always been less committed to major reforms than its sister groups, and if its member clubs slackened their efforts, the national leadership continued to support the federation's traditional interests. The best evidence of the movement's decline was the fate of the Women's Joint Congressional Committee, which had been formed in 1920 to lobby for bills in which organized women took a special interest. Although it enjoyed some success (it helped keep Muscle Shoals [a federal hydroelectric project in Alabama] out of private hands and it preserved a measure of federal support for mothers' pensions and other welfare programs), it lost more battles than it won, especially in the crucial struggle to ratify the Child Labor Amendment.

Why Women's Liberation

MARLENE DIXON

In an age of revolt and general questioning of traditional authority, it comes as no surprise that the largest oppressed segment of society should try to free itself from the restraints that have bound it over the years. Thus, in the 1960's, a new women's liberation movement was born.

The current movement can be traced to a variety of sources. For many women, the issues behind the women's revolt were defined in 1963 by Betty Friedan in *The Feminine Mystique,* a book in which she discusses the profound discontent of the middle-class, college-educated housewife who finds herself tied to a house in the suburbs and expected to find personal fulfillment through her husband and her children. Other women joined the movement as a result of disillusioning experiences in the radical student movement of the middle 1960's. Many young women activists working in the civil rights drive and in a variety of college-based organizations found themselves assigned by male associates to the stereotyped female roles, such as typing, cooking, housekeeping, and providing sexual companionship. In recent years, still another source of support for the movement has been a group composed predominantly of poor black women, the increasingly militant National Welfare Rights Organization, which is fighting to improve national welfare programs.

On occasion, the different strands of the new women's rights movement have cooperated to bring their case against male supremacy dramatically before the public eye. For instance, a broad-based coalition of groups participated in the Women's Strike for Equality on August 26, 1970, the fiftieth anniversary of the ratification of the Nineteenth Amendment giving women the right to vote. As a rule, however, the various women's groups function independently, seeking different, specific goals related to the liberation of women.

The middle-class, professional associates of Betty Friedan, who founded the National Organization of Women (NOW) in 1966, have been primarily interested in securing equal opportunity in education and employment for women. Although there are federal laws designed to protect women in these respects, they are frequently neglected or ignored. Thus the women of NOW have supported the enactment of the equal rights amendment to the Constitution first proposed to Congress by Alice Paul of the Women's Rights Party in 1923. This amendment, which forbids any sex-based discrimination by state or federal governments, has been opposed by some women's labor organizations on the grounds that it would abolish certain protective legislation that works to the advantage of women in commerce and industry. Aspects of the NOW program that have more general support from the nation's women include the establishment of free twenty-four-hour day-care centers for the children of working mothers and the provision of free abortion on demand.

Another segment of the women's liberation movement stresses what it calls "consciousness raising"—the formation of small groups of women who come together regularly to discuss their common problems and ways in which society might be changed to permit more freedom for women. According to this group, it is necessary for women to reach a heightened awareness of the discrimination inherent in the traditional sex roles before they can realize the possibilities of true liberation.

For the most part, the women of the liberation movement are seeking neither female supremacy nor isolation from men. Rather, they are seeking to define their social roles for themselves. If they are successful, their struggle may free men also from the burden of a stereotyped sex role.

The following article outlines the character and the underlying causes of the new women's movement and analyzes the cultural factors that have permitted inequality of the sexes to persist in this country.

The 1960's has been a decade of liberation; women have been swept up by that ferment along with blacks, Latins, American Indians and poor whites—the whole soft underbelly of this society. As each oppressed group in turn discovers the nature of its oppression in American society, so women have discovered that they too thirst for free and fully human lives. The result has been the growth of a new women's movement, whose base encompasses poor black and poor white women on relief, working women exploited in the labor force, middle class women incarcerated in the split level dream house, college girls awakening to the fact that sexiness is not the crowning achievement in life, and movement women who have discovered that in a freedom movement they themselves are not free. In less than four years women have created a variety of organizations, from the nationally based middle class National Organization of Women (NOW) to local radical and radical feminist groups in every major city in North America. The new movement includes caucuses within nearly every New Left group and within most professional associations in the social sciences. Ranging in politics from reform to revolution, it has produced critiques of almost every segment of American society and constructed an ideology that rejects every hallowed cultural assumption about the nature and role of women.

As is typical of a young movement, much of its growth has been underground. The papers and manifestos written and circulated would surely comprise two very large volumes if published, but this literature is almost unknown outside of women's liberation. Nevertheless, where even a year ago organizing was slow and painful, with small cells of six or ten women, high turnover, and an uphill struggle against fear and resistance, in 1969 all that has changed. Groups are growing up everywhere with women eager to hear a hard line, to articulate and express their own rage and bitterness. Moving about the country, I have found an electric atmosphere of excitement and responsiveness. Everywhere there are doubts, stirrings, a desire to listen, to find out what it's all about. The extent to which groups have become politically radical is astounding. A year ago the movement stressed male chauvinism and psychological oppression; now the emphasis is on understanding the economic and social roots of women's oppression, and the analyses range from social democracy to Marxism. But the most striking change of all in the last year has been the loss of fear. Women are no longer afraid that their rebellion will threaten their very identity as women. They are not frightened by their own militancy, but liberated by it. Women's Liberation is an idea whose time has come.

The old women's movement burned itself out in the frantic decade of the 1920's. After a hundred years of struggle, women won a battle, only to lose the campaign: the vote was obtained, but the new millennium did not arrive. Women got the vote and achieved a measure of legal emancipation, but the real social and cultural barriers to full equality for women remained untouched.

For over 30 years the movement remained buried in its own ashes. Women were born and grew to maturity virtually ignorant of their own history of rebellion, aware only of a caricature of blue stockings and suffragettes. Even as increasing numbers of women were being driven into the labor force by the brutal conditions of the 1930's and by the massive drain of men into the military in the 1940's, the old ideal remained: a woman's place was in the home and behind her man. As the war ended and men returned to resume their jobs in factories and offices, women were forced back to the kitchen and nursery with a vengeance. This story has been repeated after each war and the reason is clear: women form a flexible, cheap labor pool which is essential to a capitalist system. When labor is scarce, they are forced onto the labor market. When labor is plentiful, they are forced out. Women and blacks have provided a reserve army of unemployed workers, benefiting capitalists and the stable male white working class alike. Yet the system imposes untold suffering on the victims, blacks and women, through low wages and chronic unemployment.

With the end of the war the average age at marriage declined, the average size of families went up, and the suburban migration began in earnest. The political conservatism of the '50's was echoed in a social conservatism which stressed a Victorian ideal of the woman's life: a full womb and selfless devotion to husband and children.

As the bleak decade played itself out, however, three important social developments emerged which were to make a rebirth of the women's struggle inevitable. First, women came to make up more than a third of the labor force, the number of working women being twice the prewar figure. Yet the marked increase in female employment did nothing to better the position of women, who were more occupationally disadvantaged in the 1960's than they had been 25 years earlier. Rather than moving equally into all sectors of the occupational structure, they were being forced into the low-paying service, clerical and semi-skilled categories. In 1940, women had held 45 per cent of all professional and technical positions; in 1947, they held only 37 per cent. The proportion of women in service jobs meanwhile rose from 50 to 55 per cent.

Second, the intoxicating wine of marriage and suburban life was turning sour; a generation of women woke up to find their children grown and a life (roughly 30 more productive years) of housework and bridge parties stretching out before them like a wasteland. For many younger women, the empty drudgery they saw in the suburban life was a sobering contradiction to adolescent dreams of romantic love and the fulfilling role of woman as wife and mother.

Third, a growing civil rights movement was sweeping thousands of young men and women into a moral crusade—a crusade which harsh political experience was to transmute into the New Left. The American Dream was riven and tattered in Mississippi and finally napalmed in Viet-Nam. Young Americans were drawn not to Levittown, but to Berkeley, the Haight-Ashbury and the East Village. Traditional political ideologies and cultural myths, sexual mores and sex roles with them, began to disintegrate in an explosion of rebellion and protest.

The three major groups which make up the new women's movement—working women, middle class married women and students—bring very different kinds of interests and objectives to women's liberation. Working women are most concerned with the economic issues of guaranteed employment, fair wages, job discrimination and child care. Their most immediate oppression is rooted in industrial capitalism and felt directly through the vicissitudes of an exploitative labor market.

Middle class women, oppressed by the psychological mutilation and injustice of institutionalized segregation, discrimination and imposed inferiority, are most sensitive to the dehumanizing consequences of severely limited lives. Usually well educated and capable, these women are rebelling against being forced to trivialize their lives, to live vicariously through husbands and children.

Students, as unmarried middle class girls, have been most sensitized to the sexual exploitation of women. They have experienced the frustration of one-way relationships in which the girl is forced into a "wife" and companion role with none of the supposed benefits of marriage. Young women have increasingly rebelled not only against passivity and dependency in their relationships but also against the notion that they must function as sexual objects, being defined in purely sexual rather than human terms, and being forced to package and sell themselves as commodities on the sex market.

Each group represents an independent aspect of the total institutionalized oppression of women. Their differences are those of emphasis and immediate interest rather than of fundamental goals. All women suffer from economic exploitation, from psychological deprivation, and from exploitive sexuality. Within women's liberation there is a growing understanding that the common oppression of women provides the basis for uniting across class and race lines to form a powerful and radical movement.

RACISM AND MALE SUPREMACY

Clearly, for the liberation of women to become a reality it is necessary to destroy the ideology of male supremacy, which asserts the biological and social inferiority of women in order to justify massive institutionalized oppression. Yet we all know that many women are as loud in their disavowal of this oppression as are the men who chant the litany of "a woman's place is in the home and behind her man." In fact, women are as trapped in their false consciousness as were the mass of blacks 20 years ago, and for much the same reason.

As blacks were defined and limited socially by their color, so women are defined and limited by their sex. While blacks, it was argued, were preordained by God or nature, or both, to be hewers of wood and drawers of water, so women are destined to bear and rear children, and to sustain their husbands with obedience and compassion. The Sky-God tramples through the heavens and the Earth Mother-Goddess is always flat on her back with her legs spread, putting out for one and all.

Indeed, the phenomenon of male chauvinism can only be understood when it is perceived as a form of racism, based on stereotypes drawn from a deep belief in the biological inferiority of women. The so-called "black analogy" is no analogy at all; it is the same social process that is at work, a process which both justifies and helps perpetuate the exploitation of one group of human beings by another.

The very stereotypes that express the society's belief in the biological inferiority of women recall the images used to justify the oppression of blacks. The nature of women, like that of slaves, is depicted as dependent, incapable of reasoned thought, childlike in its simplicity and warmth, martyred in the role of mother, and mystical in the role of sexual partner. In its benevolent form, the inferior position of women results in paternalism; in its malevolent form, a domestic tyranny which can be unbelievably brutal.

It has taken over 50 years to discredit the scientific and social "proof" which once gave legitimacy to the myths of black racial inferiority. Today most people can see that the theory of the genetic inferiority of blacks is absurd. Yet few are shocked by the fact that scientists are still busy "proving" the biological inferiority of women.

❊   ❊   ❊

MARRIAGE: GENESIS OF WOMEN'S REBELLION

The institution of marriage is the chief vehicle for the perpetuation of the oppression of women; it is through the role of wife that the subjugation of women is maintained. In a very real way the role of wife has been the genesis of women's rebellion throughout history.

Looking at marriage from a detached point of view one may well ask why anyone gets married, much less women. One answer lies in the economics of women's position, for women are so occupationally limited that drudgery in the home is considered to be infinitely superior to drudgery in the factory. Secondly, women themselves have no independent social status. Indeed, there is no clearer index of the social worth of a woman in this society than the fact that she has none in her own right. A woman is first defined by the man to whom she is attached, but more particularly by the man she marries, and secondly by the children she bears and rears—hence the anxiety over sexual attractiveness, the frantic scramble for boyfriends and husbands. Having obtained and married a man the race is then on to have children, in order that their attractiveness and accomplishments may add more social worth. In a woman, not having children is seen as an incapacity somewhat akin to impotence in a man.

Beneath all of the pressures of the sexual marketplace and the marital status game, however, there is a far more sinister organization of economic exploitation and psychological mutilation. The housewife role, usually defined in terms of the biological duty of a woman to reproduce and her "innate" suitability for a nurturant and companionship role, is actually crucial to industrial capitalism in an advanced state of technological development. In fact, the housewife (some 44 million women of all classes, ethnic groups and races) provides, unpaid, absolutely essential services and labor. In turn, her assumption of all household duties makes it possible for the man to spend the majority of his time at the workplace.

It is important to understand the social and economic exploitation of the married woman, since the real productivity of her labor is denied by the commonly held assumption that she is dependent on her husband, exchanging her keep for emotional and nurturant services. Margaret Benston, a radical women's liberation leader, points out:

> In sheer quantity, household labor, including child care, constitutes a huge amount of socially necessary production. Nevertheless, in a society based on commodity production, it is not usually considered even as "real work" since it is outside of trade and the marketplace. This assignment of household work as the function of a special category "women" means that this group *does* stand in a different relationship to production. . . . The material basis for the inferior status of women is to be found in just this definition of women. In a society in which money determines value, women are a group who work outside the money economy. Their work is not worth money, is therefore valueless, is therefore not even real work. And women themselves, who do this valueless work, can hardly be expected to be worth as much as men, who work for money.

Women are essential to the economy not only as free labor, but also as consumers. The American system of capitalism depends for its survival on the consumption of vast amounts of socially wasteful goods, and a prime target for the unloading of this waste is the housewife. She is the purchasing agent for the family, but beyond that she is eager to buy because her own identity depends on her accomplishments as a consumer and her ability to satisfy the wants of her husband and children. This is not, of course, to say that she has any power in the economy. Although she spends the wealth, she does not own or control it—it simply passes through her hands.

In addition to their role as housewives and consumers, increasing numbers of women are taking outside employment. These women leave the home to join in an exploited labor force, only to return at night to assume the double burden of housework on top of wage work—that is, they are forced to work at two full-time jobs. No man is required or expected to take on such a burden. The result: two workers from one household in the labor force with no cutback in essential female functions—three for the price of two, quite a bargain.

Frederick Engels, now widely read in women's liberation, argues that, regardless of her status in the larger society, within the context of the family the woman's relationship to the man is one of proletariat to bourgeoisie. One consequence of this class division in the family is to weaken the capacity of men and women oppressed by the society to struggle together against it.

In all classes and groups, the institution of marriage functions to a greater or lesser degree to oppress women; the unity of women of different classes hinges upon our understanding of that common oppression. The nineteenth century women's movement refused to deal with marriage and sexuality, and chose instead to fight for the vote and elevate the feminine mystique to a political ideology. That decision retarded the movement for decades. But 1969 is not 1889. For one thing, there now exist alternatives to marriage. The most original and creative politics of the women's movement has come from a direct confrontation with the issue of marriage and sexuality. The cultural revolution—experimentation with life-styles, communal living, collective child-rearing—have all come from the rebellion against dehumanized sexual relationships, against the notion of women as sexual commodities, against the constriction and spiritual strangulation inherent in the role of wife.

Lessons have been learned from the failures of the earlier movement as well. The feminine mystique is no longer mistaken for politics, nor gaining the vote for winning human rights. Women are now all together at the bottom of the work world, and the basis exists for a common focus of struggle for all women in American society. It remains for the movement to understand this, to avoid the mistakes of the past, to respond creatively to the possibilities of the present.

Women's oppression, although rooted in the institution of marriage, does not stop at the kitchen or the bedroom door. Indeed, the economic exploitation of women in the workplace is the most commonly recognized aspect of the oppression of women.

Most women who enter the labor force do not work for "pin money" or "self-fulfillment." Sixty-two per cent of all women working in 1967 were doing so out of economic need (i.e., were either alone or with husbands earning less than $5,000 a year). In 1963, 36 per cent of

American families had an income of less than $5,000 a year. Women from these families work because they must; they contribute 35 to 40 per cent of the family's total income when working full-time, and 15 to 20 per cent when working part-time.

Despite their need, however, women have always represented the most exploited sector of the industrial labor force. Child and female labor were introduced during the early stages of industrial capitalism, at a time when most men were gainfully employed in crafts. As industrialization developed and craft jobs were eliminated, men entered the industrial labor force, driving women and children into the lowest categories of work and pay. Indeed, the position of women and children industrial workers was so pitiful, and their wages so small, that the craft unions refused to organize them. Even when women organized themselves and engaged in militant strikes and labor agitation—from the shoemakers of Lynn, Massachusetts, to the International Ladies' Garment Workers and their great strike of 1909—male unionists continued to ignore their needs. As a result of this male supremacy in the unions, women remain essentially unorganized, despite the fact that they are becoming an ever larger part of the labor force.

*   *   *

Women, regardless of race, are more disadvantaged than are men, including non-white men. White women earn $2,600 less than white men and $500 less than non-white men. The brunt of the inequality is carried by 2.5 million non-white women, 94 per cent of whom are black. They earn $3,800 less than white men, $1,800 less than non-white men, and $1,200 less than white women.

There is no more bitter paradox in the racism of this country than that the white man, articulating the male supremacy of the white male middle class, should provide the rationale for the oppression of black women by black men. Black women constitute the largest minority in the United States, and they are the most disadvantaged group in the labor force. The further oppression of black women will not liberate black men, for black women were never the oppressors of their men—that is a myth of the liberal white man. The oppression of black men comes from institutionalized racism and economic exploitation: from the world of the white man. Consider the following facts and figures.

The percentage of black working women has always been proportionately greater than that of white women. In 1900, 41 per cent of black women were employed, as compared to 17 per cent for white women. In 1963, the proportion of black women employed was still a fourth greater than that of whites. In 1960, 44 per cent of black married women with children under six years were in the labor force, in contrast to 29 per cent for white women. While job competition requires ever higher levels of education, the bulk of illiterate women are black. On the whole, black women—who often have the greatest need for employment—are the most discriminated against in terms of opportunity. Forced by an oppressive and racist society to carry unbelievably heavy economic and social burdens, black women stand at the bottom of that society, doubly marked by the caste signs of color and sex.

The rise of new agitation for the occupational equality of women also coincided with the re-entry of the "lost generation"—the housewives of the 1950's—into the job market. Women from middle class backgrounds, faced with an "empty nest" (children grown or in school) and a widowed or divorced rate of one-fourth to one-third of all marriages, returned to the workplace in large numbers. But once there they discovered that women, middle class or otherwise, are the last hired, the lowest paid, the least often promoted, and the first fired. Furthermore, women are more likely to suffer job discrimination on the basis of age, so the widowed and divorced suffer particularly, even though their economic need to work is often urgent. Age discrimination also means that the option of work after child-rearing is limited. Even highly qualified older women find themselves forced into low-paid, unskilled or semiskilled work—if they are lucky enough to find a job in the first place.

The realities of the work world for most middle class women— that they become members of the working class, like it or not—are understandably distant to many young men and women in college who have never had to work, and who tend to think of the industrial "proletariat" as a revolutionary force, to the exclusion of "bourgeois" working women. Their image of the "pampered middle class woman" is factually incorrect and politically naive. It is middle class women forced into working class life who are often the first to become conscious of the contradiction between the "American Dream" and their daily experience.

Faced with discrimination on the job—after being forced into the lower levels of the occupational structure—millions of women are inescapably presented with the fundamental contradictions in their unequal treatment and their massive exploitation. The rapid growth of women's liberation as a movement is related in part to the exploitation of working women in all occupational categories.

Male supremacy, marriage, and the structure of wage labor—each of these aspects of women's oppression has been crucial to the resurgence of the women's struggle. It must be abundantly clear that radical social change must occur before there can be significant improvement in the social position of women. Some form of socialism is a minimum requirement, considering the changes that must come in the institutions of marriage and the family alone. The intrinsic radicalism of the struggle for women's liberation necessarily links women with all other oppressed groups.

The heart of the movement, as in all freedom movements, rests in women's knowledge, whether articulated or still only an illness without a name, that they are not inferior—not chicks, not bunnies, nor quail, nor cows, nor bitches, nor ass, nor meat. Women hear the litany of their own dehumanization each day. Yet all the same, women know that male supremacy is a lie. They know they are not animals or sexual objects or commodities. They know their lives are mutilated, because they see within themselves a promise of creativity and personal integration. Feeling the contradiction between the essentially creative and self-actualizing human being within her, and the cruel and degrading less-than-human role she is compelled to play, a woman begins to perceive the falseness of what her society has forced her to be. And once she perceives this, she knows that she must fight.

Women must learn the meaning of rage, the violence that liberates the human spirit. The rhetoric of invective is an equally essential stage, for in discovering and venting their rage against the enemy—and the enemy in everyday life is men—women also experience the justice of their own violence. They learn the first lessons in their own latent strength. Women must learn to know themselves as revolutionaries. They must become hard and strong in their determination, while retaining their humanity and tenderness.

There is a rage that impels women into a total commitment to women's liberation. That ferocity stems from a denial of mutilation; it is a cry for life, a cry for the liberation of the spirit. Roxanne Dunbar, surely one of the most impressive women in the movement, conveys the feelings of many:

We are damaged—we women, we oppressed, we disinherited. There are very few who are not damaged, and they rule. . . . The oppressed trust those who rule more than they trust themselves, because self-contempt emerges from powerlessness. Anyway, few oppressed people believe that life could be much different. . . . We are damaged and we have the right to hate and have contempt and to kill and to scream. But for what? . . . Do we want the oppressor to admit he is wrong, to withdraw his misuse of us? He is only too happy to admit guilt—then do nothing but try to absorb and exorcize the new thought. . . . That does not make up for what I have lost, what I never had, and what all those others who are worse off than I never had. . . . Nothing will compensate for the irreparable harm it has done to my sisters. . . . How could we possibly settle for anything remotely less, even take a crumb in the meantime less, than total annihilation of a system which systematically destroys half its people. . . .

Suggestions for Further Reading

For information on the condition of women in the period before the Civil War, see Andrew Sinclair, *The Emancipation of the American Woman* ° (Harper and Row, 1965), first published under the title *The Better Half;* Eleanor Flexner, *Century of Struggle: The Women's Rights Movement in the United States* ° (Harvard University Press, 1959); and Robert E. Riegel, *American Feminists* ° (University of Kansas Press, 1963). A useful collection of documents is Aileen S. Kraditor (ed.), *Up from the Pedestal: Selected Writings in the History of American Feminism* ° (Quadrangle, 1968). Hannah Josephson examines the plight of women textile workers in *The Golden Threads: New England's Mill Girls and Magnates* (Duell, Sloan and Pearce, 1949). A study related to the role of women in American society is Bernard Wishy, *The Child and the Republic: The Dawn of Modern American Child Nurture* (University of Pennsylvania Press, 1967).

An expanded version of the essay by William L. O'Neill that is reprinted in this volume was published under the title *Everyone Was Brave: The Rise and Fall of Feminism in America* ° (Quadrangle, 1969). A history of the movement written by the leaders themselves is Elizabeth Cady Stanton et al., *The History of Woman Suffrage* (6 vols.; Fowler and Wells, 1881–1922). Two important publications by leading feminists are Charlotte Perkins Gilman, *Women and Economics* ° (Small-Maynard, 1898), and Carrie Chapman Catt and Nettie Rogers Shuler, *Woman Suffrage and Politics* ° (Scribner's, 1923). Good biographies of feminist leaders are Mary Gray Peck's *Carrie Chapman Catt* (Wilson, 1944) and Alma Lutz's *Created Equal: A Biography of Elizabeth Cady Stanton* (Day, 1940) and *Susan B. Anthony: Rebel, Crusader, Humanitarian* (Beacon, 1959).

The current women's liberation movement began with the publication of *The Feminine Mystique* ° (Norton, 1963), by Betty Friedan. A study that offers a good deal of insight into the problems of women in America is Robert J. Lifton (ed.), *The Woman in America* ° (Beacon, 1967), first published in the spring 1964 issue of *Daedalus.* Kate Millett's *Sexual Politics* (Doubleday, 1970) is a provocative analysis of the literary sources of male supremacy. Two important collections of essays on male-female relationships are Robin Morgan (ed.), *Sisterhood Is Powerful: An Anthology of Writings from the Women's Liberation Movement* ° (Random House, 1970), and Betty Roszak and Theodore Roszak (eds.), *Masculine/Feminine: Readings in Sexual Mythology and the Liberation of Women* ° (Harper and Row, 1969).

° Available in paperback edition.

A	2
B	3
C	4
D	5
E	6
F	7
G	8
H	9
I	0
J	1